Social Movements and Activism in the USA

What can we learn when we listen closely to and engage in dialogue with social movement activists?

Social Movements and Activism in the USA addresses this question for a group of progressive activists in Hartford, Connecticut, who do community, labor, feminist, gay and lesbian, peace, and anti-racist organizing. Situated within the twenty-first-century landscape of post-industrialism and neo-liberalism and drawing on oral histories, the book argues for a dialogic and integrative approach to social movement activism. The dialogue between scholar and activist captures the interpretive nature of activists' identity, the variable ways activists decide on strategies and goals, the external constraints on activism, and the creative ways activists manoeuvre around these constraints. This dialogic approach makes the book accessible and useful to students, scholars, and activists alike. The integrative nature of the text refers to its theoretical approach. Rather than advancing a new theory of social movements, it uses existing approaches as a tool kit to examine the what, how, who, and why of social movement activism.

Stephen Valocchi is Professor of Sociology at Trinity College in Hartford, Connecticut. He is the author of *Queer Studies: An Interdisciplinary Reader* (with Robert C. Corber), and has also written numerous essays on progressive social movements in the United States, which have appeared in *Mobilization, Research in Social Movements, Conflicts and Change*, and *Social Problems*.

Social Movements and Activism in the USA

Stephen Valocchi

 Routledge
Taylor & Francis Group

LONDON AND NEW YORK

First published 2010
by Routledge
2 Park Square, Milton Park, Abingdon, Oxon OX14 4RN

Simultaneously published in the USA and Canada
by Routledge
270 Madison Avenue, New York, NY 10016

Routledge is an imprint of the Taylor & Francis Group, an informa business

Typeset in Great Britain by Saxon Graphics Ltd, Derby
Printed and bound in Great Britain by TJ International Ltd, Padstow,
Cornwall

British Library Cataloguing in Publication Data
A catalogue record for this book is available
from the British Library

Library of Congress Cataloging in Publication Data
Valocchi, Stephen M., 1956–
Social movements and activism in the USA / Stephen Valocchi.
p. cm.
Includes bibliographical references.
ISBN 978-0-415-46158-0 (hbk.) — ISBN 978-0-415-46159-7 (pbk.) —
ISBN 978-0-203-87398-4 (e book) 1. Community activists—United States.
2. Social reformers—United States. 3. Social movements—United States.
I. Title.
HN59.2.V35 2009
303.48'4—dc22
2009002840

ISBN10: 0-415-46158-8 (hbk)
ISBN10: 0-415-46159-6 (pbk)
ISBN10: 0-415-87398-X (ebk)

ISBN13: 978-0-415-46158-0 (hbk)
ISBN13: 978-0-415-46159-7 (pbk)
ISBN13: 978-0-203-87398-4 (ebk)

Contents

	Acknowledgements	vi
1	Scholars and Activists in Dialogue	1
2	Theory and Activism	12
3	The Historical and Contemporary Context of Hartford Progressive Activism	34
4	What Activists Do: Developing Strategies, Conceptualizing Goals, Exploiting Opportunities	55
5	What Activists Do: Gathering Resources, Forming Organizations	84
6	What Makes Them Do It: Recruitment and Commitment to Social Movements	107
7	What Makes Them Tired: Activist Burnout and Managing an Activist Life	124
8	Who They Are: Collective Identity and Oppositional Consciousness	139
9	Rethinking Activists' Questions and Scholars' Answers	162
	Appendix	169
	Notes	173
	References	178
	Index	189

Acknowledgements

It should go without saying that this book is dedicated to the many activists in Hartford, Connecticut who shared their time with me. I am honored that these men and women gave so freely of themselves to help me sort out the many questions that have long perplexed me about working for progressive social change in Hartford and by extension throughout the United States. This project was a labor of love, since there is nothing that I love more than a good story of struggle! My only regret is that I had to stop listening to and collecting these stories and to start making sense of them. The "sense" that I made of them in the pages below is provisional and open to debate. Indeed, if there is one thing I learned from talking with progressive activists, it is that all knowledge is political and therefore subject to dialogue and contestation. It is in this spirit that I present my account of *Social Movements and Activism in the USA.*

These stories of activists and activism touched other people as well. There were several students who transcribed the interviews and retrieved statistical and historical materials for the book. Like me, they were also moved and educated by these conversations: Chase Anderson, Ben Johnson, Marc Shafer, and Judene Small. Veronica Zuniga also provided technical and word processing assistance. To all of them, I extend my heartfelt thanks!

Three people deserve special acknowledgement. My colleague, Stephanie Gilmore (now at Dickinson College in Pennsylvania), encouraged this project from the outset. She offered her always smart insights and allayed my seemingly constant anxieties. Peter Costella, my long time friend, cooked many meals for me which we both enjoyed while watching reruns of old sitcoms.

Finally, more than anyone else, Lazaros Papanikolaou lived this process with me. I am deeply grateful for his unyielding confidence in me.

Chapter 1

Scholars and Activists in Dialogue

There is a certain irony to scholarly work on social movements. On the one hand, this work relies on the lived experiences of individuals as they encounter injustice and devise ways to fight it. These activists struggle on many fronts to make sense of the world around them, convince others of the justness of their cause, and confront numerous obstacles to achieving their goals. Their actions and campaigns are the raw material for scholarly books and essays on social movements. On the other hand, the questions and debates that inform the scholarship on social movements, while grounded in this raw material, are rarely formulated and resolved *in dialogue with* the individuals who supply this "raw material." Many times scholars and activists talk past one another: scholars want the "big picture" and develop a conceptual vocabulary to bring that picture into focus while activists address immediate concerns and rely on experiential knowledge to make decisions about issues and strategies. Subsequently, we miss opportunities to benefit from each other's stock of knowledge. Each purpose is important but there may be ways to reorient the knowledge produced by each for mutual benefit.[1]

I have been reminded of this irony and these missed opportunities many times. My limited participation in various forms of collective action frequently leaves me frustrated with both the slow pace of change and the rapidity with which decisions need to be made. In these episodes, I struggle to find insights from the scholarship that can be useful for these decisions and, not surprisingly, come up empty-handed. Do we storm the president's office because the administration has not been sufficiently responsive and risk losing supporters or do we continue the less dramatic path of "more meetings" and risk "death by committee"? Do we accept management's "last and final offer" even though it is not all we wanted and risk alienating the more radical workers or do we accept the offer, define it as success, and risk cooptation? These are snap decisions, and the relevant research on these decisions either does not exist or is locked away in theoretical language and specialized methodology. These episodes of contention, moreover, do not lend themselves to the careful deliberation of scholarship by activists in areas where the research is indeed relevant. For example, social movement scholars know a great deal about the costs and liabilities of certain organizational forms for longevity, democracy, creativity, and cooptation (Breines 1989; Freeman 1973; Piven and Cloward 1979;

Polletta 2002; Staggenborg 1986; 1989). Activists rarely have the luxury of learning from and then applying this scholarship.

My most productive interactions with activists have not been "in the heat of battle" but in the relative comfort of the classroom, coffee shop or, as I hope to demonstrate in the chapters to follow, in the conversations I had with activists for this book. In these contexts, reflection, deliberation and dialogue prevail, and it is those qualities that promote mutual learning. I want to model and extend these conversations in a more systematic way, and in the pages that follow, you will read the outcome of these extended conversations about progressive activism in one U.S. city—Hartford, Connecticut—at the end of the twentieth and beginning of the twenty-first centuries. These dialogues and the commentary that contextualizes them demonstrate the intellectual benefits for students and scholars of social movements of listening closely to activists' narratives and the practical benefits for social movement activists when scholars make their research accessible to organizers and activists. We can be better students and scholars of social movements if we listen to activists; activists can be more effective agents of social change if they listen to scholars.

For these reasons, the book privileges the "voices" of activists, letting them express themselves in their own words. Their words are just as important as, if not more important than mine and the success of this effort depends on reading both in relation to one another. In practical terms, this means that the (almost) verbatim excerpts from my conversations with activists comprise significant space in the book. As Richard Flacks (2005) argues in an edited volume devoted to a similar joint enterprise, productive collaboration comes from listening closely to activists' theories of change. As Sarah Maddison and Sean Scalmer (2006) demonstrate in another similar project with Australian progressive activists, activists produce "practical knowledge" which can reorient scholars' theoretical approaches to social movements.

The other source of frustration from my involvements in collective action is in the slow pace of change. My critical and cynical temperament focuses my gaze on the limits of reform, the need for radical restructuring, and the vast resources of those in power to thwart substantive social change. I know full well how my biography and background led me to that temperament. I am not quite a child of the 1960s as my students sometimes think I am. More accurately, I am a child of the 1970s: someone who came of age during the unraveling of the civil rights, student, and peace movements. I did not imbibe the heady optimism and earnestness of that earlier period. Instead, I participated in the 1960s only vicariously through its music, drugs, and sexual liberalism. The politics I imbibed were tinged with caution and cynicism as I witnessed the demise of dreams (perhaps fantasies) of revolution and the rise of political conservatism and economic insecurity. No surprise then that I ended up a scholar trained to stand at a critical distance *from* the world even as I continue to see the value of acting *in* that world. Thus, I am naturally drawn to and stand in awe of activists who seem to have this imperative to act and the temperament to do so. For that reason, the chapters that follow not only illuminate and contextualize the "what" of progressive activism in Hartford—what it is exactly they do, how they do it, and the challenges associated with it—but also the "who" of the activists themselves—how they came to do this work, why they commit themselves to it, if and why they become frustrated and why, despite the frustration, they persist. As these chapters argue, these two sets of questions are inseparable.

Thus, the dialogic stance of the book is partly in service to scholars and students of social movements. What can we learn about the utility of our existing concepts and perspectives when we listen closely to the stories activists tell about their lives and work? What new questions do activists pose that demand the attention of social movement scholars? The book's dialogic stance is also in service to activists to help inform their work on progressive social change. How can our concepts and perspectives assist activists in understanding better the full range of options available for doing their work, the possible consequences of particular strategies and goals and the tradeoffs involved in particular courses of action? How can these concepts help activists gain a better understanding of the sources and possible resolution of some of the conflict and tension experienced while doing this work?

To begin to answer these questions, Chapter 2 presents an overview of the major social movement theories and argues that, rather than seeing these as competing paradigms, I recover the concepts that are most useful for understanding the interplay of constraint and agency, and structures and meanings that organize the dialogue between activists and scholars. I want to forge a path between activists who oftentimes insist on their agency in terms of their actions and beliefs and scholars who oftentimes insist on the constraints and structures that limit action and shape beliefs. In order to accomplish this balancing act, I describe the theoretical frameworks as they developed in interaction with the historical social movement landscape over the course of the past sixty years and examine the relevance of these frameworks for the dialogue between scholars and activists. As we will see, this interaction reveals an ongoing tension between the themes that animate the book: constraint and agency; structures and meaning.

Many of the concepts developed by these theoretical frameworks inform my historical overview of progressive activism in Hartford in Chapter 3. This chapter does several things. First, it places the activists whose stories you hear throughout the book in a long line of activism in the city and stresses the diversity of this progressive activism. Second, the historical analysis also helps us see both the uniqueness and typicality of Hartford as a setting for progressive activism. Hartford shares several economic, demographic, and political features of medium-sized cities in the United States but possesses a somewhat unique civic culture that both encourages and contains various forms of social action. Third, the historical analysis demonstrates the utility of sociological concepts to organize and analyze that history, particularly stressing the constraints and structures that shape contemporary activism and the ways in which individuals have constructed oppositional cultures and belief systems to challenge some of these constraints and structures. Finally, it introduces many of the institutional actors and activist campaigns referred to by progressive activists in subsequent chapters as they recount and reflect on their experiences.

Chapters 4 through 8 examine their experiences using the stories of activists themselves. These chapters mimic and model the nature of the conversations we had around strategies and goals (Chapter 4), resources and organizations (Chapter 5), participation and commitment (Chapter 6), activist burnout (Chapter 7) and activist identity (Chapter 8). Every chapter introduces some relevant scholarship on the topic and allows the activists to weigh in on the topic. This encounter serves any number of purposes. In some cases, it critiques the concepts; in other cases, it suggests solutions to or "ways around" dilemmas or unresolved tensions within activism. In general, this encounter is between the scholar's emphasis on "the ties that bind" and the activist's emphasis on the actions and meanings of individuals that loosen those ties. Its goal is to chasten the hubris of activists who see all things possible and counter the cynicism of scholars who see cooptation and compromise at every turn.

Chapter 4 uses this encounter to provide suggestions about strategies to move from reform-oriented goals to those that attempt institutional restructuring. Chapter 5 uses activists' stories to remind scholars of the plethora of viable social movement structures and settings. Chapters 4 and 5 present activists speaking about the goals they pursue in doing social change work, the strategies they use to obtain those goals, the resources they try to cultivate to assist them in that work, and the networks or organizations they develop to give continuity to that work. The many excerpts from the oral histories are structured by and juxtaposed with the relevant theoretical frameworks and concepts that scholars use to examine strategies, goals, resources, political opportunities, and organizations. This encounter yields several outcomes. For social movement scholars, it provides some suggestions about improving those concepts and frameworks. For activists, it provides some clues to resolving or thinking differently about some of the dilemmas and issues involved in their work.

Chapter 6 gives both scholars and activists a different way of approaching recruitment and commitment, moving scholars away from additive or monocausal understandings and showing activists the untapped resources and techniques they possess to mobilize members. The chapter features activists' personal stories about how they were recruited into and became committed to activism and the strategies they use to encourage participation in progressive activism. Unlike the way that scholars have presented that process, activists describe it not as a function of a single factor or even a combination of factors accumulated in an additive manner. Instead, we see a variety of pathways to activism, all interactively constructed across a number of biographical, social-network, and event-driven dimensions. The stories do participate in the concepts that social movement scholars use to describe these processes but they complicate and deepen these concepts in many ways. This encounter between concepts and stories provides some insights into techniques activists might use in doing their recruitment and solidarity-building work in various organizations and campaigns.

Chapter 7 uses concepts of abeyance and plausibility structures (Nepstad 2004; Taylor 1989) to point to the importance of social supports when doing activist work. In the absence of formal supports, activists talk about the informal ways they use to manage burnout and conflict within their activist work or, more generally, to balance their activism with other areas of their lives. This encounter challenges scholars to attend to these informal methods of support and activists to attend to formalizing some of these informal techniques.

Chapter 8 employs the now-popular concept of collective identity to explore progressive activism not only in terms of the strategies, goals, coalitions, organizations, and opportunities but also in terms of the ideologies or belief systems of the activists themselves.[2] For activists, it encourages a reassessment of those typical concerns (e.g. strategies, goals, etc.) in terms of the individuals who believe in them and pursue them in different ways because of their identities. By showing activists that the ideas, strategies, and goals of a campaign or organization are not necessarily precisely shared by all participants of that campaign or organization, this chapter opens up a new set of challenges for activists.

The Activists and Their Activism

As a teacher of courses on social movements, I am frequently frustrated by the scholarship available in this area. Most of it is so dense with theory, concepts, hypotheses, and statistical procedures designed for causal analysis that the excitement, the uncertainty, the full array of human emotion is squeezed out of it.[3] In order to reinsert this energy into the study of social movements, I put "front and center" the words, stories, rhetoric, and emotions of over thirty activists—men, women, young, old, religious, secular, Black, white, Latino, straight, gay, bisexual, queer—who have devoted a significant part of their lives to the sometimes exhilarating, sometimes frustrating, and oftentimes difficult work of social justice, democracy, and equality.

The result of six years of oral history interviewing, *Social Movements and Activism in the United States* gives voice to the lived experiences of men and women who work for progressive social change in the city of Hartford, Connecticut, one of many medium-sized cities in the U.S. characterized by deindustrialization, urban poverty, and increasing inequalities between city and suburb. But to locate these activists solely in a local economic context does not do justice to the diversity of the work they do. They are simultaneously local, state, national, and global activists.

These activists do peace and global justice work at the local and national level, community organizing in the neighborhoods of the city, anti-violence, anti-racist, and immigrant rights work in those neighborhoods and around the state. They work in the progressive wing of the labor movement, in feminist organizations; they engage in campaigns for lesbian, gay, bisexual, and transgender rights, and in organizing queer youth.

Although these activists work on different issues with different targets and different short-term goals and although they sometimes disagree on priorities, strategies, and goals, they reference one another when I ask them to name others in town doing similar work. In general, they talk about themselves as members of a progressive community dedicated to changing individual consciousness, the institutional practices of organizations in the city and region, the structures of power at all levels of government, and the culture of the larger society. They come from similar cultural and political traditions awakened or nourished in a diverse array of the area's institutions: colleges and universities, churches, unions, social service agencies, and neighborhood organizations. As we will see, "similarity amidst difference" is a very good way to describe the identities of these activists, their activist biographies, their activist engagements, and activist philosophies. It may also be a good way to reconsider definitions of progressive activism that tend to restrict membership on any number of criteria.

To define progressive activism in such a capacious way may appear troubling to some who object to the inclusion of one sector or another in that community. While not wanting to engage in debates about the nature of the political left or the kinds of political work that contribute to or impede a progressive movement in the United States, I do want to distance my definition from those who would define it solely on the basis of class and economic justice issues.[4] Of course, any definition of progressivism must include these issues and a political framework that acknowledges the structural inequalities generated by a capitalist system and the class divisions it produces. In an age of financial excesses, mortgage defaults, and corporate bailouts, a progressive movement must organize around a critique of capitalism.

Other inequalities and divisions are also enduring features of American society (and all western societies), most notably: race, ethnicity, gender, and sexuality. Again, in an age when some pundits are encouraging a discourse of "going beyond" or transcending race and gender, it is imperative for a progressive movement to analyze and critique this "post-racial" and "post-feminist" discourse and recognize the continued but changed significance of race and gender cleavages in twenty-first-century America.

Some on the left have contended that political attention to these cleavages prevents a broad-based social justice agenda around economic transformation and leads to a fragmented identity politics, cultural isolation or inconsequential personal empowerment. I reject this narrow view and embrace one that begins from an analysis of structural inequalities in all their dimensions and complexities. Racism is a structural source of power. Sexism is a structural source of power. Nationalism is a structural source of power. Homophobia is a structural source of power. Moreover, they are not isolated and individual in their operation but interconnected with complicated material and social psychological effects.[5] Activists who draw their motivation from or see their issues in terms of these dimensions qualify as progressive activists.

I would also want to entertain a definition of progressivism that embraces a service ethic in that definition. Again, some progressives would contest that definition since service work involves individual or even group-level benefits that may alleviate some of the distress of inequality but does not question the nature of nor directly challenges that inequality. This blanket refusal, however, does not account for the diversity of approaches to service delivery.[6] Admittedly, some approaches do abide by a strictly social work approach that sees only the individual as the cause of the problem for which the service is delivered or that locates the problem in family or community breakdown and refuses a broader structural explanation. Other approaches, like the ones included here, involve an explicitly political component to that service ethic (Gilkes1988; Sacks 1988). Included in my sample, for example, are a few individuals who deliver services to specific populations in the city and region but do it utilizing progressive principles. For example, in some cases, this role of service provision is in addition to their more traditional role of organizer who mobilizes individuals for collective action to pursue unaddressed needs or problems. In other cases, these services are delivered with a particular empowerment philosophy. This can entail political education, consciousness-raising, and behavioral change that may not lead to a collective demand on an institutional actor but does entail personal and cultural change. This change of "thinking or living differently" or "living against the grain" as one of my activists described it makes this work decidedly progressive.

Table 1 (Appendix) introduces my sample of Hartford activists, their age at the time of the interview, the number of years they have spent in activism, their race, ethnicity, and social class, and their areas of activism. This group includes 16 men and 17 women: 20 whites, 9 blacks, 3 Latinas, and 1 Latino; 11 activists are in their twenties, 7 in their thirties, 8 in their forties, 6 in their fifties, and 1 in her sixties. Five activists have extensive experience in the peace and anti-globalization movements; 4 have extensive experience in the labor movement; 12 have extensive experience in various kinds of community organizing; 5 have extensive experience in organizing around low-income or immigrant communities; 10 have extensive experience in anti-racism organizations or initiative; 3 have extensive experience in feminist organizations; 11 have extensive experience in gay and lesbian or queer-identified organizations, initiatives, and campaigns. Finally, these activists run the gamut in terms of both chronological age ranging from 21 to 60 years and activist age ranging from 2 to 34 years. There are veteran activists who have spent most of their adult lives engaged in social change work as well as younger activists who are just starting out but, despite their age, talk like seasoned veterans.

As an observer and sometime participant in local progressive politics, I had some familiarity with the progressive community in Hartford. Based on this familiarity, I assembled an initial list of three to five contacts within each area, the members of which vary by organization, gender, race, and age. I asked those "familiar" contacts to then recommend others. Based on this technique of snowball sampling, I also included in my sample an equal number of activists with whom I was unfamiliar. This technique insured that I included many of the key figures in these areas—those who do the bulk of the organizing work—without over-sampling from among my personal networks. This technique also insured variation in terms of movement sub-cultures, the organizational features of the movement area, and the social biographies of the activists who participated in that movement area necessary to represent the full range of mobilizing work performed by progressive activists.

Based on these contacts, I conducted 33 open-ended, face-to-face, and tape or digitally recorded interviews between 2002 and 2008. These interviews lasted between one and three hours and dealt with six basic questions. What kind of activism are you and have you been involved in (i.e. areas of activism)? How do you do it (i.e. the methods of their activism)? With whom do you do it (i.e. the social networks of their activism)? Why do you do it (i.e. the motivations of their activism)? How did you come to do it (i.e. the biography of their activism)? What is the relationship between your activism and other areas of your life (i.e. the integration of their activism with their lives)? These general questions allowed respondents to talk broadly about how they saw themselves as activists, the challenges, successes, and failures involved in their work, their experiences with and evaluations of social movement strategies and goals, and how they have been affected by their activism. The interview schedule is reproduced in the appendix.

Organizing the reams of transcripts produced by these interviews and observing commonalities and differences among the activists were quite challenging. Basically, I approached this task as I had approached the interviews themselves: as an encounter between activist experience and scholarly categories and concepts. With each reading of the transcripts, I found certain themes emerging around certain topics and concepts. Each chapter represents a "triangulation" of sorts between activist themes and scholarly concepts. Sociologists refer to this method as grounded theory first developed by Nathan Glaser and Anselm Strauss (1967).

This brief introduction does not begin to capture the diversity and nuance of what activists do and who they are. As the chapters that follow amply demonstrate, that is best left to the activists themselves. For now, some brief introductions help to clarify the nature of the progressive community in Hartford. For example, contrary to some accounts of late twentieth-, early twenty-first-century progressivism in the U.S., "identity" activists do not always abide by identity politics. Beth, a young queer activist who at the time of the interview was employed by a feminist organization, refuses to be defined by the identity politics of the organization:

> I largely do a lot of queer work throughout the state...but I do a lot of anti-war stuff, anti-globalization, anti-racism work and multi-issue organizing. I started hanging out with a whole different group of people that did a lot of labor issues, that did animals rights stuff, that did protesting the war, and all of a sudden I just saw that it was so much bigger than just working on queer issues, which is still really important.

Beth calls attention to one feature of Table 1 (Appendix): the number of activists who do multi-issue organizing and who see that work in terms of changing values, social institutions, or culture. Like Beth and others included here, I share her definition of progressive activism as one that encompasses many specific and diverse issues all in the pursuit of social justice, full democratic participation, equality of access and outcome, and human freedom. As we will see, this diversity also extends to the broad goals of the progressive community: some, like Beth, emphasize changes in policies and practices; others emphasize changes in attitudes and culture.

Table 1 (Appendix) also does not capture the insistence of other activists that their work be considered progressive activism and speaks to another component of the progressive community in the city. Lisa, another activist who has spent 15 years working with young Latina mothers in Hartford, encourages me to broaden my definition of activism:

> When you called and asked about activism, I was thinking—what this is really about is helping people access their own power. And helping them [do this] through education.

Lisa and others in my sample blur the traditional lines between service delivery and community organizing and provide concrete models to accomplish this blurring. As we will see, several activists blur this line by delivering needed material and social services in ways that empower individuals and engage those same individuals to think and act critically about the larger systems of power and service provision.

Table 1 (Appendix) also draws our attention to the large number of activists who have been involved in this work for a very long time: 19 of the 32 activists report involvement of over ten years! This longevity glosses over many different patterns of participation that will occupy my attention in subsequent chapters: some activists engage in activism at the grassroots without pay and without an organizational home for their entire careers while others move from volunteer activism to paid activism in formal organizations. Both these groups, however, speak of a dilemma or tension that exists in all forms of progressive activism: the tradeoffs between doing grassroots activism and organizational development. Robin started an organizing project with queer youth that has blossomed into a fairly large organization. She expresses a sentiment I hear from several long-term activists:

> I think that one of the ways that it's been activism is in training kids to go home to their own school and their own areas to make a difference there in creating the gay–straight alliances. In terms of the agency, a lot of the work that we do is working with legislators and policy stuff around same-sex marriage, around co-parent adoption, and around trying to get some teeth into the student bill of rights....We actually did more direct activism in the early years, and I feel that one of the things that's changed in ways I'm not happy with is that, as the agency has grown, I'm doing administrative stuff. I'm writing reports, you know, I'm doing grants, and the community organizing part really falls off. The first two years it really was a community-organizing project.

Like many of the veteran activists who manage to turn their activism into a career, Robin struggles with the downside of success: the fall-off in direct action and the danger that the organization ceases to straddle the line between organizing and service and becomes simply a vehicle for the delivery of services. I return to this organizing dilemma in Chapter 5.

Just as we don't see differences in participation patterns among activists in Table 1 (Appendix), we also don't see differences in activist commitment. While I will take up these differences in Chapter 6, one striking feature of my sample is the general reluctance of these activists to separate who they are and the work they do. Even for the career activists they resist this model of work from the dominant culture. Cornel, a tireless fighter against violence, drugs, and racism in the city, bluntly states: "What I do is primary and everything else is secondary." Steve, a labor activist who refuses that singular label, also refuses the separation of personal identity and work: "One thing I know, in terms of who I am, I could never not be an activist." These activists challenge models of activism based on a separation of identity and work but, at the same time, they leave unexamined the difficulties living out this all-encompassing identity. These difficulties are discussed in Chapter 7.

Lastly, my introduction does not communicate the conflicts these activists encounter even as they profess identification with a progressive community: conflicts associated with being young in some progressive organizations or being non-white or queer or a woman in ostensibly white, straight, and male-dominated organizations. Josh, a 28-year-old peace and media activist, caused quite a stir among several veterans of the peace movement who he affectionately referred to as the "freeze ladies":

> I made the flyer [for the protest] and the flyer was a take on the finale of Dr. Strangelove where he's riding a missile down, but it was Bush riding a nuke, but he was as a skeleton, and the older generation flipped.

Age is not the only dimension of difference along which conflict occurs among progressive activists. As Cheryl, an African American activist with 15 years' experience in the city, notes how race is still a source of tension in progressive organizations:

> Although they gave me chances to be in power positions, I knew I would be tokenized, I would be one of the few, so I said no.

Gender is one of the areas where Laura M., a tireless labor organizer and fierce negotiator, insists that progress has been made. Still, she battles sexism in the same way she battles for better wages and working conditions for workers:

> I've been really lucky because there's a generation of women who came before me, so I have not been the first tough broad they've seen. But I think that is basically true throughout our union. They set up a model for having a strong—strong female leadership within the leadership of the union. There's not a single banquet waitress that you want to cross! But I still get attacked for it. Like when the people from the internal opposition were here—when it was clear that the program that I was on was succeeding and the workers

were coming forward...their first attack on me was to call me "The Bitch from Boston."...But, you know, being called a bitch, there are times at the negotiating table...There's been some negotiators on the other side, because it's been almost entirely men on the other side, who I've wanted to bring a dildo to negotiations so I could take it out and put it on the table and go, "Okay, now look, I've got one too, so can we just move on?"

These and other conflicts among the activists in the sample caution against a sanguine view of progressive movements as immune from the biases of the "outside" world. As I will argue in Chapters 5 and 8, these conflicts are common in all formal organizations but are dealt with differently and have different personal and organizational consequences because they take place in a fairly close-knit progressive community.

When activists have the chance to define themselves we find even more difference and nuance than can be reported in any standard sociological description of samples and populations. But these self-definitions also cannot be taken at face value. They need theoretical context and historical context, a task I turn to in the following two chapters.

Chapter 2

Theory and Activism

Concepts and frameworks exist to organize reality.[1] They help us wade through a diverse and seemingly complex social world. They call attention to the crucial aspects of that world and suggest how those aspects might be related to one another. What concepts and frameworks help us understand the social world of progressive social movements in general and their specific dynamics within Hartford Connecticut in the contemporary period? This chapter identifies and describes these theoretical frameworks with their associated concepts. It also evaluates them according to how they resonate with the stories activists tell about their work and lives. In Chapter 3, I utilize many of these social movement concepts to make sense of the history of the city and how that history affects progressive activism.

Theoretical frameworks are composed of logically related propositions that are built on empirical observations of commonalities across a number of cases and that explain some question or questions about a phenomenon (Abbott 2005). The frameworks discussed below, for example, address the "why," "how," "who," and "what" of activism. What they don't always address is the "so what" of these frameworks. In other words, what is the utility of these approaches for activists and for an activist-oriented knowledge of social movements?

Even as I review these standard frameworks for understanding activism and social movements in this chapter, I do not want to avoid this "so what" question. How can these frameworks assist activists in making explicit the unconscious motives or unexamined strategies of themselves or their targets? How can they help call attention to significant aspects of the contexts of activism, the potential costs and benefits of various kinds of activism, and the day-to-day dilemmas and larger tensions experienced when doing social movement work?

Before I proceed, one example may clarify how social movement concepts and frameworks can address this "so what" question. Many of my activists discuss their thought processes in convincing or persuading others to participate in activism or in developing a media strategy to accompany a particular campaign. Social movement scholars have developed the concept of "framing" to capture the several essential elements of these efforts (Benford 2000; Johnston and Noakes 2005; Snow et al. 1986). As we will see below, this concept is part of a larger theoretical framework that asserts the importance of culture and interactively constructed meaning for addressing many questions of social movement analysis. The concept of framing calls attention to the ideas, meanings, and cultural scripts used to define a problem, map the causes of the problem, and suggest ways to address the problem (Snow and Benford 1992: 137). The concept and the theoretical framework on which it is based suggest that this process is carried out either consciously or unconsciously utilizing some notion of "resonance," that is, utilizing ideas, cultural values or moral concerns that people can relate to and hopefully be moved by. Even as it resonates with aspects of the dominant culture, however, it pushes up against that culture and encourages us to challenge that culture in significant ways.

Sociologist William Gamson utilizes the framing concept in his university-based Media Research and Action Project [MRAP] which works with activist organizations to help bridge the academic–activist divide. In research on the media discourse on nuclear power, for example, he and André Modigliani (1989) identify the "interpretive packages" or frames used by the media to describe the industry, the energy crisis, and the Three Mile Island accident in 1979. Particularly useful is their identification of themes and counter-themes used by the media which have varying degrees of resonance with the public (e.g. technological progress, energy independence, public accountability). This research becomes part of a larger strategy of assisting activist organizations in their media campaigns. If we know how the dominant society frames an issue, then activists can use that knowledge in their own framing strategies. Framing also assists in the internal work of solidarity building as Charlotte Ryan (2005), another MRAP member, shows in her research and activist work with a coalition against domestic violence in Rhode Island. She shows how participants in the coalition brainstormed about the dominant frames used by both themselves and the media around domestic violence. Through a process of interaction amongst themselves around these different frames, they produced a media strategy that "play[ed] within the dominant culture but yet [broke] with it in significant ways" (Ryan 2005: 133).

As Gamson's work at MRAP makes clear, the concept of framing begins to address that "so what" question about theoretical frameworks, since it helps activists think about the different ways their messages need to be "packaged" for different campaigns or actions. As the work at MRAP shows, the concept simply helps activists think more explicitly about the multiple dimensions of an activity that they do almost instinctively. When I asked activists how they go about choosing their framing strategies, most rely on past experience or on consensual decision making. Equipped with the knowledge of how framing activities have operated in many different mobilizations, scholars can share with activists their knowledge of the limitations and trade-offs of particular framing strategies. For example, which framing efforts are most important or necessary first steps: those aimed at building membership, raising consciousness among members, getting media attention, or counteracting the framing efforts of opponents? Further, if I personalize an issue to appeal to legislators, does that undercut my efforts to represent the issue as social, shared by many, and thus in need of a collective, institutional solution? In these ways, the insights of scholars from research on framing can be brought into the discussion.

Not all scholarly concepts and the theoretical frameworks sociologists work with are that immediately useful. For the most part, sociological theories of social movements attend to the large questions of emergence, development, change, and decline. Some of these are designed to help us understand why big bursts of activism occur at some times and not others (e.g. Piven and Cloward 1979; Tarrow 1994; Tilly 1978); some ask these same questions but for smaller, more localized, and perhaps more continuous forms of activism (e.g. Dugan 2005; Lopez 2004); some are designed to help us understand how activism—the issues, the techniques, the goals, the people—has changed over the years (e.g. McAdam *et al.* 2001); some help us identify the kinds of people likely to participate in activism (e.g. Klandermans 1997; McAdam 1988). Finally, others help us understand the "internal life" of movements, both the structures and cultural processes that facilitate and impede activism (e.g. Hirsch 1990; Taylor and Whittier 1992). I address all of these questions below, organized into six somewhat coherent frameworks that address the why, how, who, and what of activism: strain theory, resource mobilization theory, political opportunity theory, cultural approaches, oppositional consciousness framework, and new social movements theory.[2]

In this way, I employ a fairly standard method of reviewing these frameworks. I provide a genealogy of these frameworks, describe the contexts in which these frameworks developed, identify the strengths and weaknesses associated with each, and evaluate the utility of each framework. These frameworks stake out different positions along a continuum that is the defining feature of the sociological perspective. On the one end of the continuum, sociologists speak of the importance of social structure. There are forces that exist around us, above us, and even in us that make our lives not entirely our own; there are patterns and "pressures" that induce those patterns; and they operate somewhat independently of our conscious awareness. On the other end of that continuum, sociologists speak of the power of human agency. Even though structures shape individuals, constrain and shape behaviors, predispositions, and attitudes, these structures are the creation of individuals as they make decisions, interact with others on the basis of shared interests and attitudes, and create social forms that sustain, reproduce and, most importantly, change society. Each framework on social movements participates in this duality. Some focus more on the structure side—the rules, roles, resources, ideas, values, and norms that shape activists and activism while others focus more on the agency side—the decisions, interests, beliefs, emotions, and processes of interaction that change those structures and help create new ones.

This standard method of review, while necessary, is not enough to bring those frameworks into dialogue with activists. These frameworks, after all, were developed in the service of scholarly knowledge not in the service of social change. To rectify this, we must situate these frameworks in dialogue with activists. We must ask: how do these frameworks help us make social change? Do they tell us what forms of social change are most effective for building a progressive society? How do they understand the sources of the inequalities or grievances that lead people to action? What courses of action do they suggest to change those inequalities and alleviate those grievances? These questions and this challenge make the structure/agency duality productive for an activist sociology.

Strain Theory

The earliest formal framework utilized by sociologists did not distinguish social movements from other types of collective behavior such as fads, panics, and mobs (Buechler 2004; Marx and McAdam 1994). Labeled the strain theory of collective behavior, this framework called attention to societal strain or major structural changes that create grievances or problems of living for large numbers of people. Changes such as rapid industrialization and urbanization, large-scale migration, and economic depression are mentioned as examples of these societal strains as the causes of the subsequent personal strain on individuals (Smelser 1962). The reference to personal strain (as well as social strain) is deliberate because the societal changes do not immediately result in externally directed dissatisfaction and grievance. Initially, these grievances are internalized and lead to confusion and alienation, according to this framework. Anomie, the sociological concept used to refer to normlessness, is an important feature of this theoretical framework. With anomie, the guidelines you once used to provide for yourself and your family no longer "deliver the goods"; alternative guidelines or norms begin to exist and you are unsure which set you should follow. In addition, the groups you relied on for social and economic support no longer exist, having been disrupted or destroyed by these large-scale processes. The eventual outcome of this personal strain is some sort of collective action.[3]

Given this understanding of how large-scale social change affects individuals and groups, it is not surprising that this theoretical framework conflates many conceptually different forms of collective action. Mob behavior, fads, social and moral panics as well as organized and sustained protest are all viewed as social psychological adjustments or responses to societal strain. This understanding also predisposes the framework to seeing collective action as spontaneous, irrational, and undirected.

The strain theory of collective behavior emerged in the 1950s at a very different historical moment from our current one. The United States was enjoying an era of unparalleled economic growth and political dominance after having endured the conflicts and calamities of the Great Depression and after defeating the brutal Nazi regime and containing, albeit provisionally, Soviet totalitarianism. When people thought about social movements, they usually thought of these totalitarianisms which delivered misery to so many. In the United States, we felt that economic growth was "lifting all boats" and creating not only social stability but also a value consensus among most Americans. We were confident that our democratic and capitalist systems were the models for the peaceful resolution of political differences and we exported them, sometimes forcibly, around the world.

Sociology participated in this historical moment by developing consensus-based theories of society. The strain theory of collective behavior was one prime example. This theory saw conflict as the temporary response to large-scale social change that would soon dissipate as economic growth addressed economic grievances or as conflict became addressed in mainstream democratic institutions. Implying or in some cases explicitly stating that this conflict was psychological in nature only added to the view that the normal state of affairs was consensus and equilibrium.[4]

For several obvious reasons, this framework has gotten a "bad rap" by many sociologists. First, we see the inadequacy of using a single framework to understand such wildly disparate phenomena as activism, moral panics, and mob behavior. While these are all examples of collective behavior that originate outside "normal" politics, the source and the causes of this behavior are very different from one another. Activism typically hails from below by groups with some level of collective consciousness about their actions. Moral panics are typically engineered from above by cultural elites who trigger social anxieties and project them onto vulnerable groups (Gusfield 1962; Rubin 1984). Mob behavior is in itself a problematic concept but typically references some sort of spontaneous collective response to an external event and is triggered by the intensity of close physical contact. In these ways, activism is conceptually different and requires a theoretical framework that, among other things, calls attention to the social causes of the grievances and the response of the group mobilizing to address those grievances.

In addition, several crucial steps are missing as the framework moves from structural dislocations to individual responses to those dislocations. Surely, one response to social strain can be a sense of uprootedness but that response is not the only one. To represent it as such gives the impression that all activist energy derives from a psychological response to this alienation. In other words, that response is fundamentally emotional: expressions of discontent that are therapeutic or pathological in nature but definitely not political, deliberative, and rational.

The strain theory also views collective action as attempts to find alternative groups or networks because social change has severed individuals' previous ties to one another. Collective behavior then feeds off the alienation caused by social strain and prevents individuals from becoming reintegrated into the social order by using the procedures of democratic politics (Kornhauser 1959). Related to this is the final problem with the framework: that is, the equally problematic assumption that social ties to others are inevitably severed by social change or social dislocation. Another response could be using those existing ties to weather these changes or using those ties to resist these changes.

Despite these many problems, there is something to be salvaged from this framework in the concepts of structural dislocations and deeply felt grievances. For sociologists and activists who want to get at the root cause of things, structures and structural change are where we look. As the overview of the historical and contemporary context of Hartford's progressive activism provided in Chapter 3 points out, several key structural dislocations such as depression, deindustrialization, immigration, and gentrification played key roles in the development of progressive collective action in the city. The strain theory of collective behavior does draw our attention to these phenomena even if it is more interested in mapping the social psychology of people's responses to them than in analyzing the precise nature of these dislocations and their various consequences for people's lives. Other frameworks, particularly the new social movements framework discussed below, give a more central role to these large-scale social changes and how those changes affect both the nature of the demands and the organizing structures activists create and use to press those demands.

As discussed in much more detail in Chapter 4, activists themselves acknowledge many of these changes when they puzzle over or strategize in the face of the loss of good jobs and the proliferation of bad ones, the unbridled power of the war-making national state, or the neglect of the city's neighborhoods in favor of a gentrified downtown. Jack, a particularly astute community organizer, recognizes the challenges of some of these changes for neighborhood-based activism:

> It's scary in New England, if you don't have a college education you are doomed to not making it...The gaps are getting worse between the folks with real good jobs and the folks that are in the service shit jobs. So we have to figure out how to win like the unions did forty years ago, it's just going to be a new play. We have to figure out how we get living wage jobs, how we get benefits, I mean, we're moving away from employers providing healthcare benefits. That's a scary thing because our whole system is based on that. So in the whole healthcare field, and the wage field, the economic pressures are moving away from us and making it harder for our folks to really gain. They're losing. And so those are some fights that are worth fighting, but I can't say right yet we've got a handle on exactly how to win them.

Clearly, there is a place for the concept of social dislocation in a theoretical framework that is both intellectually rigorous and practically useful.

Additionally, these activists would insist on a role for deeply felt grievances as a motivator for collective action, although not in the way that strain theorists represent them. The interviews I conducted with activists were chock full of various emotional responses to social dislocations and other structural inequalities: anger, sadness, pain, hope, passion, to name a few. Whether they are discussing strategy and goals (Chapter 4), participation, commitment, and burnout (Chapters 6 and 7), or the nature of their activist identities (Chapter 8), these emotions well up and are entangled in most of what they do. These same activists would recoil, however, at the suggestion that these emotions are pathological or evidence of an anomic relation to the world around them. To the contrary, these emotions are rational responses to real inequities and are generated not in isolation but in interaction with similarly-feeling others. Regina captures perfectly part of this dynamic in response to my question about emotion:

I'm really slow to anger. I'm angry, but it's kind of a mellow anger. My anger makes me think, "What am I going to do about it?" My anger is scheming... scheming more than steaming. And so right away I start to look for solutions or actions.

Emotion and strategic action do not work at cross purposes. Like many of my activists, Regina stresses how emotions are strategically employed as part of a strategy of political and cultural change. The chapters that follow illustrate this limitation of the strain theory of collective behavior even as they hold onto the notion of *"deeply felt"* in any definition of grievances.

Resource Mobilization Theory

Of course, activists do not wait for social dislocations to engage in collective action. A second framework, resource mobilization theory, acknowledges both the impatience and commitment of activists and addresses some of the limitations of the strain model of collective action.[5] The resource mobilization framework does not concern itself too much with the broad structural changes or social dislocations highlighted in some other models. Unlike strain theory, its emphasis is on human agency and the conditions that give rise to collective displays of that agency. As others have pointed out, the resource mobilization approach addresses the "how" rather than the "why" of collective action.

Resource mobilization theory starts with an assumption very close to most activists' hearts: the notion that grievances are always with us (McAdam 1982: 21). Therefore, there is little reason to analyze broad structural changes at the root of these grievances. According to resource mobilization theory, we always have grievances that are socially caused. The challenge for activists and the intellectual puzzle for scholars become how those grievances get turned into collective action and social change. The focus is less on those structural changes and more on the dynamics of mobilizing to address the grievances resulting from omnipresent inequality.

The resource mobilization framework foregrounds the concepts of resource aggregation, organizational structure, and the relationship between the organization and its environment as key to social movement success (McCarthy and Zald 1977). As described below, this framework conceives of social movements like any kind of collective endeavor with its attendant challenges of funding, recruitment, agendas, and engagements with other actors from the social environment.

Not surprisingly, this framework was developed and became dominant in the 1970s as scholars, many of whom were participants in the social movements of the day, became increasingly dissatisfied with the negative assumptions and connotations of the dominant strain-based approaches to collective action. These scholars did not see new grievances bubbling up as the result of dramatic social dislocations but long-standing grievances of racism, segregation, and discrimination finally being directly confronted by new activism. They did not see alienated or anomic individuals taking to the streets with anger and without forethought but politically engaged individuals consciously and rationally using the resources at their disposal to calculate and strategize about tactics, goals, and allies. They did not see crowds but organized masses. They did not see spontaneous eruptions but carefully planned campaigns (Morris 1984; Payne 1995).

Armed with these observations and their dissatisfaction with strain theory, scholars systematically studied a whole host of mobilizations connected to social movements. These studies found that the key ingredient of a successful mobilization was the aggregation of resources. Those groups that were able to procure, organize, and deploy resources in strategic ways were better able to gain concessions from elites as compared to those who were not as successful. Further, these resources took several forms: economic resources of money to finance campaigns, infrastructural resources such as meeting places, materials, and technology to enable the day-to-day business of these campaigns; and organizational resources such as settings or social networks to provide the membership base and leadership cadre for these campaigns. This theoretical model reimagined social movements not as disorganized phenomena on the margins of society but as organized and strategic phenomena in the mainstream. It did this by viewing them like any other formal organization that must maneuver and succeed in a variety of environments.

The frequently studied civil rights movement provides the prototype for scholars who came to support the resource mobilization framework and thus serves as a good illustration of the components of this theoretical framework. The reorganization of southern agriculture, the subsequent urbanization of the south, and the migration of African Americans to those cities in both the north and the south increased the amount of resources going into highly segregated black communities (McAdam 1982; Piven and Cloward 1979). Black churches and schools grew in these communities and became the organizational settings for the resistance, mobilization, and strategizing of the movement (Payne 1995). These organizations contributed the constituencies for struggle, the money for bail, flyers, and travel; the foot soldiers for door knocking, picketing and praying; and the leaders for the public face of the movement. Deeply felt grievances did not suddenly materialize. They were of centuries-long duration; the key to success was the aggregation and use of resources. Also key was the strategic use of those resources by analyzing and then targeting the appropriate environments to leverage concessions from elites in these environments. Some of this research called attention to the strategic use of northern liberal allies or the strategic use of the divisions between national political elites concerned with allaying crisis and winning elections and local elites concerned with maintaining the Jim Crow system of racist power in the south (Oberschall 1973). Other research stressed the successful mobilization of the indigenous resources within African American communities and the power of organized masses to pressure elites (Morris 1984).

Political Opportunity Theory

Closely related to the resource mobilization framework and in some sense an extension of the idea that social movement actors are rational and strategic beings who must successfully negotiate their social environment is the political opportunity framework.[6] This framework foregrounds the political environment within which movements emerge and develop as key to the success of social movements. The political environment has been defined in many different ways in this theoretical framework: electoral alignments and shifts, ideological differences among different branches of government, division of power among these different branches of government, and popular crises of confidence in an existing political regime (Tarrow 1994: 85). Regardless of the definition, the political environment with its internal weaknesses and instabilities and its different sets of interests and allies associated with it, is key because it provides opportunities for activists to unsettle the prevailing balance of power and gain some concessions from elites. In this way, concepts of resources and opportunities frequently coexist in this framework.

From this research in the political opportunity framework, we have gotten the concept of protest waves or protest cycles (Tarrow 1994: 153). The exploitation of political opportunities opens up the space for large-scale protest from a number of different groups. This heightened period of activity generates its own particular dynamics involving increased participation, national attention, competition among protest organizations, the decline of some of these organizations, the absorption of others into mainstream politics, and the repression of others by the state. Besides the particular dynamics associated with social movements in a protest wave, the larger point and one contribution of the political opportunity approach is a distinction it makes between the vast majority of collective action that does not occur inside these protest waves and collective action that does occur in these historically exceptional periods.

Using the example of the civil rights movement again, many scholars see the mobilization of resources as a necessary but not sufficient cause of the emergence, development, and success of the movement. As alluded to above, part of the genius of many of the struggles of this movement was the ability of organizers to correctly "read" the political opportunity structure: to know when and how to play one elite against another and how to use allies to put pressure on political elites. Some of the most notable campaigns of the civil rights movement—the Montgomery Bus Boycott of 1956 and the Freedom Rides throughout the South in 1960, for example—explicitly played on these elite vulnerabilities emphasized by the political opportunity framework. The bus boycott depleted the profits of the bus company that then pressured local political officials to resolve the crisis. The freedom rides created a confrontation between southern politicians who would not ensure the safety of the riders and national officials who had to (at least rhetorically) abide by the constitutional principle of racial integration in interstate travel (Morris 1981; 1993). In these examples, the indigenous resources of the movement interact with the political opportunity structure of the U.S. state to inform strategy and goals.

Research using these frameworks has produced many of the concepts that are the standard fare of social movement analysis. As already mentioned, material resources, social movement organizations, and political opportunity structures are foundational. Other concepts or dynamics, perhaps not so immediately obvious, also derive from these approaches. For example, some research in these traditions has demonstrated the importance of pre-existing organizations or social networks which may not be directed to social change or collective action purposes but serve as "breeding grounds" or "training centers" for social movement activists; what one sociologist, Aldon Morris (1984), refers to as local movement centers. In the above example of the civil rights movement, the black church clearly served that role. Other research on the emergence of the feminist movement has pointed to the women's caucuses of the Democratic Party that brought women together, taught them specific organizing skills, and encouraged but then thwarted their political activity (Costain 1992).

While this concept assists in understanding the relationship between organizations and the environment prior to the onset of a social movement, research has also identified other concepts and dynamics useful in examining that relationship once in the throes of social movement activity. One particularly important dynamic is known as the radical flank effect and involves the relationship between social movement organizations on the one hand, and their relationship to elites in their environment on the other hand (Haines 1988; 1984). This involves two sectors or organizations in a campaign or a movement fighting for a similar goal: one group demands the goal using traditional interest-group tactics; the other group pursues a more disruptive set of strategies such as public demonstrations, civil disobedience, and radical rhetoric.[7] The encounter with elites to meet the demands is made by those engaged in lobbying and education. They employ some version of: "we are the reasonable one, give us what we want or else you will have to engage the radicals." It is a strategy to deliver progressive goals by playing the radicals against the reformers in the movement's encounter with elites.

Another closely related dynamic also involves a social movement organization and its interaction with elites and is known as elite channeling or social movement cooptation (Jenkins and Eckert 1986; Piven and Cloward 1979). This interaction involves negotiations between the challenging organization and elites whereby elites meet some of the challenger's demands in return for certain concessions from the challenger. Research that has documented this dynamic finds that these negotiations result in the transformation and decline of the outside challenge. It results in either the decline of protest, the increased formalization of the organization or the incorporation of social movement leaders into the ranks of elite organizations. Depending on one's political perspective, some researchers see this as success and the incorporation of social movement concerns into the operation of normal politics while others see is as cooptation and a way for elites to stave off greater challenges and preserve their continued dominance.

Not surprisingly, the resource mobilization and political opportunity frameworks "feel" right to many progressive activists since these frameworks resonate so strongly with these activists' day-to-day activities. The stories activists tell about their work are often about tracking down funding and applying for grants, procuring meeting space and developing leaders, and spending countless hours "reading" the political landscape—activities highlighted by the resource mobilization and political opportunity frameworks and discussed at length in Chapters 4 and 5. Jack, who has done organizing in the city for 31 years, stresses one aspect of the resource mobilization framework in his evaluation of the past and present state of community organizing:

> Foundations back in the 70s were putting up money for organizing, for neighborhood organizing...They were just doing it kind of like as a flavor du jour back then but they have not stuck with it. And so it is very difficult to find foundation dollars right now for community organizing, very hard. And that's really made a difference in terms of how much neighborhood organizing goes on.

As we will see in Chapter 5, anxieties about funding are such a constant for many progressive organizations that it sometimes went unmentioned during my conversations with activists.

Labor activist, Laura M., employs the strategizing implicit in the political opportunity framework when she describes how her union took advantage of the different interests among different political elites in forcing management to abandon its intimidation tactics during a union organizing drive:

> You grab that community, in this case it's Hartford, but it's also the college... You know, the professors were involved, and the students were involved, and we were dragging the politicians into it...Because [the college] stepped in and said to Marriott in front of us, and they never do this in front of the union, and said, "I want it done. I don't want my professors running around going to demonstrations. I don't want the students involved in demonstrations. I don't want that stuff to happen on my campus anymore, I want this done."

As Laura M. implies and elaborates further in Chapter 4, many activists would reject a passive role in terms of these political opportunities. Instead, they see themselves as creating opportunities rather than merely exploiting already existing ones. Either way, activists embrace the fundamental assumption of these frameworks that activism is about organizations oriented to changing policy and influencing the state. As Sidney Tarrow (1994) summarizes so cogently, social movements are "politics by other means."

These frameworks of resource mobilization and political opportunity are especially valuable for activists in that they are well-suited as road maps through several organizing dilemmas, thus addressing the "so what" challenge for these scholarly frameworks. This is not surprising in light of the activist origins of these theoretical frameworks.

One example illustrates the utility of both the resource mobilization and political opportunity frameworks as guides for activism. In research on the women's movement, scholars have found that different organizational structures promote different social movement activities and are associated with different sets of costs and benefits. Organizations that are more centralized with formal membership lists and clear divisions of labor are best suited for policy advocacy and policy change and less suited for consciousness-raising or for recruiting new people with new ideas into the organization (Staggenborg 1989). Organizations that are more decentralized and more fluid in terms of membership and the division of labor have different strengths and weaknesses. They encourage creativity in strategies and goals and build group solidarity but are less adept at engaging in the policy-making process (Reger 2002). In addition, other research also on the women's movement argues that the effectiveness of different organizational forms depends on the political opportunity structure. More centralized organizational forms are most effective in relatively open opportunity structures which provide leverage for these organizations to exert their claims. More decentralized forms of organization are better suited to relatively closed opportunity structures which provide little opening for external claims making (Costain 1992; Whittier 1995). In a sense, social movements find it difficult to do policy-directed work in times of closed or limited political opportunities; thus they turn their attention to other goals such as consciousness raising, public education, or other cultural goals (Whittier 1995). Research such as this can be very useful to activists as they discuss what they want to do, how they want to do it, and the possibilities of success and failure.

Even while activists see some of their work as consistent with the claims of the resource mobilization and political opportunity frameworks, their motivations, actions, strategizing, and goals are more complex than what can be captured by these frameworks.[8] We need to temper this image of the constantly calculating, organization-building, opportunity-seizing activist. Activists "act" for many different non-instrumental or utilitarian reasons ranging from religiously or politically informed values, moral claims, group loyalties and identities (Gould 2002; Hirsch 1990; Jasper 1997; Rupp and Taylor 1999). Laura M., the labor activist quoted above, is motivated by "the class war" between workers and managers and the "need to organize ever greater numbers of workers." Lisa, who organizes young Latina women, says: "a big motivator for me was the Gospels, and listening to what Jesus is saying we ought to be doing." These two excerpts suggest that large portions of what they do and why they do it are written out of these theoretical frameworks. For example, activists speak not only of building organizations and changing power structures but of changing themselves and others on both a personal and cultural level.

In these ways, activists give voice to some of the limitations of these frameworks and suggest the need for frameworks that deal more centrally with the role of culture and interpretation in social movements. Since these "newer" frameworks all focus on the meanings, ideas, and symbolic systems created in the process of social interaction, I refer to them as cultural frameworks. In doing so, I include in this cultural framework some approaches that others have treated separately, namely the symbolic interaction and social construction approaches. All these approaches, however, foreground the contingent nature of meaning formation as accomplished through interaction with others. While seeing these processes of interaction and interpretation as important, I want to foreground the cultural products of these efforts: the meanings and ideas of activists, the symbolic demands of movements, and the identities of individuals that are both causes and consequences of collective action.[9]

Cultural Theoretical Frameworks

One way to understand these frameworks is in comparison to the resource mobilization and political opportunity frameworks from which they partly emerged. Resource mobilization and political opportunity frameworks downplay the non-cognitive factors that lead people to engage in social movements and ignore the important social psychological processes that take place within individuals upon participation in social movements. Partly because they see grievances as always present, these frameworks also see the ideas that transform grievances into public or actionable issues as a purely organizational or political problem and not one embedded in culture, emotion, and social interaction (Jasper and Goodwin 1999). Individuals act not only according to self-interest or material interests but also on the basis of social interests that emerge in the process of interaction with others. These interests may entail group solidarity, ideological conviction or personal identity support (Hirsh 1990; Mansbridge and Morris 2001). Because the resource mobilization and political opportunity frameworks see movements as focused mainly on instrumental action, they do not consider the ways that movements help construct identities or how an individual's identity or biography gives shape to social movements. Movements may be as much about changing people's understandings of themselves and the world around them as about changing laws and policies. These frameworks declare the importance of culture as an important resource in the mobilization of social movements, as something created in the process of social movements, as consequential for internal dynamics of social movements, and as an important goal of social movements (Rochon 1998).

Like previous theoretical frameworks, these cultural frameworks also emerged as a result of several historical developments. As the U.S. political landscape became less hospitable to progressive organizing in the 1980s, scholars began to notice that, while some forms of activism declined, other forms proliferated. This "newer" activism involved life-style, consciousness-raising, and identity-based concerns and did not necessarily have the state as its target. Upon closer inspection, scholars realized that these supposedly new types of activism had always existed and this insight led them to question the adequacy of frameworks that saw activism mainly as "politics by other means." This questioning led these scholars to a vibrant intellectual tradition in European social movement study, new social movements theory. This theory saw the state as that which activists resisted, not necessarily that which activists wanted access to or something from. In addition, this tradition defined social movements as, first and foremost, symbolic and interpretive phenomena, a set of meanings, discourses, and action projects that challenged the dominant culture (Taylor and Whittier 1995). In these ways, culture began to be taken more seriously by U.S.-based social movement scholars.

Several concepts have emerged from these frameworks that both resonate with activists' experiences and provide guidance to activists in doing their work. I introduced this chapter with one of these concepts—framing. This dynamic process of cultural packaging clearly illustrates the importance of ideas and social meanings for social movement scholars and also for activists who must think through the multiple dilemmas and tradeoffs involved in organizing an action or mounting a campaign. Again, labor activist, Laura M., describes a framing strategy during a particularly contentious struggle to organize hospitality workers in a major hotel in Hartford:

> We made the campaign high profile. There was one camp of people bringing the presidential debates into town and saying, "This is how we're going to save Hartford." And our theme was really consistent, "*We* are Hartford." You know, if you want to save Hartford, you don't have a debate come into town, because when the debate leaves, what's left? We're what's left! So if you want to save Hartford, what you've got to do is approve the ability of the people who live and work there to make a living. And so [we put] workers' future out front and center of the debate. No pun intended...

Although Laura's framing strategy was directed mainly at the media, there are multiple audiences that must be considered in deciding on a framing strategy: your already-recruited constituency, the constituency you want to target, sets of influential allies and bystanders, and particular targets.

Framing strategies may differ depending on the audience and each strategy has different sets of costs and benefits. In addition, there are typically three components to framing. A diagnostic dimension frames the problem; a prognostic dimension frames the solution; and a motivational dimension tells us why we should care and be moved to act (Noakes and Johnston 2005: 5–6). As we will see later, activists routinely engage in framing activities but do not typically think of these multiple dimensions in their decision-making process. Nonetheless, this concept and others from this framework provide new ways of thinking about the challenges of turning personal troubles into public issues by acknowledging the creativity and agency of individuals and groups and their active use of culture in engineering this shift.

A second concept—collective identity—has emerged from these cultural frameworks and is related to framing in its attention to meanings and motivations. Instead of focusing on the packaging of the movement to relevant audiences, the concept of collective identity focuses instead on the processes that create a sense of "we-ness" among social movement actors: how we "package" ourselves vis à vis our relationship to the movement. Collective identity refers to the incorporation of the frames, discourses, and ideologies of a particular social movement into the social psychology of the individual, affecting her/his values, and cognitive, behavioral and emotional dispositions (Gould 2002; Howard 2000; Polletta and Jasper 2001; Stryker *et al.* 2000). It also refers to the relationship of the individual to other similarly thinking and feeling individuals such that they all consider themselves part of the same group or community (Taylor and Whittier 1992). Conversely, collective identity also implies a conscious awareness of and sometimes antagonistic relationship to other groups or communities the individual perceives as not sharing the same activist commitments, understandings, and memberships (Gamson 1997). This collective identity, moreover, is not static but formed and changed in interaction with many significant others and events: opponents, leaders, allies, protest events, etc. (Einwohner 1999; Robnett 2005; Taylor and Whittier 1992).

This concept has been the most productive one to emerge from these cultural frameworks. It has given scholars a way to move beyond the admittedly dubious assumptions of resource mobilization and political opportunity frameworks that individuals join social movements for self-interest or narrowly instrumental reasons. The concept of collective identity captures the uniquely social reasons for social movement participation. The process of collective action may create group-based solidarities, or pre-existing social cleavages based on race, ethnicity, gender, or sexuality may provide the building blocks and initial entry into collective action. In any event, the concept of collective identity gives scholars a way to understand social movements not simply as "different kinds of formal organizations" or "politics by other means," as depicted by resource mobilization and political opportunity frameworks but as more open-ended, ephemeral, multi-faceted social formations.

Along those same lines, this concept also adds some nuance to accounts of the inner workings of social movements. Resource mobilization and political opportunity frameworks call attention to the decision-making processes, the strategy sessions, the debates over goals, etc., and how different organizational structures facilitate different internal processes. Again, the collective identity concept encourages us to view those internal processes as both instrumental and expressive in nature, as a function of resources and opportunities but also of group understandings and how those understandings affect decision making, strategy, goals, etc. (Valocchi 2009).

The utility of this concept is glaringly obvious from my conversations with activists. These are highlighted in Chapter 8 where I discuss activist identities. Discussions of strategy and tactics, activities, goals, allies are almost never only about those things; they are also about who these activists are; how they define themselves; how they see the nature of the project they are engaged in; and how they feel about what they are doing. For Carolyn, another veteran activist who entered activism through second-wave feminism in the 1960s, "who she is" and "what she does" are deeply connected:

> So, for me, as a feminist lesbian, that's [i.e. building coalitions] challenging. Because I stay committed to my issues, and yet I realize that I may be in a setting working on an issue that have many folks who are not going to agree

with just basically who I am, let alone my rights, and won't make those connections between racism, sexism, homophobia, poverty issues. But I guess my commitment is to always be very—I am the same person.

Not surprising in light of Carolyn's comments, if there are internal conflicts and tensions about the direction of a movement, many times these are due to the different collective identities embraced by its members. In these ways, cultural meanings, biography, collective identity intermingle with questions about resources, organizational structure, and political opportunities.

One final observation can be gleaned from my conversations with activists which is relevant to the cultural frameworks on social movements. Stated bluntly, culture also can be used as a resource or an opportunity. Many of my activists have few of the necessary resources that these other frameworks see as crucial for successful social movements. They have no money, no infrastructure, no emergent leaders; all they have is a sense of injustice and a pre-existing collective identity. As Luz, one of the several grassroots activists in the city, succinctly states:

> I was just doing stuff 'cause it was good to do. We needed to do it in order to get what we needed. It was as simple as that. People say you need to look at this or that. For me it's: "what you want; what you need; how you gonna get."

Furthermore, these endeavors may not always result in sustained activity directed toward changing the state or the practices of mainstream institutions but they nonetheless may be oriented toward other forms of social change. These activists do not stand around analyzing the opportunity structure to identify vulnerabilities to be exploited but nonetheless engage in action which may indeed create vulnerabilities where there were none. In these ways, the cultural frameworks with their associated concepts resonate quite strongly with the identities, dispositions, and activities of progressive activists. Scholars can carve up activists' worlds into discrete chunks and, indeed, this carving up may be useful for analysis, but if we forget about "the chunks we left behind" and do not reinsert them into the analysis we do both ourselves and activists a disservice.

Oppositional Consciousness Framework

A closely related theoretical framework defined by Aldon Morris and his collaborators (1992; 2001) as the oppositional consciousness approach does not dismiss the importance of collective identity, framing or the other concepts that highlight the interpretive processes and collective meaning making that individuals use to engage in collective action. Instead, it insists that structural inequalities shape the kinds of cultural work that takes place prior to and in the development of social movements. In this way, it brings together some of the concerns of strain, resource mobilization, and political opportunity approaches about large-scale structures of inequality with the concerns of the cultural approaches about how individuals and groups understand and interpret the consequences of those structures.

This oppositional consciousness framework focuses on longstanding institutional cleavages in society that create the preconditions for an oppositional consciousness. Cleavages such as class, race, ethnicity, gender, and sexuality precede individual instances of collective action and exist for historical and contemporary reasons. In many cases, these cleavages become the building blocks for future collective action and for the development of a collective identity that undergoes change as a result of that collective action. As mentioned above, it is the structural corrective to cultural approaches to collective action in that the oppositional consciousness approach pays attention to "how objective structures of domination interact with subjectively experienced domination to produce collective action" (Morris and Braine 2001: 24). According to this framework, structural systems of inequality generate unequal power relations and encourage the creation of an oppositional culture by the subordinate group. This oppositional culture provides the symbolic and discursive resources for an oppositional consciousness necessary for the creation of a social movement. Although there may be other bases of collective identity that precede or are created in the process of social movements, these structurally rooted cleavages are oftentimes catalysts.

In addition, the oppositional consciousness created by systems of inequality is quite complex and can be mobilized by activists in different ways. The oppositional consciousness framework captures this complexity by borrowing the sociological concept of intersectionality from feminist theory and applying it to social movements (Collins 1991; Crenshaw 1995). Intersectionality is the matrix of an individual's identities and social locations along the dimensions of class, race, ethnicity, gender, and sexuality. It is a matrix because any one individual can occupy structurally different positions on these dimensions. A white lower-class straight woman, for example, possesses different "bundles of penalty and privilege" (Collins 2006: 244) as a consequence of her positions on the different hierarchies of power and identity mentioned above. Thus, it refers to a system of power that allocates life chances and economic opportunities based on an individual's location along these various hierarchies. But it is also an indicator of individual identity in that it refers to a social psychological construct that communicates a subjective awareness about who one is and how one is compelled to act (Collins, 1991; hooks 1981; King 1988).

We will see the operation of this dynamic throughout the book but particularly in Chapter 8 that focuses on activist identity. As Carmen, a poor Latina activist, states in that chapter:

> Once I learned my roots, and I started realizing what oppression was, and how our culture has been oppressed for so many...way beyond six hundred years. And what racism was, and how internalized racism begins...that [my organizing] began!

The interplay between the structural and subjective components of intersectionality is "where the action is" for the oppositional consciousness framework. Carmen's elision between her identity as Latina, her subjective awareness of this identity, and her interest in organizing suggests that one's oppositional consciousness influences the content of one's social movement politics. How an individual chooses to construct an intersectional identity affects a whole host of social movement outcomes: strategies and framing, goals and coalitions (Bernstein 2005; Kurtz 2002; Stockdill 2003; Valocchi 2009).

Oppositional consciousness informed by structurally based identity interests and issues features prominently in some activists' stories of what they do and why they do it. For the most part, activists see these identities as essential components of themselves. Of course, they do not always understand the ways that institutionally and culturally imposed processes of labeling create the identities that then become the rallying points for their collective action. This scholarly framework points not only to the inequalities in resource distribution and material benefits as a result of the hierarchies of class, race, ethnicity, gender, and sexuality but also to the oppressions built into the naming process itself. Activists readily understand how to mobilize to address those resource and material inequalities; they are less certain about how to productively oppose the label, categories, and identities that support those inequalities. The identities, even if they are defined as subordinate and exist only in relation to the dominant identities, give them a place from which to exert their claims. As we will see in Chapters 4 and 8, the activists who come closest to this understanding are those with intersectional identities wedded to a deep coalitional politics.

New Social Movements Theory

Like the oppositional consciousness approach, a final theoretical framework also integrates both structural and cultural factors into an explanation of why social movements emerge and how they develop. This framework, referred to somewhat awkwardly by the moniker "new social movements theory," was referred to briefly above in my discussion of the European influences on U.S.-based cultural approaches.[10] It is not surprising then that it dovetails with many of the assertions of the cultural framework, most centrally with the concept of collective identity. It situates this analysis, however, within a macro-historical account of the structural causes of social movements. For example, according to new social movements theory, social movements in the developed capitalist world tend to be more identity-based and post-materialist in nature, hence the term "new" social movements (Melucci 1989). This difference between the old and new social movements tends to be exaggerated, however. Older movements such as the labor movement has as much to do with building a collective identity as with demanding a redistribution of power in the workplace (Calhoun 1993). Newer movements such as the gay and lesbian movement have as much to do with the extension of tangible material benefits as they do with changing the meanings of the categories of "gay" and "lesbian"

(Bernstein 2002). Nevertheless, the distinction draws our attention to the changes in the modes of production and consumption of the economy and in the changing nature of the state's intervention into civil society as causes of social movements (Buechler 2000: 45–51).

In some sense, this new social movements framework returns scholars back to the macro-historical changes that give rise to and shape the nature of social movements and collective action first developed in strain theory. Although the ideas of strain theory have fallen out of fashion (and for some very good reasons), the "baby"—its emphasis on structural causes—was thrown out along with the "bathwater" of individual pathology, irrationality, and anomie. The new social movements framework recovers and complicates this old assertion that changes in the broad social, political, and economic environments are causally related to the emergence of (somewhat) new forms of social movements and collective action. The other frameworks that have dominated scholars' thinking—the resource mobilization, the political opportunity, and the cultural frameworks—focus more on the how, what, and who of social movements and give short shrift to this other important question of "why."

The specific answers to this "why" depend on which new social movement scholar you listen to. For some, it is a more nuanced variation of strain theory with its emphasis on the social dislocations associated with industrialization, urbanization, immigration—now updated to account for the additional strains associated with a post-industrial, information-based, service-oriented society. Globalization, mass-mediated forms of communication, and state expansion figure centrally in this version creating more diffuse yet more insidious forms of inequality (Hirsch 1988; Steinmetz 1994).

Analyses of urban social movements from this framework focus on the rise of cities as centers of multinational information processing and coordination, the coalitions formed between corporate elites, real estate interests, and government to ensure favorable business conditions in the city, and the transformation of the physical and social environments of the city as the structural preconditions of urban movements (Castells 1983). These movements typically entail attempts to gain more services, goods, or jobs to compensate for the negative consequences of these structural developments. Just as important, these movements entail the creation, consolidation, or reconfiguring of a collective identity among the participants in collective action. You get a glimpse of some of these "big processes" at work in Hartford in the comment below by Steve, who has been involved not only in labor struggles but in neighborhood, peace, and gender equity struggles over the past 30 years:

> The two most loaded words in the city, the two most politically potent words in the city for a good 10–15 years were neighborhood and downtown. Neighborhoods meant, and it was a class and race thing, neighborhoods meant the people who lived and died in this city who struggled to raise their families. Who are homeowners or renters, black and white and brown. And downtown

were the people who owned all the best property, none of whom lived in the city, were all white and all rich...It meant not necessarily the physical space, it meant those people.

In this quote, Steve captures, albeit obliquely, the processes of globalized capital, post-industrial consumerism, and the intersection of these interests with place-based real-estate interests. Steve also captures perfectly the identities produced by these processes that are also part of this new social movements perspective.

For other theorists of this framework, these systemic changes involve the domination of large-scale bureaucracies that tend to hide power relationships and monopolize knowledge and information. Although the institutions referenced are science, the academy, corporations, and the state, this version of the new social movements framework emphasizes the knowledge systems or cultural discourses produced by these institutions (Melucci 1996). Thus, the strains and the grievances produced by these institutions are not necessarily economic or material in nature but cultural; the result of the increased colonization and commodification of an individual's identity and life space. Thus, movements emerge as much to escape the state as to get something from the state; they emerge to create free spaces or carve out autonomy from private or state actors who encroach on civic space; they create their own identities to assert a set of interests and meanings apart from the knowledge created by these "colonizing" institutions (Melucci 1989).

These forms of resistance may be more symbolic and expressive than material and political. The participants in these movements may adopt protest tactics that are more personal in nature like living outside "colonized spaces" and/or actively creating non-colonized spaces in urban or rural areas. These tactics have been described as prefigurative politics to capture the idea that they are aimed at prefiguring the desired political change on a large-scale level by living and acting according to different norms, values, and ideals in one's personal life (Breines 1988). This sense of "being in the world differently" is communicated by Julia, who cut her activist teeth in the global justice movement in San Francisco and now heads an activist theater group in Hartford:

> We operate according to 100% straight consensus which blows people's minds. Sure we have disagreements but we are really well trained in it we have been doing it for a long time. We came together with affinity. We came together... when I was learning through the global justice movement what an affinity group was and how much easier that makes it when you have affinity and we truly have affinity. We have great, great love for each other. We have no doubt that we are in it for each other's good. So we are all on the same page for the grander stuff anyway.

These politics stand in contrast to the politics of "old social movements" referred to as strategic politics, a more instrumental, material, and policy-oriented way of achieving social change.

Activists do not typically use these concepts of "colonizing life worlds," "commodification," or "prefigurative politics" to situate either themselves or their activities in the city's progressive movement or in the general environment of the city, the nation, or the globe. And, they do not tend to think about the large-scale structural features of their environments when reflecting and acting on some aspect of those environments.

It is quite possible, however, that I have missed some of these activists who travel "below the radar screen" since they are, by definition, groups of private actors whose activities only periodically enter the public consciousness. I am reminded that I have missed these activists by Justin. Although he declares himself an animal rights activist and directs at least some of his attention to changing institutional practices, he spent most of his time talking about the importance of "living differently" and resisting the intrusion of the scientific, medical, and pharmaceutical industries in our lives:

> I am vegan in the sense of not wearing leather, not buying products that are tested on animals, not eating animals....completely divorcing yourself from any industry or process....If we win, and we turn everyone vegan, factory farms go out of business, people who test on animals need to get new jobs, people stop wearing clothing and producing clothing that's made from animals. That all stops. So veganism is the goal. You know, when we talk about the goal of animal rights, it's veganism. Universal veganism is the goal. Because that's what saves lives.

Clearly, Justin would be comfortable with the concepts of commodification and colonizing life worlds from the new social movements framework to make sense of his activist identity.

Conclusion

The six theoretical frameworks described and evaluated in this chapter can be best represented as different understandings of the structure/agency dualism of the sociological perspective introduced at the outset of the chapter. Some frameworks emphasize the structures that generate grievances like strain theory and new social movements theory while others emphasize the agency of individuals to exert some independent control over those structures like resource mobilization and political opportunity approaches. Some of these approaches see structures not necessarily in material terms but in cultural terms and stress the meanings, discourses, and identities that define grievances and goals of collective action. The cultural approach, the oppositional consciousness approach and some versions of the new social movement approach share this construction of the structure/agency dualism. Together these frameworks communicate themes of "constrained choices" and "created structures" that nicely capture this dynamic interplay between structure and agency.

I started this chapter with the caveat that these theoretical frameworks concern themselves with the big processes of social movements: emergence, development, change, denouement, and decline. In this way, there is a "disconnect" between these concerns and the more immediate concerns and questions of activists. I have tried to provide openings in these scholarly frameworks for activist concerns. Suffice to say, however, that, for the most part, activists do not concern themselves with the big picture. They do not see how the large-scale institutional and cultural changes that have occurred in the city, region, nation, and world have changed the landscape and possibilities of collective action and social movements. They do not sit around and wait for favorable opportunities but tend to see issues or grievances in much the same way as the resource mobilization framework: as always present. These activists also tend to see their available strategies and tactics—what scholars call repertoires of collective action—as fixed and stable and not in relation to power relationships embedded in historically specific structural arrangements.

Part of this "blindness" involves the general demands of organizing collective action: few activists have the luxury to ruminate on how globalization and its diffusion of power centers makes certain kinds of space-specific organizing ineffective, for example. Part of this involves the reluctance of scholars to complement their analyses of changing circuits of power with practical suggestions for interrupting these circuits. These observations return us to sociology's orienting duality of structure and agency and remind us of how difficult it is to see connections between the complex social structures and their impact on individual and group conditions.

In Chapters 4 through 8 I use many of the concepts highlighted by these scholarly frameworks to make sense of the multifaceted work of Hartford's progressive activists and the complex nature of their activist identities. Rather than arguing that one of these theoretical frameworks does the "best" job in accounting for the similarities and differences in the organizing of progressive activists or for the outcomes of their activism in Hartford, I focus on using these frameworks as roadmaps through the dilemmas, tensions, persistent conflicts, and ambivalences expressed by these activists as they talk about strategies and goals, resources and organizations, commitment, burnout, and the nature of their activist identities Before moving to that discussion, Chapter 3 situates Hartford activists and their activism in their contemporary and historical contexts. The concepts derived from the theoretical frameworks guide the analysis as they call attention to the important processes that make Hartford an ideal setting to investigate the limits and possibilities of progressive activism in the United States.

Chapter 3

The Historical and Contemporary Context of Hartford Progressive Activism

C. Wright Mills, an activist sociologist of the late 1950s, reminds us that individuals' "private troubles" need to be situated in broader "public issues" (Mills 1959). Actually, it was less of a gentle reminder and more of a stern call to arms during a time when sociology was becoming increasingly detached from the world around it. Sociology, he said, needed to be concerned with the intersection of biography and history, particularly with those large-scale social processes that cause misery for the many and luxury for a few. Heeding this call, just as relevant in the early decades of the twenty-first century as it was in Mills' day, requires we situate this group of activists within both a local and national historical context. This is necessary because, to paraphrase another activist intellectual who was writing in the nineteenth century, Karl Marx (1972), these activists craft strategy, articulate goals, respond to adversaries, form coalitions, etc., and therefore make history but not under conditions of their own choosing.[1]

To this famous maxim, I would add that activists' very sense of themselves as social actors is also shaped and limited by both their own histories and the contexts within which they find themselves. This is not meant to diminish the extraordinary efforts of individuals who in many ways work "against the grain" of the world around them. It is meant to empower more fully these activists by placing their work in a longer and larger tradition than they themselves may realize. More importantly, it is also meant to describe the landscape of possibilities for understanding oneself and acting as a progressive activist in the current moment. Which activist paths are well-trodden? Which are more risky? Which participate in the "local" status quo of social change efforts? Which challenge that status quo?

The perspectives of C. Wright Mills and Karl Marx are important for the study of social movements for another reason as well that will become clearer throughout this chapter. While the theoretical frameworks of social movement scholars call our attention to many of the important concepts and dynamics in the study of social movements, they sidestep a crucial concept that is part and parcel of all these frameworks. Marx and Mills direct our gaze to the role of power in virtually all features of social life. Marx's famous analyses of the rise of industrial capitalism in Europe argued that capitalist elites, due to their ownership and control over the means of production, exert pervasive influence over virtually every sphere of social life (Marx 1967). Mills' emendation of Marx's view of power does not deny the crucial role of economic power derived from the principles of private profit and labor exploitation but adds other dimensions of power not derived from these principles (Mills 1956). In Mills' analysis of the United States, he argues that those who control the means of coercion and administration in society, and they may be heavily influenced by capitalist elites but do not necessarily have the same interests and concerns, also exercise disproportionate power over social life. In his analysis, various sectors of political elites also dominate American society.

These analyses of power are invoked here for a simple reason. Our social movement frameworks do not give enough attention to the complexities of power in the emergence, development, and consequences of social movements. The operation of power underlies the central concepts of the six frameworks outlined in the previous chapter. Marx and Mills implicitly challenge those frameworks to dig deeper and interrogate, among other things, the sources of the social strain or the forces that have constructed the post-industrial economy, the resources that elites use to channel or limit the efforts of social movements, and how cultures, even cultures of opposition and other collective identities, are influenced by the resource restrictions and dominant belief systems constructed by elites.[2]

In these ways, scholars can make contributions to activist work. As stated above, one contribution would be situating their work in its historical context, thus providing some information on the landscape of possibilities for action. This chapter describes this context using the concepts and theoretical frameworks from the sociological study of social movements. I use these concepts and frameworks in an eclectic manner. Instead of choosing one of these frameworks or advancing an alternative framework that works best for understanding the dynamics of progressive activism in Hartford, I argue that all of these frameworks have something to offer both scholars and activists. The goal is not theory testing or causal analysis using techniques of co-variation and statistical control. Neither is the goal to do away with theory and concepts altogether in historical analyses of activism.

Instead, the spirits of C. Wright Mills and Karl Marx insist that we bring theory and activism into dialogue with one another for the purpose of meaningful and effective social change. What are the public issues behind our private troubles? What are the social conditions that shape our collective responses to those private troubles? What are the constraints and limits to our collective responses to those troubles? How has power shaped those social conditions and our response to those conditions? In these ways, theory is in service to activism, and activism can be informed, nourished, and changed by theory.

Setting the Stage: Hartford and its Grievances

Hartford is a medium-sized city of 124,554 (CERC 2008) located in the center of the state of Connecticut in the New England region of the United States. Typical of many medium-sized Northeastern cities, Hartford has experienced population decline, profound deindustrialization, and high levels of poverty and unemployment over the past 25 years which have, in turn, produced ongoing grievances about jobs, housing, crime, and schools (Simmons 1994: 3–10; 2008). Between 1970 and 2000, Hartford's population fell from 158,017 to 121,578, a 30 percent decline (U.S. Census Bureau 2000). Between 1970 and 2002, the number of workers employed in manufacturing fell from 20,030, 14.9 percent of the city's nonagricultural labor force, to a staggering 1,646, 3 percent of the city's nonagricultural labor force (U.S. Census Bureau 2000; 2002, Table 1). In 2002, Hartford's poverty rate was 32 percent compared to a state-wide average of only 8 percent. In 2007, 9.7 percent of Hartford's labor force was officially unemployed more than twice the rate of unemployment in the state. Hartford's median household income was $27,611 compared to the statewide average of $61,879 (CERC 2006). Obviously, Hartford is a poor city and, to these dire statistics, could be added others such as infant mortality, illiteracy, and crime rates. I recite these statistics not to repeat the often heard narrative of a forlorn city but to suggest the many challenges as well as opportunities facing Hartford's progressive activists. Strain theorists talk about economic and social forces that disrupt people's routines and affect the quality of their lives. There are social strains aplenty in the city.

Also typical of other U.S. cities, Hartford's deindustrialization was accompanied by a rapid out-migration of the predominately white middle class and an almost as rapid in-migration of African Americans and Latinos. In 1960, Hartford was 80 percent white; in 2007 that percentage was reversed such that 80 percent of Hartford's population is now non-white, mainly African American and Latino (CT. State Data Center 2007). One exception to this white out-migration, at least until the 1990s, were white middle-class gays and lesbians who formed a core of the LGBT and feminist movements in the region and who became coalition partners for other forms of progressive collective action in the city (Monteiro and Mann 1991). Again, strain theorists talk about the disruptive impact of migration patterns and, indeed, the rapid in-migration of non-whites into an unwelcoming city did produce its share of grievances. And, as the resource mobilization framework suggests, a core of white liberals with their economic resources and social capital assisted in providing resources for collective efforts at social change.

Hartford is somewhat unique in that it is a poor and predominately non-white city bounded by wealthy and predominately white suburbs that are politically protected from being incorporated into the city boundaries. In addition, as the state capital, Hartford is home to many government buildings that do not yield tax revenue to the city. The city also is the site of many colleges, universities, hospitals, clinics, and social service organizations whose property is also tax-exempt. In all, more than one-third of Hartford's property is tax-exempt (Burns 2006: 29). Of course, the city maintains the infrastructure and incurs the direct and indirect costs of providing these services even though they are used by everyone in the region.

Other comparisons between city and region are also stark: the suburban poverty rate of 9.3 percent was less than a third of the city's rate; the suburban unemployment rate of 2.5 percent was half the city's rate and its median income of $57,927 was over twice the city's median household income (U.S. Census Bureau 2005).

While other cities in the Northeast responded to population and resource shifts by annexing inner-ring suburbs, a provision in the state's constitution prohibits such a response, and the distribution of state assembly seats that disproportionately favor suburbs and small towns has thwarted the few efforts to alter this arrangement (Fraser 1988). These stark geographic, economic, political, and racial inequalities are a powerful symbol used in many forms of activism throughout the city. Drawing from the cultural framework of social movements, we see activists using these inequalities to engage in framing strategies that draw on themes of injustice and inequity to motivate participation and gain media attention.

Another potent symbol is the profound inequality between the central business district to and from which many of the wealthier white suburbanites commute, and the neighborhoods that contribute relatively few workers to the predominately financial, insurance, and investment industries in the downtown except as janitors, security guards, and food service workers. In 2000, 37,720 men and women—67 percent of the entire Hartford workforce—commuted into the city, most of them heading to the downtown or to two insurance companies just west of the downtown (CERC 2002a). Also in 2000, four out of the five top contributors to the city's tax rolls were insurance, finance, real-estate industries, many of which are also located in this area. Collectively, they contributed 11.2 percent of the city's revenue (CERC 2002b). Similar to other U.S. cities nationwide, Hartford has experienced a significant growth in the lower-wage service sector in the past decade. Between 1997 and 2002, for example, the percentage of Hartford workers employed by the service sector (health care, social assistance, arts and entertainment, and recreation, food and hotel services) grew from 25 to 34 percent (U.S. Census Bureau 2006). Service workers in Hartford, as in the entire state of Connecticut, are more likely to be nonwhite, female, and employed on a part-time basis (Regan 2007: 1, 8). New social movements theory with its emphasis on the changes that take place in post-industrial cities provides a way to understand this set of inequalities and the subsequent demands to address those inequalities. It also helps us understand another aspect of the city that has bedeviled activists: the globalized nature of the new economy and the multi-layered, far-flung, often hidden nature of power.

This brief profile of the contemporary city's inequalities reveals the variety of racial, ethnic, class, gender, and regional grievances that have fueled progressive activism in Hartford over the past two decades. Grievances are central to sociologists' talk about social movements. Private troubles and public issues are rife in this accounting of Hartford's contemporary context and, as we will see in later chapters, these grievances get "picked up" by activists and "spun" in particular ways illustrating Marx's insight of individuals (in this case, activists) creating history but not under conditions of their own choosing. Delving deeper into the historical context, however, reveals both the roots of some of these grievances as well as the institutional and community-based infrastructure that spawned and shaped the specific responses to these grievances by Hartford activists. Accounting for these causes of this progressive activism requires a synthesis of many of the theoretical approaches to social movements.

The Historical City I: Group Building, Oppositional Consciousness, and a Culture of Benevolent Control

Anyone familiar with the Northeast region of the United States is familiar with cities like Hartford that rose to prominence in the late nineteenth century on the strength of early industrialization made possible partly through profits from the slave trade. Hartford's location as a trading port on the Connecticut River, as a major stop on a stage line between New York City and Boston in the eighteenth century, and as an important railroad center in the nineteenth century gave it an economic importance in excess of its size (Weaver 1982). During the nineteenth century, its location and its economic opportunities also made it one of several ports of entry for successive waves of European immigrants: German and Irish beginning at mid-century and southern and eastern Europeans at the turn of the twentieth century (Stave, Sutherland with Salerno 1994).

Beginning in the interwar period with the tightening of immigration laws, and the subsequent decline of cheap European labor, Hartford became a destination for African Americans from the South and Latinos primarily from the island of Puerto Rico looking for work and a better life. Both groups found work in the shade tobacco fields just north of the city and in the many manufacturing plants throughout the city. While the wages were, on average, higher than in the South or in Puerto Rico, their experiences with racial and ethnic discrimination on these jobs ensured that these wages were lower than those for whites (Pearson 1976; Spivey 1994). African Americans were also at the bottom of the employment queue in manufacturing; European immigrants if available were given first preference (Lieberson 1983; Tuckel *et al.* 2007). As strain theorists point out, it is not always absolute deprivation that leads to grievances but relative deprivation: how your deprivation compares to similarly situated others.

Although these characteristics don't begin to exhaust the relevant background to contemporary activism in Hartford, they do supply some of the demographic scaffolding on which a rich history of labor, civil rights, and racial and ethnic organizing was assembled. For social movement scholars, the common background, modes of incorporation, experiences, and grievances are the crucial aspects of this scaffolding that produce the rich history of activism. These scholars are very interested in the different ways in which groups are constructed, especially those groups that are marginalized or denied equal access to resources and citizenship. As emphasized by the cultural approach to social movements, the commonalities of experience oftentimes become the basis of a collective identity. When these commonalities intersect with already existing social cleavages such as class or race, this identity can develop into an oppositional consciousness as suggested by the oppositional consciousness theoretical framework.

Hartford's manufacturing base was rooted in machine tools, aircraft engines, typewriters, and armaments and, throughout the last half of the nineteenth and first half of the twentieth centuries, its industrial working class comprised the recent white immigrants to the city—Catholic, Jewish, "ethnic," and sometimes racially and politically suspect (Valocchi 2002; Wilson 1993). Similar to other Northeastern manufacturing cities, the class structure in manufacturing also involved a stratum of factory owners and managers who hovered over their employees at work, from their brownstones on the edges of the factory district or from their homes on the hills in the southern part of the city. Also similar to other cities, Hartford had its share of working-class militancy and labor radicalism. Low wages, long hours, and oppressive factory conditions gave rise to strikes, marches, leafleting, unionization, and even election campaigns by pro-labor, socialist, or communist candidates in the decades between the two world wars (Lenzi 2003; Pennybacker and Kershaw 2004; Saul 1998). As early as 1909, city fathers were so concerned about this militancy that they constructed the state armory and arsenal at the edge of the largest factory district in the city as a way to protect the downtown from "working class revolt" (Lenzi 2003). Few factors are as crucial for creating a sense of mutuality and shared grievances than situations of relative powerlessness. The concept of oppositional consciousness comes to mind: an awareness of common interests opposed to the interests of another more powerful group. That this oppositional consciousness was crafted and sustained in various kinds of organizations from nascent unions to the Communist party reminds us that resources, infrastructure, leadership, etc., all stressed by the resource mobilization framework, were also important in the creation of this oppositional consciousness.

We can see more clearly these processes of group formation, the inequalities associated with it, and its potential impact on oppositional culture and consciousness by examining Hartford's history of immigration and industrialization. This history also shows us that this oppositional consciousness was contradictory in nature. While there may have been some who desired a dramatic refashioning of city, state, or national institutions, most just wanted equal access to those institutions.

As in other Northeastern cities, European ethnics achieved upward mobility through patronage jobs in city and state government, factory and construction work and, with the New Deal in the 1930s and the expansion of national social programs in the 1940s, social security, subsidized mortgage benefits for homeownership, and education benefits for veterans. For the most part, African Americans and Puerto Ricans were not so lucky.[3] Job and housing discrimination greeted African Americans and Puerto Ricans with their arrival in the city. National programs discriminated against racial minorities either in the qualification for or administration of these programs. Factory work was decreasing in the decades following World War II just as these groups were gaining a foothold in jobs, and as unions were becoming less racist (Wilson 1980). In addition, city government was restructured in 1946 to eliminate ward-based representation thus diluting the growing electoral power of African Americans since racial segregation forced them into one or two election districts (Pawlowski 1991). The restructuring also professionalized city agencies which greatly reduced the amount of patronage available to both African Americans and Puerto Ricans (Janick, 1975: 84–5; Pawlowski 1991). In these ways, C. Wright Mills' "big processes" and "historical shifts" operated to create group-specific life chances and sow the seeds of oppositional consciousness. As we will see in the next section, however, many of the organizations formed and the campaigns mounted that embodied this oppositional consciousness were aimed at access and inclusion rather than radical restructuring.

Hartford was not a typical manufacturing city. Predating industrialization and complicating the class and political structures of the city was an insurance and banking sector that generated even greater profits for its owners than did manufacturing and relied on a middle class of educated, white, Protestant residents of the city as its workforce (Weaver 1982). Given their longstanding history in the city since the late eighteenth century, insurance and banking elites bound together by a common Congregationalist faith controlled local politics. These economic elites communicated values of thrift and careful calculations of risk tempered by a sense of civic and moral responsibility (Walsh 1996).

This culture of benevolent control permeated many social institutions and influenced how elites handled discontent, disadvantage, and misfortune in the city (Walsh 1996). Despite the many twists and turns in the local and national economy, these elites remained prominent in the civic and political life of the city for over a century (Neubeck and Ratcliff 1988: 306–7). At least until the mergers and reorganization of the insurance sector in the 1990s, these insurance company executives and the few civic leaders closely tied to these executives were dubbed "the Bishops" (Filer 1986). The Bishops exercised the real power in the city and were considered the embodiment of this culture of benevolent control (Filer quoted in Burns 2006: 30). This structure of power, partly economic, political, and cultural, affected the kinds of collective action that emerged, the kinds of individuals who participated in it, the resources available to it, and the outcomes of this collective action.

Another aspect of this structure of power that also affected the historical development of social movements was its religious dimension. Undoubtedly, these values of thrift and civic responsibility derived from the austere forms of Protestantism of Hartford's Yankee elites; the early financial institutions of the city were established as extensions of the Congregationalist Church. The Protestant Establishment in Hartford had a strong sense of themselves as the "chosen" leaders and protectors of the city. This leadership was not simply about political and economic control but also about private benevolence stemming from an interpretation of Protestant theology in changing economic and social circumstances.

In the late nineteenth century with industrialization and immigration from both rural Connecticut and Europe, this Establishment found itself surrounded by new religions, new ethnic groups, new social problems, and potentially new challenges to its leadership. In the face of these developments, this Establishment carefully repositioned itself in the social and civil life of the city. In essence, it took a somewhat more prominent public role, forming groups and activities that both performed valuable social services and communicated Protestant values. Most importantly, the church leadership started a variety of benevolent organizations to address poverty, prostitution, child welfare, tramping (i.e. homelessness), and the like. It brought its considerable resources to bear on addressing social problems consistent with its values of moral probity, thrift, and individual responsibility (Walsh 1996).

Probably the best example of this service ethic and the culture of benevolent control is the Hartford Foundation for Public Giving founded in 1925 by trust officers at two prominent banks as a way to channel old WASP money into a centralized fund for charitable giving (Weaver 1975: 116, 118). This foundation has been the major source of private funds for social service and community development projects in the city and, in some instances, for progressive activism (Donahue 1999). When the Hartford Foundation celebrated its seventy-fifth anniversary in 1990, it was the tenth largest community foundation in the United States (Donahue 1999: 63).

These unique features of Hartford's political economy bring to mind two familiar concepts used in the resource mobilization framework of social movements: material resources and elite channeling. Although most discussions of resources for activism focus on their utility for facilitating collective action, Hartford's culture of civic responsibility and private benevolence reminds us that resources, especially external resources, can be a double-edged sword. Quite simply, they can provide help, address grievances, and take the edge off the inequality described earlier. But, there may be a price to pay. They can also channel more militant activism with radical goals into more cooperative efforts at reforming existing institutions. In this regard, Mark Twain, the famous novelist, essayist, satirist, and Hartford resident, referred to Connecticut as "the land of steady habits" to account for "the State's prudence and careful conservatism" (Fraser 1988: 13). The careful use of corporate resources may be one important ingredient cultivating these steady habits and ensuring that conflicts and tensions do not upset long-standing power relationships in the economy and politics. We see that dynamic repeatedly in Hartford's history of activism. In this environment, some collective action is for incorporation into the system on equal terms. Even activism stemming from explicitly oppositional cultures are transformed into more accommodating forces as these individuals who possess some form of oppositional consciousness utilize elite resources and engage in the compromises necessary to keep organizations running and benefits forthcoming.

The Historical City II: Opportunity Structure, Economic Shifts, Organizations, and Urban Landscapes as Sites of Power

Although labor militancy and union activity were features of the industrial landscape beginning in the mid-1930s, the staunchly pro-business elites fought fiercely against the right of workers to organize throughout the first half of the twentieth century. On the eve of the Great Depression, for example, Hartford was the headquarters of the open shop movement in Connecticut with employers, government officials, and newspaper editors in agreement to keep unions out of the city's factories and construction industry (Valocchi 2002). As a result of unprecedented militancy both nationally and locally, the labor movement established an institutionalized presence in the city but that presence was limited to manufacturing and government (Simmons 1994). To this day, unions remain fiercely resisted in insurance, banking, and financial services (Wilson 1993). The consolidated power that both Marx and Mills emphasize constituted the status quo and limited the kinds of collective action that took place during this time. As the political opportunity framework reminds us, however, this status quo can be interrupted if "the conditions are right."

As noted in Chapter 2, this framework stresses the importance of any number of structural or episodic factors that create shifts or instabilities in power alignments and thus provide openings for mobilization by challenging groups. Applying the concept to this historical discussion, the Depression-era instabilities created nationwide labor militancy that also reverberated in Hartford. These shifts in the national political opportunity structure were only partially mirrored at the local level since the cozy relationships between insurance elites and political elites went undisturbed by these national instabilities.

This uneven opportunity structure during this pivotal moment has contemporary consequences for the economic landscape confronted by subsequent generations of activists, another reason why history or, in C. Wright Mills' phrase, "the intersection of history and biography" is important (Mills 1959: 4). As the manufacturing sector declined beginning in the mid-1960s, work in health care, government, and hotel and restaurant services grew (Moody 1988). These sectors did not have a history of labor activism, and the post-World War II labor movement put most of its energy into servicing its already existing membership rather than organizing the unorganized. Although some of the unions in the declining manufacturing sector made headway in these new areas, most notably in the public sector, other unions specifically for service sector workers in health care, custodial, hotel, and restaurant services made inroads with models of organizing that focused on the needs of a historically low-paid, predominately female and non-white workforce (Clawson 2003: 43–50). These unions were energized by the social movement activism of the 1960s which sought a closer connection between the working class and other movements for the poor and people of color (Clawson 2003: 92). Local chapters of the Service Employees International Union, representing health care, government, and custodial workers, and the Hotel and Restaurant Workers (now an affiliate of UniteHere), representing cafeteria and food service workers were important participants in this resurgence. Along with public sector unions, they emerged as the most active union presence in this growing economic sector in the city (Rhomberg and Simmons 2005).

This history illustrates not only the utility of the concept of political opportunity structure as important to understand the labor activism of the twentieth century but also of concepts from resource mobilization theory. As the history summarized above suggests, opportunity structures (either open or closed) were not the only important factors shaping labor activism. In addition, the specific nature of the organizations formed was also important in shaping the nature of that activism in the post-World War II period. In this regard, resource mobilization theorists would focus on the concept of social movement organizations—bureaucracies with their own internal dynamics partially independent of the opportunity structures—that also shaped social movements.

We see this dual understanding of union organizations played out in the history of the labor movement. As the working class institutionalized its gains from the protests and militancy of the 1930s, entered into permanent collective bargaining agreements in the 1940s, and was subjected to the Cold War purge of labor radicals and communists in the 1950s, a business unionism took hold of the movement (Moody 1988). This unionism was better suited to securing gains in wages and benefits for its existing members than it was for committing resources to organizing new members, especially as the legal and political environment grew more hostile to union organizing in the 1970s and 1980s. Ironically and unfortunately, these existing members who were benefiting by a union presence were in the rapidly declining manufacturing sector.

This interaction between these social movement organizations and the economic changes in the post-World War II period helps explain some of the profound poverty in the city. It also helps explain why most labor progressives are located in the aforementioned service-sector unions and why these unions have turned to coalitions with neighborhood and community groups to construct mutually beneficial strategies and agendas (Rhomberg and Simmons 2005). We would be hard-pressed to find a better example of Marx's axiom of activists making (or trying to make) history but not under conditions of their own choosing. It is also a good example of how a synthesis between concepts derived from the resource mobilization and political opportunity approaches best explains the structure and functioning of labor activism in Hartford.

So much of the inequalities activists react to in cities is embedded in the physical makeup of those cities: how space, architecture, housing, and ultimately wealth are distributed across urban landscapes. As the profile of contemporary Hartford in the introduction to this chapter makes clear, issues of contested space figure prominently in Hartford's history of activism. Unlike other "manufacturing cities" where business owners' wealth is displayed in large houses in separate neighborhoods but not necessarily in the central business district, the concentration of insurance and banking with their imposing buildings and white-collar workers in the downtown area presented and still presents a stark contrast to the working-class, racially and ethnically inflected neighborhoods.

In the early part of the twentiethth century, these neighborhoods consisted of multi-family tenements. As more areas of the city were developed in the inter-war and post-World War II periods, better-off members of the working and middle classes moved into single-family detached housing in the southern and northwestern sections of the city (Pawlowski 1973; Stave 1979: 36–40). This process of wealth concentration was solidified in 1962 with the elimination of the last downtown residential neighborhood and its replacement with Constitution Plaza, a series of office towers for the Travelers Insurance Company. Spearheaded by the Chamber of Commerce and financed with federal urban renewal monies, this project displaced Italian, Polish, and African American residents, and eventually became a symbol for many residents and some neighborhood activists of the self-serving corporate interests of economic elites (Kern 1992; Kuzyk 2003: 60–3).

These tensions were again unleashed in 1975 by the release of a confidential memo from a planning consortium of the major corporations in the city that outlined an ambitious program of downtown development and neighborhood displacement (Cruz 1998: 102–6). This involved, among other things, slowing the growth of Puerto Rican immigration to the city, relocating to the periphery of the downtown those who were already in the city, and developing a rural area of the state as a new town primarily for African Americans from Hartford (Neubeck and Ratcliff 1988: 321–4). Unlike the earlier urban renewal, this effort was never realized due to the vociferous outcry by many sectors of the city, especially the increasingly politicized Puerto Rican community.

Subsequent conflicts over urban space in the 1980s met similar fates in the face of organized neighborhood activism. An extensive skywalk project that would allow downtown office workers to float above the sidewalks of Hartford's downtown was significantly scaled back and an expansion of downtown office space was linked to a fund for neighborhood revitalization (Neubeck and Ratcliff 1988: 311–20; Simmons 1994: 59; People's History 1995: 102). These historical examples point to the importance of geography and urban space not only as the context of social movement activism in the city but also as a crucial part of how grievances are framed, strategies are developed, and targets are identified in social movement activism. In this way, concepts from new social movements theory alert us to the changing nature of grievances in post-industrial cities.

Histories of Hartford Activism I: Pre-existing Organizations, Moderation, Militancy, and Elite Channeling

Most of the historical discussion thus far deals with the preconditions of activism, opportunity structures, group formation, and elite power. These features of the city's post-World War II social context—some common to most U.S. cities; some unique to Hartford—have yielded rich histories of activism. Prior to the migration from the South, the small African American community established many self-help organizations to cope with social and economic marginality. Many African American churches served this purpose and functioned not only as places of worship but as sites of political consciousness raising and service provision (Harris 1999; Miller 1994: 39). During the Great Depression, for example, one of these historic churches started a feeding project run by the congregation for needy members of the north end neighborhoods of Hartford that, at the time, were composed of African Americans and Italians (Valocchi 2002: 56). But, as alluded to above, we get very little insight into the nature of activism simply by examining its preconditions. As resource mobilization and new social movement theories as well as the cultural approaches to social movements stress, we need to examine both the nature of the organizations out of which activism emerged as well as the nature of the new organizations formed as a result of the activism.

Hartford also had an extremely active branch of the NAACP founded in 1917 in response to an ultimately unsuccessful effort to segregate the schools (Jones 1995).

While the organization generally favored behind-the-scenes letter writing and lobbying as strategies against discrimination, it remained an urgent voice of social change in the city. Until the 1960s, the NAACP as well as other established members of the black community chose a strategy of "quiet negotiation" often working in conjunction with state government or individual employers to combat discrimination throughout the city (Close 2001: 228). During the early years of the civil rights movement ministers once again took the lead in campaigns for open housing, access to jobs and job training programs and against policy brutality but their efforts were quickly eclipsed by more confrontational strategies of various groups and organizations from the African American activist community (Close 2001: 244–8; Jones 2003). One such group was the Black Caucus, greatly influenced by the black power philosophies of Malcolm X. This moderate/militant dynamic produced a more aggressive NAACP in the city as reflected in the tireless leadership and subsequent successes of its President, Wilbur Smith (Close 2001: 249–53). This dynamic was also reflected in the response to a series of riots in 1968 and 1969, with visible rifts between the church-centered civil rights leadership and a group of younger activists from the neighborhoods and the white-dominated student movement.

Several important concepts from social movement analysis emerge from this highly telescoped history of African American activism in the city. We see the importance of pre-existing organizations, ones not centrally dedicated to activism, as providing finances, leadership, and constituencies or supplying the cultural ideals for activism. In the context of social strains or changes in the political opportunity structure and the subsequent activist stirrings, these organizations were not equipped to accommodate this activism and new organizations developed. For example, the local NAACP and the Interfaith Ministerial Alliance, designed for individual advocacy, support, and service purposes, served as pre-existing organizations of the civil rights activism in Hartford, providing meeting space, membership, money, and a language of integration and incorporation. As that activism grew, new organizations emerged that focused solely on civil rights concerns. The resource mobilization and cultural frameworks focus our attention on these organizational developments: resource mobilization theory stresses the material nature of organizations and cultural frameworks see organizations as embodiments of ideas, symbols, and rhetorical resources.

This dynamic gives rise to another frequently noted by scholars of social movements: the divisions between moderates and militants in many mobilizations for social change. Oftentimes invisible to outsiders, the interactions and conflicts between the two factions affect the direction and outcomes of social movements with at least some segment of the moderate activists being taken into mainstream organizations or electoral politics.

Money from the federal government's War on Poverty program fed, at least temporarily, the activism of the late 1960s and early 1970s and contributed to this tension between moderates and militants (Piven and Cloward 1979: Chapter 5). This money, coupled with local foundation money from the corporate community, channeled the militant street activism into organizational development and service delivery. The Hartford Foundation for Public Giving, for example, funneled large amounts of money into the North End of Hartford, the site of the riots, and helped establish one of the major social service organizations in the city, Community Renewal Team (CRT), that still operates today (Donahue 1999: 32; Weaver 1982:130). CRT was the site of not only service provision but activism, especially in the 1970s. This activism also led to greater participation in electoral politics. Here again we see how internal and external influences on a politicized oppositional culture encourage accommodation and incorporation into mainstream institutions, albeit somewhat altered institutions.

The early subordinate relationship of African Americans in the 1950s and 1960s brokered by the Italian and Irish American politicians who continued to dominate city government gave way to a more independent relationship as 1960s activists turned to mobilizing a growing African American electorate and as white flight to the suburbs accelerated in the aftermath of the riots. In 1980, Hartford elected its first African American mayor, Thurman Milner. In 1987 another African American, Carrie Saxon Perry, became the first African American female mayor of a major U.S. city.

This history of the denouement of the civil rights/black freedom movement in the city nicely captures several concepts in social movement scholarship. Mentioned earlier, the concepts of resources and channeling prove important here since the elite response to the riots and related militancy was not mainly police repression although there was that. The funding provided in the wake of the militancy provided seed money for organizations. While it may have also fueled further collective action in the short run, it channeled that insurgency into the electoral system, opened up some job opportunities in local government to African Americans and, in so doing, contributed to the decline of non-institutionalized insurgency.

Puerto Ricans in Hartford also have a long history of activism rooted in struggles for cultural identity, economic opportunity, and political access. The cultural, economic, and political struggles are closely connected. The early activism of Puerto Rican women to get Catholic masses conducted in Spanish and to organize the annual Puerto Rican Day Parade occurred alongside the more conventionally political struggles of gaining a voice on City Council and the Board of Education (Cruz 1998; 52–66; Pawlowski 1991). As stressed by the cultural approaches and oppositional consciousness framework of social movements, Puerto Ricans' assertions of identity recognition were simultaneously cultural and political in nature. They were made to gain resources from mainstream institutions to build that identity through bilingual education, and equal access to housing, and jobs.

Like African Americans, Puerto Ricans took to the streets to protest police brutality, slum housing, and urban renewal that threatened to displace large numbers of Puerto Ricans. Also like African Americans, this activism involved both moderate and militant voices. Some of this activity was organized by the Puerto Rican Socialist Party which was devoted to the independence of Puerto Rico as well as to local struggles for jobs, housing, and non-racist representations in local culture. Some members of this group participated in the first Puerto Rican community organization in the Frog Hollow section of the city, Vecinos Unidos, and battled landlords, employers, City Hall, and eventually even the neighborhood organization of which they were a part (Cruz 1998; People's History 1995: 29–32). Resources from government, corporations, and a small but significant Latino professional middle class channeled this activism into cultural and social service organizations that provided programming, bilingual language classes, and affordable housing, and monitored the needs of the growing Latino community (Donahue 1999).

This history of Puerto Rican mobilization in Hartford reminds scholars of the importance of culture as an important goal of social movement activity. Although the distinction between "politics" and "culture" can be exaggerated—changing laws frequently requires and results in changing culture and changing culture frequently requires changing laws—scholars emphasize this distinction to signal the different approaches activists use to make social change. We see its utility in the case of Puerto Rican activism in the city.

Puerto Rican electoral activism had to negotiate its way between an entrenched local machine dominated by white ethnics and another new challenging group of African Americans (Cruz 1998; Pawlowski 1991). Until that political machine lost power, African Americans and Puerto Ricans were positioned against one another in elections for town committee, the board of education, and city council. The cooperation hammered out with the decline of white ethnic political domination was always tentative and short-lived. Most of the conflict between African Americans and Latinos occurred in mainstream politics as they vied for elected offices (Cruz 1998: 95–8). Most of the cooperation occurred in grassroots organizations since both groups confronted a similar set of economic and social deprivations (Bonelli and Simmons 2004: 18–20).

The exception to this pattern and the onset of a brief period of cooperation at both the electoral and grassroots levels occurred in 1991 when Puerto Rican activists allied with several progressive activists from the African American political community, organized labor, and the gay, lesbian, and bisexual civil rights organization to gain control of City Hall for two years (Bonelli and Simmons 2004; Simmons 1996). This historical moment in the city's political history illustrates the utility of cross-movement coalitions stressed by both the resource mobilization and political opportunity approaches to social movements as a strategy to aggregate resources and exploit vulnerabilities among political elites in order to gain access to power. And, as the few accounts of this coalition mention, its short-lived nature as a ruling coalition stemmed from, in part, the hostility it encountered from downtown business interests.

The return to a more competitive pattern of political maneuvering following the discrediting of this progressive ruling coalition was fueled by a profound downturn in the local economy in the late 1980s followed by the reorganization, downsizing, and loss of jobs in the insurance sector in the early 1990s. A shrinking pie made each claim on a slice of that pie consequential and an invitation to conflict (Simmons 1996: 166). Despite these developments, Eddie Perez, a former gang member, turned neighborhood activist, turned college community relations officer, turned institutional development president, cobbled together a coalition of Puerto Ricans, African Americans, and white liberals to become the first Puerto Rican mayor of Hartford in 2001. As evident from this political biography, Perez was able to capitalize on his relationships in the progressive activist community, the politicized Puerto Rican community, and institutional stakeholders from across the city. Unlike the earlier progressive coalition of the 1990s, this mayor devoted more time to courting the corporate community and promoting efforts to revitalize the downtown, essentially continuing a process of urban conservatism in the aftermath of the short-lived progressive coalition of the early 1990s (Simmons 1998).

This recent political history once again reminds us of the forces that are brought to bear on the long process of activism and on the oppositional culture and consciousness that initially fueled it. For some, the opposition was strategic to gain entry; for others it was serious attempt to change social institutions. Sociological concepts, such as elite channeling and moderate/militant flank effects, allow us to better understand how an oppositional culture can be transformed into a culture of incorporation.

This recent political history also reminds social movement scholars that power is probably the most important (and most neglected) concept we have in our scholarly lexicon. The power of collectivities, both inside and outside the democratic polity is one kind of power that social movements have available to them. The power of organized capital and the leverage that corporate elites exercise at various levels of politics is a more daunting form of power. The interplay between the two is "where the action is" for activists and social movement scholars alike. This interplay reminds us, once again, of Marx's dictum of making history but not under conditions of our own choosing. It teaches us the sobering lesson that the more powerfully situated in terms of economic resources have more options and fewer obstacles to make history than do the rest of us.

Histories of Hartford Activism II: Churches, Colleges, National Movements, and a Culture of Benevolent Control

The activists who form the core of the progressive community and whose voices you hear in this book are not only drawn from the working class and non-white racial and ethnic constituencies as implied by the historical overview thus far. Several of these other activists speak directly about the values and programs of the predominately white Protestant and Catholic churches as springboards for their activism. Others speak of particular kinds of educational experiences in colleges and universities that communicated progressive ideals or exposed them to activists in the local progressive community. Just as the unique features of the local context and history of labor, African American, and Puerto Rican activism dovetailed with national movements and developments, the context for the essentially middle-class white activism participates in a larger history of 1960s-era activism which transformed colleges and gave rise to identity-based social movements rooted both in urban areas and on college campuses.

Once again, we see the importance of the concept of pre-existing organizations in the form of colleges and religious institutions as contributing the "raw materials" for social movement activism. We also see the intersection of these organizations with national-level social movements. The political opportunity framework gives us the concept of cycles of protest or protest waves that help account for the rise of these pre-existing organizations as hotbeds of activism and for the proliferation of protest across different groups and issues out of these organizations.

Given what we know about Hartford's Protestant Establishment, it may be somewhat surprising that Hartford's religious institutions contributed to progressive activism in the city. Religion, commerce, and politics were closely connected in the construction of a local elite and in the development of a political culture defined by values of individualism, sobriety, and civic responsibility (Janick 2002; Walsh 1996; Weaver 1982). This civic orientation involved engagement in but not substantial change of the city. Even as the political power of this establishment diminished throughout the twentieth century, this civic orientation persisted and was mimicked by other Protestant and Catholic churches and Jewish synagogues. Several of these churches and synagogues developed urban ministries to address problems of poverty, race relations, homelessness, and nuclear war, and out of these ministries some progressive activism emerged. This tension between a civic and a progressive engagement reminds us that some pre-existing movement organizations may be contradictory in nature. Organizations that are part of the power structure can spawn elements that seek to subvert that structure. Religious institutions were sources of philanthropy and services but for some (several of my activists included) they were also sources of ideals that led to progressive activism.

Another consequence of Hartford's legacy of great wealth and civic responsibility is the concentration of institutions of higher education in the area. Despite the city's relatively small size, it is home to four colleges, a teaching seminary, and the state university's schools of social work, urban studies, and law. Similar to the situation of the church, the schools provide resources, networks, and ideas that have sometimes supported an activist relationship to the city and the larger society.

Since the 1960s, the colleges in the area have been home to periodic bursts of activism that both reflected and affected developments in the larger society. The protests against the Vietnam War and military recruitment on campus, and in support of the Black Panther party in Connecticut mobilized virtually all the campuses in the area and had effects on the structures of these institutions including these institutions' relationships to the city (Knapp 2000: 340–65; Stave 2006; Weaver 1982: 128–30). In response to racial tensions at their rural campus 25 miles outside Hartford, the University of Connecticut, for example, initiated an Urban Semester Program in December 1968 located in the city (Stave 2006: 149). Undergraduates who participate in the program spend a semester living in the city and working for a variety of city agencies. The University of Connecticut, both its rural and urban branches, has periodically engaged in progressive activism since that time: in the 1980s against U.S. support for the apartheid regime of South

Africa; in the 1990s against the college's use of sweat-shop-produced apparel; and in the post-9/11 era, against the U.S.-sponsored war in Iraq (Stave 2006: 239–46).

This dynamic was also evident in the smaller schools located directly in the city. Students at Trinity College, for example, staged a sit-in outside a meeting of the Trustees in the spring of 1968 to demand action on a set of policies to expand scholarships for black students and to support "faculty initiatives to develop courses in urban affairs...and for community development efforts" (Knapp 2000: 344, 351). Activism around similar issues of racial diversity and the college's relationship with the city has bubbled up periodically since that time.

Scholars in the resource mobilization and cultural approaches point to colleges and universities as one type of pre-existing movement organization. And when local insurgencies in these organizations intersect with national-level movements they become hotbeds of activism due to factors identified by these approaches. These organizations provide access to resources such as money, meeting space, and technology. Common settings and networks among students make mobilization relatively easy. The demographic and attitudinal characteristics of students (e.g. middle class, liberal, unencumbered by jobs and family obligations) make them more likely to participate in activism The college setting promotes a cultural ethos that encourages engagement and critique. As the Hartford story indicates, these local "hotbeds" become even hotter when they intersect with national-level social movements.

Also similar to the situation of the church, these educational institutions are also part of the power structure of the city and state so that the activism which sometimes emerged from its essentially middle-class faculty and students was tempered by the official actions of the institutions. Even as these colleges were hotbeds of student and faculty activism around civil rights and anti-war issues in the late 1960s and early 1970s as well as local issues of racism and poverty in subsequent decades, some of these institutions continued to encroach on urban neighborhoods for their building programs. In the late 1990s, for example, Trinity College located just south of two of the poorest census tracks in the city, acquired state and privately owned land on the eastern edge of campus to build a "learning corridor" of educational facilities for the Hartford region (Trinity College Bulletin 2008: 8). This redevelopment effort involved the displacement and relocation of some homeowners and renters. The promise of low- and moderate-income housing that accompanied the original version of the project never materialized, and some land that was cleared of derelict housing on the streets adjacent to the "corridor" remained vacant. This occurred simultaneously with the development of an urban curriculum with a civic and service orientation, although some aspects of the curriculum did become opportunities for student activism in the city.

Once again, this narrative drives home the importance of the concept of power for social movement scholars. As this historical overview makes clear, powerful actors were cloaked in the culture of civic responsibility and public benevolence. This cultural discourse associated with the colleges' institutional power had contradictory effects. The institutions trying to gain control over land, housing, and redevelopment were also producing some of the activists who resisted these attempts.

These schools also provided one organizational context for the emergence of gay rights activity in the area. One of Hartford's direct links to the New York-centered gay rights movement was an older Trinity College graduate, Foster Gunnison Jr., described by another activist in 1971 as "the only dedicated gay activist who smoked cigars, wore three-piece Brooks Brothers suits, sported a crew cut, and spoke in an accent vaguely redolent of some upper-crust private school" (Duberman 1993: 270). Other personal ties that existed between New Left college students and the more liberationist-oriented activists in New York gave rise to gay liberation fronts on the campuses of both Trinity College and the University of Hartford (Distelberg 2007: 13; Marotta 1981). As in other areas of progressive activism in the city, a more reformist and accommodationist approach to issues of homosexuality and gay rights coexisted with a more militant and radical approach.

Prior to the arrival of gay liberation, the city had a gay rights organization in the form of the Kalos Society, organized by Canon Jones, a Protestant minister. Given the centrality of a kind of benevolent Protestantism referred to above, it is not surprising that gay organizing and activism in Hartford during the late 1960s and early 1970s were closely linked to clergy and churches (Distelberg 2007: 2). These efforts ran the gamut from hosting social events and guest speakers, educating professionals and doing peer counseling to lobbying politicians to prohibit antigay discrimination. The merger of the Gay Liberation Front and the Kalos Society in the summer of 1970 did not produce a more radicalized gay politics in the city nor did it purge those politics of its religious connections. If anything, it pushed the organization away from a therapeutic or counseling ethos and toward a more traditional reform-oriented identity-based orientation. In this case of interaction between the national movement and the local context, unlike that of the student movement that preceded it, the local culture of gay advocacy tempered the more radical impulses coming from the national movement. The interaction between national-level movements and local manifestations that existed in previous activism existed here as well. This case shows how the local context matters in this interaction.

The Kalos Society became the foundation for the major gay civil rights organization in the state. Between 1984 and 1991 this organization, reconstituted as the Connecticut Coalition for Lesbian and Gay Civil Rights, mobilized for and ultimately won a state-wide civil rights bill utilizing a variety of strategies from lobbying and education to direct action (Monteiro and Mann 1991). A unique feature of this mobilization was the relationships fostered between the organization and the broader progressive community in the state, pointing to the importance of social movement coalition building as propitious for social movement success, a concept highlighted by the strategic considerations of the resource mobilization approach (Bonelli and Simmons 2004). This brief moment in the late 1980s and 1990s led to a closer relationship between the bar culture and political activity and proved fortuitous in early education surrounding AIDS. The bars were also sights of voter registration, recruitment to the gay rights organization, fundraisers, and celebrations (Bonelli 1996).

Since that time, the popularity of the drag and vogue scene in the city with its predominately non-white membership yielded several "houses": kin-like groups of gender queer performers and house members who sponsored fundraiser balls for HIV disease and breast cancer (Liesgang *et al.* 2004). This scene helped make the transgender community more visible among the city's traditional LGBT organizations, and transgender activists pressured these organizations to push for the incorporation of gender identity and expression as part of the state's civil rights protections. Social movement scholars would again note the importance of culture—in this case "drag" and "ball culture"—for creating social change. This social change involved challenging attitudes and assumptions about sex and gender.[4] It also involved using cultural performance as a vehicle for more political forms of change such as HIV prevention and education. The cultural frameworks of social movements alert us to the various ways in which culture is implicated in social movements; in this case, as both a strategy and a goal.

Most of the efforts of gay rights activism, however, continue to be framed in terms of traditional lesbian and gay civil rights particularly with the successes of an organization that focuses on family rights especially marriage for same-sex partners. As the national-level gay and lesbian organizations narrowed their agendas to overturning the military ban on gays and lesbians and passing same-sex marriage laws, many local organizations jumped on the bandwagon (Ghaziani 2008: 210–16). In the Hartford case, however, the policy and reform focus was already in place from the earlier battle for a state civil rights bill. Unlike the earlier civil rights organization, the "marriage right" was fought without substantive ties to other progressive organizations. Unable to gain same-sex marriage through the legislature, marriage equality organizations supported a lawsuit by six same-sex couples who sued the state, arguing that the denial of marriage constituted a violation of the state constitution. In October 2008, the State Supreme Court found in favor of the couples and Connecticut became the third state in the country to allow gay and lesbian couples to marry.

Conclusion

The activists whose narratives are featured in the following chapters experience and are motivated by many of the economic and social inequalities that began this chapter. They also come to their work at the end of the historical narrative sketched above. But this narrative is not only important as a "prelude." By telling this narrative attentive to the myriad concepts and dynamics from social movement theory, we can situate activists' stories in the local context and see the aspects of this context that are common to many other cities in the United States. When the concept of power is added to this conceptual toolkit, we see what is also unique about this local context. Quite simply, the historical construction of elite power in

Hartford was one of benevolent control. This culture affects many aspects of the activism from its initial formulation and the shape it takes to the ways in which elites and the public respond to it. For contemporary activists, this historical context suggests where to look for resources, the associated dangers of accepting those resources, and the kinds of organizations that participate in or push up against the culture of benevolent control.

This review of the historical context of contemporary activism makes six important points. First, the large- and small-scale processes alluded to above, things like discrimination in housing, education, and employment, deindustrialization, entrenched poverty and its associated social problems, migration and suburbanization, and the loss of political patronage created a host of grievances affecting people's lives that were unmet by "normal" democratic politics or the "normal" workings of the capitalist market. Second, many of these same processes produced not only these private troubles and public issues but also conditions favorable to group building. And, at least some of that group building involved the development of an oppositional culture and consciousness.

Third, these groups utilized many pre-existing organizations to turn private troubles into public issues and social action. Organizations in the city, such as the churches, schools, unions, ethnic and racial groups, or social service organizations provided the resources and ideas that moved people to act in more progressive ways than intended by the mandates of these organizations. But these same organizations were also products of a political culture in the city that stressed cooperation over conflict and service over activism. This tension shaped the kinds of progressive activism that emerged and proved successful in the city.

Fourth, these groups also took advantage of some favorable political opportunities. Chief among the political opportunities turning private troubles into public issues was the Depression era economic instabilities and the 1960s-era national social movements. The Depression created an auspicious organizing environment for labor unions. The 1960s protest wave spawned local service and advocacy organizations as well as local versions of national insurgencies. Fifth, the response to that collective action was shaped by the "velvet glove" of benevolent control in the civic sphere and the "iron fist" of corporate resistance in the economic sphere, although clearly the former form of control was more deeply embedded in the political culture. Social movement organizations embodied both moderate and militant postures in their strategies and goals but, owing to the periodic benevolence of elites and their control over resources, these organizations veered decidedly in the direction of moderation. Seventh and finally, the urban context itself, particularly the symbolic and economic uses of architecture and land helped shape the specific nature of social movement demands. Many concepts from social movement scholarship are necessary to explain this rich history of Hartford's progressive activism.

This overview also returns us to C. Wright Mills' exhortation about history and biography and about large social processes and individual life circumstances. It also illustrates the constraints under which current activists operate:

the conditions "not of one's choosing," again paraphrasing Karl Marx. The progressive activists working in the city in the early part of the twenty-first century are products of this context and conditions in manifold ways but, as we hear in the following chapters, they are also active agents who change this context and these conditions.

Chapter 4

What Activists Do: Developing Strategies, Conceptualizing Goals, Exploiting Opportunities

Community organizing is about letting the people decide...helping people clarify their self-interest, giving them the kind of information they need to do that: who they need to talk to, what they want to do about an issue. (Alta, 53-year-old white middle-class female)

If you go to knock on somebody's door and say, "Have you got a problem?" The response has always been the same, "Yeah, I've got a problem." And of 20 doors, you can get 10 who will say, "Yeah, let's do something about it." (Jack, 58-year-old white middle-class male)

To me what I love about [community organizing] is sitting down with a woman who has never once written a letter in her life, and just the fact that she can go to the state capitol and testify on her behalf. Or go to a state legislator and tell him, "You're screwed up; I want this...!" And just to someone who has a third-grade or a fifth-grade education, a woman that, like I am, has been oppressed all her life, come out of that shell and learn to say, "I want change. I am going to stop being the victim. And this is time for us to take over. Enough is enough!" (Carmen, 42-year-old working-class Latina)

And that's what Rootz [the HIV intervention program that organizes young men of color who have sex with men] does: understand the cultural barriers and what makes these guys take risks. The group has looked at the cultural barriers for Latino men which is machismo, which is religion for the African American and West Indian population. A lot of them had this fear that because they were having sex with men, because they were bisexual, because they were gay, that they were going to go to hell so why should I use a condom. (David, 26-year-old West Indian working-class male)

It [the demonstration] was just one of those events that really showed some good solidarity between labor unions, student groups, global activists....It's just an overwhelming feeling of solidarity and overwhelming support when you can get together with people who are like minded, that are willing to stand up and walk beside you as strangers, but you're not [strangers], because you're united by these ideologies. And it's just such an empowering feeling. So, if nothing else, even if every battle doesn't win a piece of legislation, it doesn't matter because you're getting people together, getting them energized, and that's part of the thing. (Kevin, 25-year-old white working-class male)

What we have to do is go out and organize ever greater numbers of workers because we're in...a class war. So we have to get more soldiers on our side in order to win that war. (Laura M., 34-year-old white middle-class female)

I think it's [the goal] about shifting power in our society. I think it's about equal access to resources. Education, universal healthcare, childcare, all those things. When I think about [single issues], I'm like, "alright, this is what they want to do." And they're taking this privileged identity and they're saying, "Let's make it even more privileged." And so, instead of working on something like same-sex marriage, I think we should all together, holistically, be working on universal healthcare, childcare, all that as a way that everyone can equally access all these things....I really believe in multi-issue organizing and recognizing the connections between different. (Beth, 25-year-old white working-class female)

Well, the first time that the bill got introduced on second parent adoption, I mean, there was some work, some grass roots actually, of course, went on, but after we lost we knew we needed to beef that up. And, so that's when we increased the efforts, and in fact, we had lots of house meetings with legislators and their constituents who supported the second parent adoption bill. It was such a powerful lobbying effort. So, we just continued the same kind of grass roots organizing efforts once we moved to marriage. (Ann, 43-year-old white middle-class female)

This is my second term as town committee member and, as a spokesperson in our district, we have not used our positions to address priorities of the community. And what I've decided to do over the last several months is that we actually meet with different constituent groups, and we say, "Hey look, what are the priorities from you?" We're working with other constituent groups and saying, "Hey, look. Bring your priorities to us. We're not trying to supplant your power, or override you, or anyone else." But if you bring to us, the town committee members, and say, "Look, these are the priorities of the community," then we'll tell elected officials. And we've made the process as transparent as we possibly can. We're going out in the community letting folks know that is what time it is in North Hartford. (Andrew, 44-year-old African American working-class male)

It was back in fall of I think it was 2002, the tipping point for me was the buyout of the *Courant* [the city's newspaper] by the Tribune Corporation and having it be the paper of record for the city. We felt like we needed to create something new and having Hartford people tell their stories that weren't being reported. So the idea of joining that bandwagon [the independent media center], jumping on and opening up one here in Hartford, just expanding that independent media movement. So that's what sort of motivated it. And I hadn't been really involved in media before, it just sounded like a new exciting thing. (Josh, 28-year-old white working-class male)

When individuals who, for whatever reason, find themselves working for social change and seek assistance on how to do it, they typically do not look to sociological frameworks or scholarly research. Most just learn by doing but some consult the variety of organizing manuals and handbooks or attend the few organizing institutes that now exist.[1] Typically, these manuals and institutes draw from activists' experiences and present guidelines, criteria, or checklists on the varying components of the organizing process (e.g. Loeb 2004; Shaw 2001). Topics such as "developing a strategy" or "organizing new constituencies" give pointers on developing long-term and short-term goals, identifying constituencies, allies, and targets, and creating organizational structures that encourage outreach as well as action. These suggestions are useful and some of them dovetail with the concerns of social movement scholars who examine many movements in many contexts to find patterns in strategy development or organizational structure.

None of these training venues or sociological frameworks, however, captures the indeterminacy, creativity, and emotion involved in doing progressive activism. The excerpts that introduce the chapter speak to this richness—the sense that doing activism is as much a craft as a set of technical skills, and that rules for organizing are honored more in their breach than in their application. Just as importantly, these excerpts tell us that *doing* activism is also about *being* an activist. For many, doing activism is a form of testimony and a necessary component of their identities. That is, activists' thinking about what to do and how to do it is filtered through their identities and biographies.

This chapter explores the "what" and "how" of progressive activism through the prism of activist stories. As suggested by the above excerpts, this chapter focuses on the broad topic of strategies, tactics, and goals while the next chapter focuses on resources, opportunities, and organizations. This chapter reports on how progressive activists describe and manage the many dilemmas and challenges involved in determining strategies, tactics, and goals. I develop two typologies developed from social movement scholarship that are useful in discerning the series of tradeoffs or balancing acts that activists engage in, oftentimes unknowingly, when they choose among a variety of possible goals and the variety of strategies to achieve those goals. By listening closely to the activists themselves, I also suggest ways of resolving these dilemmas and tradeoffs.

Additionally, these accounts of how they organize and what they organize around speak to the importance of combining many of the concepts that come from the different theoretical frameworks discussed in Chapter 2. As we will see, structural considerations of resources, interests, and opportunities and cultural considerations of meaning, framing, and identity frequently coincide and intermingle in these discussions. All this discussion returns us to the central concerns of the book: what scholars can learn from activists; what activists can learn from scholars.

Before proceeding, we need to acknowledge the diversity of approaches to organizing among Hartford's progressive activists. These activists do not typically abide by any one pattern of organizing. As the accounts that introduce the chapter indicate, activists see many different strategies and goals as important to progressive organizing. Jack's and Alta's brief descriptions of what they do typifies an approach to community organizing developed by Saul Alinsky, a labor and community organizer in Chicago for several decades beginning in the mid-1930s. It can be summed up by the slogan: "Let the people decide." The strategy for organizing is four-fold: appealing to self-interest, aggregating that self-interest into an agenda, transforming that agenda into a set of problems that need to be solved, and collectively pressuring the decision-makers to address these problems (Valocchi 1996). Broad democratic participation is the strategy and whichever demands emerge from that process become the goals of the organizing.

Carmen's account of her approach to community organizing does not assume that individuals are always well-positioned to recognize their self-interest because group oppressions may prevent individuals from doing so. Thus, her approach emphasizes personal empowerment. Not surprisingly, she is also more skeptical than Jack and Alta that decision makers will respond to neighborhood pressure and is more willing to use direct action to achieve group goals. Carmen's organizing has led her to believe that low-income women who do not have a voice in mainstream politics are also disempowered in other areas of their lives as well. Her strategy for social change is empowering women in both the personal and political realms but clearly the ultimate goal is to challenge structures of political power traditionally defined. Confronting a legislator, interrupting a session of the Connecticut General Assembly, bringing welfare mothers to one of the largest employers in the area demanding jobs—all of which Carmen has done—are the goals of her activism. Her way to achieve those goals is by consciousness-raising attentive to the class, ethnic, and gender-based marginalization that keeps women from realizing their power.

David's description of one of his organizing efforts with young men of color also stresses the importance of education and consciousness-raising and derives in part from his personal identification with the men he is organizing. Unlike Carmen, however, who sees this organizing as a means to an end—acquiring jobs, welfare, day care, etc.—David sees consciousness-raising—changing the way people understand themselves—as a perfectly defensible progressive goal.

Kevin's account of the strategies and goals he uses in his short but busy career as a progressive activist also emphasizes personal empowerment but it is an empowerment created in the process of collective action rather than as a precursor to collective action. This particular strategic focus stems from the goals he values as an activist—building solidarity and establishing alliances among disparate constituencies within a progressive coalition. These goals loom as large as the other set of more traditional goals he and others like him emphasize such as ending the war or protesting police brutality. There is an implicit recognition on his part that protest strategies can serve many purposes and that the "big" progressive goals such as anti-racism and anti-militarism are ideals very rarely realized especially in the current political moment.

Laura M. refuses to get bogged down in the politically possible. Although she shares with Kevin a progressive vision of the world built on a redistribution of power, she insists that the best way to realize that vision is through class struggle, achieved through aggressive use of traditional and nontraditional techniques of organizing workers into labor unions.

Beth also works toward a similar set of progressive goals as Kevin—universal health care, affordable day care, ending the war, etc., and also subscribes to a similar set of strategies such as alliance building to achieve those goals. Beth's strategic thinking derives from the initial standpoint of her activism in lesbian, gay, and transgender issues. For her, the point of the alliance building and collective solidarity is to move from single-issue, identity-based goals to multi-issue and inequality-based goals. In this respect, she differs dramatically from Ann, another LGBT activist, who values the painstaking education and lobbying work necessary to extend the same sets of marriage rights available to heterosexual couples to same-sex couples. Working in another issue area of city politics, Andrew also stresses the importance of working within the political system but sees himself as a thorn in the side of the political establishment even as he aspires to become part of that establishment.

Josh values the importance of political work of many of these activists; indeed he rubs elbows with them at demonstrations and rallies, and on campaigns, door knocking and fundraising. He, however, combines that activism with the hard work of getting out an alternative newspaper and putting together an alternative radio show that unabashedly foregrounds a progressive perspective on many of the local, state, and national issues. This cultural activism is his attempt to alter the "political common sense" of people who would not otherwise be moved by other forms of activism.

Captured in these ten excerpts are many different understandings of progressive social change and how to accomplish it: changing laws and institutional practices; changing attitudes and culture; personal empowerment; creating cross-identity multi-issue coalitions; engaging in disruptive tactics; forming organizations to pressure elites. How can we make sense out of these different approaches to progressive organizing and how can we understand the advantages and disadvantages, costs and benefits of each goal and strategy?

Since most of the theoretical frameworks discussed in Chapter 2 focus on more general (and scholarly) questions of social movement emergence, development, and decline, they cannot be applied directly to these more specific (and activist-oriented) questions. Some of these frameworks, however, do take seriously what goes on inside social movements, inquiring into the resources and political environments of movements as well as the internal organizational and identity concerns that influence decision making. In addition, some of the research that assesses the utility of these frameworks yields insights useful to movement activists and to the development of a classification scheme for assessing strategies, tactics, and goals.

Talking about Goals

Combining the concepts and insights from these frameworks, social movement goals are best viewed along three dimensions: the extent to which the activism seeks to extend power to narrow or broad constituencies (Bernstein 1997; Gilmore 2008), the extent to which the activism seeks reform or radical restructuring (Piven and Cloward 1979; Rimmerman 2002), and the extent to which activism is directed to changing laws and practices or changing culture and consciousness (Cohen 1985; Rupp and Taylor 2003). We can revisit the comments of Hartford progressive activists which introduce this chapter in terms of these dimensions and examine the advantages and disadvantages, costs and benefits, associated with each type of social movement goal.

Many social movements are focused on a particular constituency or group and seek to extend rights, services and various types of recognition to that group. The feminist, civil rights, and gay movements can be seen as movements geared toward extending power to these identity-defined groups. By contrast, other social movements attempt to cast their nets more broadly by making demands that are more universalistic in nature or that appeal to constituencies that have multiple identities or interests but may share a common situation of relative powerlessness (Rimmerman 2002). Each of these approaches is associated with advantages and disadvantages. The research on the feminist, civil rights, and gay movements reveals that, while substantive gains were made in each of those areas, these gains affected mainly a privileged segment of women, blacks, gays, and lesbians. Furthermore, there existed various kinds of exclusions within those movements that ensured that the issues that emerged and the ways they were framed would cater to this specific constituency.[2] At the same time, other research shows the challenges of organizing for broad constituencies—getting everyone to agree, asserting a winnable demand, keeping individuals committed for the long haul. This organizing is most successful when the opposition is weak, when sufficient consciousness-raising has taken place within the movement to discourage resentments or divisions, and when the goals are framed in a way that resonates with multiple constituencies.[3]

The experiences of Ann and Beth in the movement for same-sex marriage fit neatly into this first dimension of social movement goals: Ann works on a goal for a narrowly defined group denied access to rights and benefits while Beth works on goals directed to broad groups of non-privileged people. What is absent from their comments, however, is any indication of how to accomplish the successful movement from single-issue/single-identity to multi-issue/multi-identity goals. In particular, how do you keep people with varying interests, issues, and identities together? In general, how do you avoid the pitfalls identified by the research on these types of movements?

Cheryl, another Hartford activist who identifies explicitly as someone who crosses multiple identities as a disabled, African American, bisexual woman, provides an idea of how she accomplishes this shift so fraught with pitfalls in her anti-racist organizing:

> How do I frame the conversation?...finding out why people are the way they are, why they are saying things the way they are saying them. There needs to be another level of understanding...and doing it with white people. You know, that we can't do this without white folks' support. So that's also the struggle and frustration is you do need to have a—to frame a conversation in a way that it's acceptable for white folks to deal too, and also bringing them along and getting them to acknowledge their own sense of racism without putting them off and alienating them because we still need everybody to do this.

By dealing frankly with identity differences and pointing to the varying amounts of "penalty and privilege" associated with race and other social differences, Cheryl attempts to move beyond the differences and identify goals that resonate with various constituencies. Her particular approach to this is through consciousness-raising which, as we see below in the discussion of strategies and tactics, can be combined with more action-oriented strategies to accomplish this shift from a single-identity to a more multi-issue, multi-identity goal.

A slightly different way of resolving the dilemma surrounding single versus multiple issues and goals does not involve holding together different people in the same organization or campaign but using certain activists as bridges between organizations or campaigns with different goals and constituencies. As a neighborhood organizer, Janice was supposed to stick to her own geographical boundaries and do "block watch" work. Rejecting that approach, she violated these tenets and organized across these boundaries and identified common issues:

> While I was working in the neighborhood, I went to the homeowners last. [Before that] I went to the two housing projects (outside the neighborhood) and started meeting with folks out there that had never heard of our organization and they didn't have anything and at the same time, the housing authority was not doing anything with the sidewalks, and it was just a mess and they had scandals and it was this whole huge thing. And in the housing projects the tenants said, "We can't forget our cousins, our aunts, our family members, who live in the other housing projects." So we organized them too. All of the political people said "(Big Gasp) how dare she organize some other community" but all of the other people were like "yes thanks because my aunt lives over there or my Tio." And it was an amazing thing to see young, old, Spanish, black, Rastas, Muslims hosting a meeting; and asked questions that [the university in the area] didn't want to talk about, the city didn't want to talk

about, and the housing authority didn't want to talk about. And they were able to get I think it's something like 1.8 million dollars that was already allocated, that the Hartford Housing Authority was not spending and they have new sidewalks out of that meeting and the homeowners have streetscapes.

Although Janice was still organizing around neighborhood and community issues, she refused to abide by the narrow turf restrictions accompanying that organizing. By doing that, she was able to bring different kinds of Hartford residents together—different races and ethnicities, different ages, and homeowners and public housing residents—around a broader set of issues than simply the policing of streets.

Steve, currently a labor organizer in the city, describes this method as he talks about coalition building between the labor and peace movements during one of the major labor actions of the 1990s against a large manufacturer in the city:

> For four and a half years we helped the Colt strike. I'm thinking half way through it that we have every group in the world supporting it except peace activists. Well, of course peace activists don't support the Colt strike because Colt makes M16s and M16s are shipped to El Salvador! Well I figured that's my job then...Where can we find the common ground? And we did! I thought it was important to bring them in and get them thinking about how important this was. And also, to have Colt talk about economic conversion where you take nuclear power plants and nuclear weapons plants and you convert them... Ain't gonna happen in my lifetime not without an entire change! But that doesn't mean we shouldn't be talking about it and I felt guilty not talking about it when in fact I was a peace activist long before I was a union activist.

Steve attempted to build a coalition for a single-issue goal—support for the strike—and at same time build support for a broader-based long-term goal—economic conversion away from the production of weapons in the state. His legitimacy in making this move comes from his previous work in peace activism. Several activists crisscross the terrain of progressive activism which provides them with the knowledge and the authority to build coalitions around broad-based multi-issue goals. Unlike Cheryl's consciousness-raising approach, this technique for delivering concrete benefits for specific groups while building a campaign among multiple groups or identity configurations involves a strategy that relies on action-oriented strategies.

A second set of goals entails the nature of the demands made by a movement: whether they are reformist or radical in nature. Even though this determination is very tricky, some scholars see the value in this distinction since it calls attention to how the movement sees itself in relation to the dominant society (e.g. Rimmerman 2008; Warner 1999). Some groups may desire to include previously excluded groups within existing laws, legislation, or organizational practices. Giving gays the legal right to marry or providing neighborhood groups with easy access to city hall are two examples of these reformist goals. They do not alter, however, the structure of marriage or its relationship to the dominant culture, as in the case of gay marriage, nor the structure of decision making in the city and its relationship to the broader set of business relationships involved in this decision making, as in the case of community organizing. It is in this regard that the distinction between reform and restructuring makes sense. Not surprisingly, research on various historical movements suggests that radical restructuring is the exception not the rule when social movements develop goals (Piven and Cloward 1979). To the extent that restructuring becomes an explicit goal, it oftentimes comes when movements' efforts at reform are repeatedly frustrated. This was the case with the civil rights movement in the mid-1960s as the tactic of nonviolence and the goal of integration were met with violent resistance in the South and only symbolic support in the halls of Congress (Allen 1992; Marable 2007).

Other research suggests that, even when radical restructuring is not an explicit goal of a movement, something approximating it can occur almost as an unintentional consequence of a prolonged series of reformist goals (Duggan and Hunter 1995). Again, the same-sex marriage issue is relevant here. Some have suggested that the extension of gays into the institution of marriage would radically change that institution. It would lead to an erosion of the sex-role distinctions and inequalities built into the institution, would push the institution further into the civil or secular sphere and away from the private or religious sphere, and would encourage a cultural re-imagining of the idea of family. This move from reform to restructuring is most likely to occur when individuals who favor more radical goals can be convinced to remain in the movement during the period of prolonged reform. Correspondingly, individuals who prefer reform must be convinced to remain in the movement even though their immediate interests were met and participate in the pursuit of each additional increasingly radical reform.

The example of AIDS activism in Hartford and Connecticut provides a limited example of this dynamic. John, a progressive activist in the city for over a decade, witnessed the transformation of the political environment for HIV/AIDS services, outreach, education, and advocacy:

> It has taken a long time on the AIDS stuff. We have managed to get the legislature to make up for Ryan White shortfalls but that was like years and years of building activists in the AIDS community to mobilize them for something that was a crisis situation. Now we have the Connecticut Aids Resource Coalition and that is a very good model because they have become the statewide spokespeople; they also have a state and local agenda. They are like the organizational embodiment of the activism....You have victories where people feel emboldened. You can't say "we can win this now then we can add later" if the base isn't hearing it. You have to listen to the base!

As John is describing this reform/restructuring dynamic, he mentions an important factor in the success of this dynamic in changing the way that HIV/AIDS is handled in Connecticut. John's almost offhanded comment: "You have to listen to the base" suggests that democratic decision making is important to keep everyone interested in the piecemeal reforms. This notion of democracy, moreover, is much more interactive than our traditional top-down notion since it involves an element of education and dialogue between the base and the leadership. Directly related to this, he also mentions another factor equally important in keeping individuals committed for the long haul—an organization with a resource stream and leadership to monitor the past successes and push for the present and future successes. Whether this shift in the state's approach to HIV/AIDS is truly radical is debatable. Regardless, John's comment points to ways to move movements along from piecemeal reforms to successive reforms that build toward benefits and structures not imaginable at the outset of this process.

In addition to democratic decision making and organization as necessary to move goals in a radical direction, some activists in the labor movement in Hartford stress another dimension as equally important. This dimension can be best expressed as education through action. In the extended epigraph to the chapter, Laura M. embraces a radical goal for her progressive organizing—a redistribution of power— but does not suggest how to move workers to get there. Jeremy, another labor organizer, describes this process:

> The essence of what I do is pushing workers to fight...to fight the boss....Most people, and not to sound demeaning toward workers, but most workers are not raised to, were not taught to fight. They go to school and they're taught when to turn in their homework and when to show up, and hall passes to go to the bathroom, and then they have detention when they do something wrong. They get to work and they have to show up at certain times, and punch in their hours. Then all of a sudden, "Okay you want to change your life?" you've got to be responsible for something other than your job and your kid. That's incredibly hard. That's what organizing is.

By "pushing workers to fight," they will learn that confrontations with power yield victories. More importantly, they yield changes in workers' consciousness that then get them to keep on fighting. Kevin, in his description of the anti-war march in downtown Hartford at the beginning of the chapter, hopes for a similar outcome. In these ways, education through action imagines ways to work on reformist goals in such a way that puts individuals and their interests in interaction with others, particularly with those who oppose their interests. This process of interaction and the "exchange" of information that takes place changes those individuals and their interests pushing both in more radical directions.

The third distinction in this discussion of social movement goals also involves the nature of the changes demanded. This dimension differentiates between the more concrete, easily measured, demands of changing laws, practices, and policies and the more abstract but equally important demands of changing people's attitudes and the larger culture's image of a particular group or issue.[4] For example, AIDS activist groups have fought for legislation that includes people with AIDS under the protections of the Americans with Disabilities Act—clearly a change in a law. Others have focused on the cultural arena, protesting the media's representations of people with AIDS, and educating the public in order to reduce the stigma surrounding the disease. Of those activists who introduced this chapter, Josh's work in the independent media movement represents the cultural goals that movements can pursue. Alta and Jack, who do community organizing, represent activists who pursue the concrete legislative and service delivery goals of progressive movements.

Like the other dimensions about goals discussed by scholars, this distinction is never clear-cut or neat: attempts to change laws may also involve education or be limited by cultural assumptions about what ideas can be brought into the state; attempts to change the content of the culture may also involve changing the rules, procedures, and policies of the institutions that produce and disseminate that culture. Still, this distinction is valuable since each of these targets is associated with its own set of challenges. Scholars point to the almost inevitable "watering down of demands" that takes place once these demands enter the legislative arena and must compete with better-resourced and better-networked organized interests. They also point to the precariousness of the gains in policies and laws if the culture does not support these gains or if there is not effective enforcement of these laws. For social movements focused on cultural goals, scholars point to an opposite set of problems. How do we know that the education or performance is truly changing attitudes? How do we know that those changed attitudes get people to act in more progressive ways?

Perhaps as a way around these dilemmas, Hartford progressive activists primarily pursue the more instrumental goals of changing policies and institutional practices. Of course, they hope that achieving these goals will result in cultural change. Josh, for example, quoted in the introduction to this chapter, has worked assiduously in many campaigns to change college policy, combat policy brutality in African American communities, and as a community organizer. His ultimate hope is for large-scale cultural change, even if it is vaguely defined:

> I think this world could be better and a lot of people are suffering because of the inequalities of this current world. And I'm in position to change that and to prevent this further inequality in the future. And also, do I want her (pointing to his recently born daughter) to inherit that, and do I want the world to be a better place?

Even Josh's recent work in alternative media is narrowly focused in that it caters to the progressive niche and does not disturb the boundary between the alternative and mainstream.

One notable exception to this pattern is the work of Julia who is the director of an activist theater company in Hartford. Whether it involves creating theater with prison inmates or with city and suburban area students, performing street theater or producing main stage theater with progressive themes, this work clearly eschews the dominant tendency of changing laws and practices and embraces, in Julia's words, "creative activism for change." Julia's reflections on this work give us the opportunity to examine the challenges of focusing on the cultural goals of progressive activism as well as to assess the relationship between these goals and the more traditional policy-oriented goals of progressives in Hartford.

Julia first talks about how cultural activism is an important progressive goal by distancing it from the traditional goals of the Left:

> I do think that the Left grossly underestimates the power of theater and any type of creative activism for change. I do think a creative action, even a simple creative action, just goes so much further. Number one, because it's clever and people like it. Number two, it's a talking point. Number three, it can get media attention. Number four, it gets away from those people who would shut down when they heard "protest" and there's plenty of people that just shut down. It's something they don't want to do or something they don't want to even hear about really. Whereas if you do—again even simple creative action...it just has a huge effect so it really breaks out of that...The Left loves to talk, loves to speechify and loves to hear themselves speechify and I can't stand it and I tune out. At a rally I want to hear 5 minutes. That's it! Then I want to move or listen to music or watch something cool or I want to march or whatever it is but speaker after speaker after speaker kills me! And bottom line is when we are doing anything theatrical we get people outside the people who came that day to see the protest. It's entertaining.

Interestingly, part of the importance of producing culture in the form of theater, music, and art is not only about the challenge to the dominant meanings about an issue or an idea but also about building a larger audience or constituency for your message. In Julia's words, it attracts "people outside the people who came...to see the protest." This comment speaks to another aspect of cultural goals also noted by some research on social movements: movements with these goals are more effective as recruitment tools than are ones with traditional policy goals that strike many people as little different from mainstream politics.

This discussion, however, begs the question about the effectiveness of these cultural goals for progressive social change. Julia gives two answers to this question. The first answer deals with the particular ways in which her theater company creates, performs, and evaluates any of their cultural products. These ways involve an intensely interactive relationship between "the art" and the people, groups, and organizations that are the subjects of that art:

> There is "do they get it?" that's one question. Are they going to do something about it, is another question. I can work on "do they get it" and one way I do that is involving people in our process so they give us feedback along the way and that's a big part of what we do so it makes a big difference....It depends on what the project is. For instance, our plays in the park series this summer is about health care. We've interviewed 30 people and creating our play is based

on that. About a couple of weeks after we open the plays in the park series we will invite those interviewees back plus other community neighborhood members to see a preview to discuss it: what they are seeing and what they are getting and not getting. So that's one of the best ways that we can try to get a handle on what it is people are getting.

This technique provides a way to monitor whether people's understandings are changing as a result of the performance. As Julia continues, it also serves as a way of building support for the progressive movement in the city:

The third part of it is to keep whatever it is within a movement. So you keep these people you interviewed involved and coming to shows and talking to their friends and bringing them to shows and getting involved; and in this case [health care] there is a campaign [so get them involved in] what the campaign is doing.

This support extends not only to these individuals involved in the performances but to organizations in the city:

We spend a lot of time making partnerships with organizations. They are not necessarily activist organizations, a lot of times they're schools; they are faith-based groups, community centers, anything. We define partners as anything, from bringing in a group from somewhere to come see a piece or doing something grander, like this summer it's the Universal Health Care Foundation of Connecticut. It's basically a commission for these plays. So it really ranges from a tiny organization that we are doing something with or having a trade with or they are coming to see our show or come to do a workshop with, to the Universal Health Care Foundation...They are usually pretty grass roots but they really can range.

Despite the distinctions she initially makes between the traditional Left and her cultural activism, she consciously connects this activism back to that Left by recruiting new people, networks, and organizations into the political orbit of the progressive movement in the city.

The second way in which Julia talks about the effectiveness of cultural change is in terms of changing the political common sense of the society. She embraces the belief that somehow these challenges to culture that her theater group plays a small part in creating make ideas that were once seen as beyond the pale of legitimate political discourse seem more commonsensical. And, that common sense gets incorporated into the policymaking process:

I started to think about this [question of the role of culture in social change] through the piece we are working on now for our next main stage play...It's all about the history of the War on Poverty. What I got from interviewing is an understanding of looking back on history. I see certain presidents and their policies and what they stood for and what they didn't stand for. But what you realize for instance was the fact that Nixon, his policies were far more progressive than Clinton's and it wasn't because Nixon was such a great guy we all knew that. It was because the people forced him with different ideas. So, when we say the people's movements, it doesn't have to be what we, the people on the Left, call a movement. It can be an attitude, a feeling. They don't know they are part of it. I have hope about that.

Captured here is a powerful statement about the power of cultural change and its important if evanescent relationship with more traditional forms of political change.

When most other Hartford activists incorporate cultural goals of attitude change into their activism, it is directed at specific groups rather than at the general culture. This focus then enables activists to do identity-change work in specific communities or even among their own social movement constituency. It is consciousness-raising in the sense of moving an already defined but passive group into a position of empowerment as illustrated by Cornel, an activist in the virtually all Black North End of Hartford, a community with a history of "promises made, promises broken."

I think first people have to see leadership. For so long in that section of town the leaders have sold out...So the first thing we do is show people what we're doing so they can feel gut level that what we're doing is sincere. They don't see you selling out...I think you have to demonstrate also what it is that you claim that you're doing. So by going out doing certain things, standing up to the oppressor, people say, "Well, he's not just talk."

The shift in Black people's understanding of themselves that Cornel is interested in is accomplished through action "not just talk."

Another kind of cultural work performed by Cornel through his activism preventing drug dealing in North End neighborhoods is identity shifting in nature. It is an explicit strategy to reframe the meaning of the word "Black" whereby certain standards of conduct and behavior and not simply phenotypic traits are necessary for inclusion in the community:

We need to get rid of these men [drug dealers] who are oppressors even though they have the same skin color we have...to get away from that thinking: that these are our brothers. You are not my brother if you shoot down our children.

Similarly, David, the AIDS activist quoted in the introduction to the chapter, does education with young men of color which encourages identity reconfiguration: shifting the meaning of black or Latino away from any homophobic associations and broadening the definition of these identities to include more fully young people of non-heterosexual desires and orientations.

Conclusion

The different goal dimensions that scholars use can assist activists in thinking about goals more complexly. Scholarship shows that goals oriented to narrow constituencies or single-identity groups carry risks of exclusion; those oriented to broad constituencies carry risks of the loss of continuous support or commitment. Goals oriented to reform risk alienating important elements of the movement yet radical demands are rarely recognized by elites. Goals that focus on changing laws, policies, and practices deliver immediate and concrete benefits but may be ephemeral or limited if not accompanied by changes in "ways of thinking" about the issue. Activists can think about goals in this way: as a series of costs, benefits, and tradeoffs.

Also important, the stories that activists tell about their goals can inform the theoretical frameworks sociologists use to understand social movements. In general, the frameworks discussed in Chapters 2 and 3 spend too little time theorizing the decision making around social movement goals. Research using these frameworks, however, has identified sets of dilemmas or tensions that exist on those three dimensions of social movement goals and listening closely to activists can provide assistance in resolving these dilemmas. For example, some of my activists discuss the importance of consciousness-raising or coalitional work within social movements as a way of simultaneously valorizing and minimizing differences between groups. Others discuss the importance of the democratic process and action-based empowerment as a way of constructing agendas that are both reformist and restructuring in nature. Still others discuss the importance of cultural change, either targeted to the general society to reframe popular understanding of social issues or to a particular group or constituency to reconfigure the meaning of identities in the context of working on other more policy-oriented and practical goals. Both types of cultural goals take place with some degree of reference to policy change or to progressive networks that engage in policy change. In these activists' minds, policy change and cultural change go hand in hand.

Talking about Strategies and Tactics

Sociologists pair these goals with a corresponding set of strategies and tactics. Oftentimes, the distinctions between goals and strategies can get fuzzy and confusing since one person's means can be another person's ends. Consider Carmen's and David's approaches to activism from the introduction to the chapter. Carmen sees consciousness-raising among low-income Puerto Rican women as a means to mobilize for acts of civil disobedience or community organizing while David sees consciousness-raising among men of color as important for the interpersonal work of identity transformation. Nonetheless, these two types of strategies entail different motivations, likely outcomes, costs, and benefits. It is important to discuss them as conceptually different and to explore how and why they are combined in practice.

We can think of tactics and strategies as traversing two continua that yield three different types of strategic activity.[5] Strategies can traverse a talking/acting continuum such that social change is achieved through discourse or action and an insider/outsider continuum whereby activists direct their claims to those internal to the movement and the political system or outside those arenas. These dimensions capture several of the dynamics highlighted by the theoretical frameworks discussed in Chapter 3. The structural frameworks of resource mobilization and political opportunity stress actions, whether internal or external to mainstream politics, which affect policy and institutional practices. The cultural frameworks of collective identity, oppositional consciousness and new social movements stress discursive strategies, whether internally or externally directed which affect identity and attitudes.

These continua yield three general strategies to achieve social change. The first set I refer to as internal tactics or self-referential tactics since they are not necessarily directed at conventional or unconventional politics but are designed to communicate a discursive message to potential movement members or targeted publics. These consist of activities such as anti-racism workshops, street theater or festivals, and basketball tournaments to promote HIV prevention. The second set is insider tactics situated within the bounds of conventional politics such as lobbying, press conferences, and demonstrations that do not disrupt public routines. The third set is composed of outsider tactics seen as disruptive by the public and outside the bounds of conventional politics such as disrupting legislative hearings, blocking traffic, demonstrating outside the homes of corporate officials, or other forms of civil disobedience. Similar to our discussion of social movement goals, this typology enables an examination of the challenges associated with each type and allows a dialogue between the findings from social movement research and the activists themselves about the challenges associated with different types of strategies and tactics.

The scholarship that focuses on the first set of strategies of education and consciousness-raising for social change sees this process as slow or not as effective as more dramatic tactics and strategies (Burstein 1985). There is an implicit assumption in this work that changing people's attitudes is much more uncertain than changing the laws that compel behavior (Rochon 1998). We have already seen this assessment in our discussion of education and consciousness-raising as social movement goals.

One of the critiques made of the civil rights movement prior to the 1960s, for example, was that it relied mainly on a strategy of "changing hearts and minds" and could not effectively address the entrenched institutional racism of American society. The alternative strategy proposed the use of protest, lobbying, etc., in order to change laws and institutional practices as quickly as possible. This strategy would in turn produce changes in attitudes. As mentioned earlier, it is difficult to measure the effectiveness of this strategy of education and consciousness-raising. How do we know the education is having an impact? Related to this, where is this strategy directed? Is the education targeted internally to the members of the social movement or is it directed outward to the public and the culture at large? Does the education need to have a tangible impact on behavior or is attitude change in itself an acceptable social movement outcome?

We have already seen one way that Hartford activists deal with these questions of education and consciousness-raising, that is by treating these organizing strategies not as a means to an end but as explicit goals of collective action. Whether consciously or not, Hartford activists have expanded the definition of progressive activism beyond the boundaries of legal reform, structural change, and even class-based social change and embrace the idea that changing the ways people think about themselves and the world around them is a laudable progressive act.

There is another set of scholarship that stresses the importance of education and consciousness-raising internal to social movements as a precursor to the pursuit of social movement goals. This scholarship references the concept of collective identity discussed in Chapter 3 as a necessary precursor to collective action. There must be some notion of group-ness—defined in terms of interests, boundaries, ideas, and emotions—in order for most kinds of goal-oriented mobilization.

My activists would both agree and disagree with this assertion. Some notion of the collective is necessary for any kind of joint activity but the nature of that collective and the kinds of education and consciousness-raising work required depends on the goals being pursued.

Contrast the approaches to organizing in the introduction to the chapter to see this variability. For example, Carmen engages in time-consuming empowerment strategies with poor women of color as a prelude to collective action while Alta simply helps individuals access their self-interest to solve a specific problem. Carmen cultivates a deep sense of collective identity rooted in gender, racial, and ethnic oppression: in her words, to help a woman "who has a third grade or a fifth grade education, a woman that, like I am, has been oppressed all her life, come out of that shell and learn to say, 'I want change'." Other activists also stress the slow, long, uncertain work of this kind of consciousness-raising. Laura L., for example, also focuses on the empowerment strategy of activism:

> Organizing is very, very slow. You just sit with people in their kitchens, and you listen and get to know their lives, and then you agitate around what they're angry about and how they're being treated by their landlord or by the city or by whatever, you know, whomever...But the most important thing is "the clicks," like when people get it, they start getting it. "We are being"—they don't use the word but it is "oppressed": "The capitalist upper class is the enemy, and we are all—I have something in common with that person who is a different color or race than me, even though she or he is poor and I'm not, we're being kept down by this big capitalist class."

And, as Laura L. notes throughout her interview, the "clicks" are about coming to an understanding of oneself not as a homeowner or a neighborhood resident but as a member of a marginalized class, racial, ethnic or gender group. Another community organizer, Janice, a protégé of Laura, expresses this transformation from personal to political power: "it's a very thin line between empowering and becoming a power house!"

By contrast, Alta cultivates a place-based and an interest-based sense of collective identity: in Alta's words, "...letting the people decide...helping people clarify their self-interest." Another activist is even more explicit about the nature of the collective identity cultivated by this type of community organizing. Karen tells a story of how she was recruited into organizing and in the process reveals the kind of collective identity she builds:

> What do you like about your neighborhood? And that's how he [the organizer] started the conversation. And then he went on to say if there was anything you could fix, what would you fix in your neighborhood? And how would you fix it? And I use that to this very day...I think [neighborhood organizing] makes a huge difference. Just the fact of letting people know that you can come together with your neighbor and with other people on your street and change whatever it is you want to change...So my mantra back then is what have you got to lose? What have we got to lose? We have nothing to lose, it's not like we have politicians knocking on our door, what have you got to lose? And once you say that to people and they understand it, it's like yeah, what do we have to lose? So again people were able to come out more.

People "come out" as residents of neighborhoods with high levels of poverty, absentee landlords, crime, drugs, and the lack of police protection, and a dearth of public services.

Each of these education and consciousness-raising strategies comes with its own set of organizing challenges. As Laura L. is quick to mention, this identity-based kind of consciousness-raising tends to be "very, very slow" and requires a fairly long-term commitment on the part of both the organizer and the members. But the payoff for that work, as Laura L. also mentions, is "the clicks" that occur in people's heads. These transformations are both personal as well as political. This change in consciousness oftentimes results in a change in the circumstances of one's personal life and in the willingness of an individual to act in public and political ways. One specific story that Laura L. tells illustrates this connection between personal transformation and the imperative to act:

> One woman, she was on state, she was involved with a drug addict, this guy who was a drug addict, I mean her life was mess. So I door knock. She said her life was a mess. And then after a couple years of organizing she got out of welfare, she went back to work, I mean, she found a job, she dropped the drug addict, she got into a healthy relationship, her life's just totally, totally

changed....So those clicks when people start getting it and that takes a long, long time, but they start putting it all together and they start saying, "Yes, I deserve to be at this table to make these decisions." They stop feeling hopeless and they feel like they do have a stake in their lives, like they can make change. And that's just amazing when you see that happen. And it's very exciting. Just all those clicks start happening and it makes it all worth it.

So, even though this strategy is time-consuming and uncertain, it not only creates an oppositional consciousness but an activist identity. The imperative to act does not have to be created anew but becomes an essential part of who that person is.

The strategy of organizing on the basis of self-interest has a different set of challenges. It is also time-consuming but, unlike the identity-based strategy, it does not attempt to do any deep transformative work. Of course, personal transformation can be an outcome but the main purpose of this strategy is to get something tangible done: a service delivered, a law passed, a program expanded. As Alta insists in her excerpt from the beginning of the chapter, the specific goal is determined by the individuals trying to come to some agreement on their collective self-interest: "community organizing is about letting the people decide."

The tradeoff with this strategy lies in the limits of self-interest as a principle for organizing since it encourages a definition of social change in terms of specific neighborhood problems with no larger account of the causes of these problems or an analysis of whose particular self-interests are being addressed in the process of decision making and whose are being left out. This danger is voiced by Josh, a brief member of a Hartford community organization that subscribed to this strategy:

> I was an organizer for a while in the South End, and kind of a real tough thing for me. I mean I got a lot out of it especially an analysis of power, learning about power. We're trained through the national training and information center in Chicago. I mean, real hard core Alinsky. And I mean Alinsky is all about whatever they want to work on, you're going to fucking work on. And it's like what? [organizing against] fucking Mister Softee [trucks]! What the fuck man? And then you have a system where it is always feeding into the police. Got a problem? We're going to organize you folks, and what we're going to get is more police and more militarization and more men of color in prison, and that's what is defined as victory in neighborhood organizing when I was doing it. It's all about feeding back into the system and creating more dependency on law enforcement, and that was like bread and butter. You always had police at your meetings, situations where police would take over the meeting and, you know, they'd become the de facto organizers. I mean they're not organizers, but they're the ones who take all the questions and they've got all the answers and they fill you with all the sweet honey in your ear that they want to hear.

If we read this strong critique of community organizing alongside the somewhat different strategy of education and raising consciousness described by Laura L. and

Carmen, we can understand the dangers of this Alinsky-inspired strategy attacked by Josh. This strategy does not explicitly cultivate a larger sense of collective identity embraced by Laura L. and Carmen. Consequently, individuals remain self-interested and are not encouraged to develop any larger understanding of themselves beyond being members of the same neighborhood.

Returning to the assertion of sociologists that social movements require collective identity on the part of their members in order to mobilize and pursue social change, activists show us that there are many different kinds of "we's" or senses of group-ness that provide the motivation and the grievances for action: from the relatively thin understanding of a collective built on self-interest to a thicker understanding of a collective built on historically constructed identities of class, race, ethnic, or gender marginalization. Each strategy yields action with different sets of consequences, risks, and tradeoffs.

Finally, most activists who use strategies of education and consciousness-raising to promote progressive social change use the metaphor of battle, as do virtually all of the activists I talked with. Of course, that makes a great deal of sense since, to paraphrase the nineteenth-century abolitionist, Frederick Douglas, "power concedes nothing without a fight." One exception to this pattern was voiced by Julia, the head of the activist theater company described earlier in the chapter. While she still holds onto the notion of "battle" and "opponents," she grapples with a new understanding of activism that is emerging from her work:

> The thing that happened over the years that I am very proud of is—taught it by the art—is to see something from another person's perspective. I was taught that through art because you become something else or because you are telling a story and you want to really tell the story and so you need to see multiple perspectives. You have to empathize, you have to believe that this person feels what they are doing is right or okay or just. I think that it helped me in my activism to try to understand why people do what they do. And why organizations do what they do and governments do what they do. That's one thing I think I have gotten better at over the years. So this idea of empathy...to try to understand....Don't get me wrong I love to fight! I am sure you can tell that about me. [But most strategies] rely on not understanding your foe...and I think we could see more success if we tried to understand. [That doesn't mean] I won't protest because that's negative. I can do battle if the moment demands it. And even understanding them I can use it against them if I need to. It doesn't mean necessarily it's this wonderfully altruistic thing.

This model of education and consciousness-raising is quite different from other activists in that it is not directed to a specific "disenfranchised" group or even to the culture at large. In some sense, it is directed at those with power in order to understand their motives, interests, and the methods they use to hold onto that power. This understanding becomes a battle tactic, as alluded to by Julia. Although never fully developed, Julia's theater-based strategy of empathetic understanding could be extended in a more interactive or dialogic direction. If the "powerful" and their allies could be compelled to empathetic understanding, who knows what impact that would have on "the balance of power" in future fights? Suffice to say, this strategy is not a common one among progressive activists.

A second set of strategies used by Hartford progressive activists in the pursuit of social change involves lobbying, political campaigning, running for office, and other forms of interest-group politics. Recall the introductory quotes of Andrew describing his progressive constituent work in the North End of the city and of Ann describing the campaign for same-sex marriage as examples of this second set of strategies. Each activist sees this somewhat mainstream political work as necessary to deliver a progressive policy outcome (same-sex marriage, in Ann's case) or a shift in the balance of local power (progressive control of the Democratic town committee, in Andrew's case).

Some social movement scholars see these tactics in the pursuit of progressive goals as limited in their effectiveness because they are not so different from the tactics used in the normal process of interest-group politics. Only rarely can these tactics get lawmakers to make significant progressive change since progressive lobbyists have to compete with their more influential and wealthier counterparts from business, organized religion, or other agents of the status quo. Because compromise is a necessary part of interest-group politics, protest groups must engage in that compromise which many times results in the channeling of the protest into legitimate political activities. In addition, recruitment to collective action that utilizes these types of strategy and tactics also resembles recruitment into interest-group politics. There may be an initial flurry of interest but then this interest dissipates as campaigns are won or lost. As a consequence, some individuals who may be interested in more dramatic tactics or radical change fall away and other individuals, finding that their specific reason for joining has been met by the campaign, also cease their involvement.

Research on these types of strategies reveals that they are most effective when they take place within favorable political environments. Recall our discussion of the political opportunity framework from Chapter 2. If there are some vulnerabilities in the normal political process resulting from electoral shifts or increased political participation, these vulnerabilities may give previously disenfranchised groups access to the decision-making process. In this case, strategies such as lobbying, campaigning, and third party leverage can convince political elites to act differently and in a more progressive direction.

My activists would both agree and disagree with this research finding. Those who disagree are usually activists who do not use insider strategies to accomplish their progressive goals so they are less attentive to or interested in what is politically possible. Many of them are activists who deliver services in politically progressive ways. David, one of the activists who introduced the chapter, falls into this category. His activism around HIV/AIDS entails delivering services, planning events, lobbying for more money, and empowering individuals. Another "service" activist is Chris who works with the Catholic Worker organization in Hartford which delivers a variety of services to the economically impoverished North End. This work does not require access to nor is it dependent on the political structures of the city, state, or federal governments. As a matter of fact, it exists almost in spite of these political structures:

> Our work includes taking in homeless folks to share our living space with us. And over the years we've had all sorts of different folks from all circumstances stay with us. Folks with—that are homeless, refugees, kids that are too young to live in shelters, people that just got out of prison. You name it they've stayed with us. We work with children in our neighborhood, have tutoring after school for them, weekend programs, summer camps, try to give them an alternative to the gangs. Try to give them a reason to have hope, to stay in school, to show them love and affection, and provide them with good food, fresh fruit, things like that. We have several different food ministries, helping people in the neighborhood with food... We also help people with furniture. We collect furniture and make it available to people. There are kids in this neighborhood that don't have beds to sleep on. Folks that don't have refrigerators and stoves and things like that. So we get the furniture and make that available to them. A lot of our work though is ad hoc...Last week...a man was beating a woman, and so it's running down and stopping that. Also, last week the police with guns drawn were in our driveway kicking a man, so some of the folks stopped them from kicking him.

This service delivery, moreover, is infused with a progressive philosophy:

> Another part of our work is trying to bring issues of poverty, violence—in the neighborhood, violence abroad—to our base of support which is largely white and largely suburban. Trying to build some bridges between the neighbor-hoods and the suburbs, but also to try to build some bridges between some of the distant lands we've traveled to...to bring our peace efforts to those folks. You know, the charitable work we do, working with kids, housing homeless folks, is work that Middle America can wrap their mind around to support, and it gives us an entrance to a basis of relationship to make connections to deeper issues of injustice, and you know, structural causes of poverty and prejudice, and also causes of war.

Unlike the activism that has preoccupied scholars of social movements, progres-sive activism in Hartford spans initiatives and campaigns that are not only oriented to the traditional political structures of power. Thus, they cannot be understood in terms of gaining influence in or being closed out of those structures of power.

There are other activists who also do not take their cues from the political envi-ronment but they still see their work as having some relationship to that environ-ment. These activists do not necessarily "read" the political opportunity structure then act accordingly, as the scholars would have it. Instead they see their activism as altering the balance of power in that opportunity structure in fundamental ways. Of the activists cited in the introduction, Laura M. and Josh would fall into this category. Laura M.'s labor organizing activities and Josh's media activism are obviously influenced by the political context but their strategies and tactics are geared toward rearranging political power on their own terms and in the long term. They are not trying to identify system vulnerabilities to obtain some immediate policy change or an increase in resources. In reference to her motivation for her tireless labor organizing in a hostile political environment: Laura M. states: "We have to get more soldiers on our side in order to win that [class] war." Each organizing victory, and there are some despite the many barriers to success, changes that political environment thus opening up that structure in a progressive direction. Thus, activists do not simply react to political opportunities, they create them.

There are still others who quite explicitly weigh the costs and benefits of acting against the realities of the politically possible. These are the activists who rely exclusively on this second set of strategies and who would agree with the assessment of scholars that movements are most effective when they exploit vulnerabilities in the political environment. Their internal processes of decision making take into account the political context and what is politically possible to accomplish in that context. Ann's carefully considered legislative strategy on same-sex family policy in the wake of a defeat of a second parent adoption bill illustrates how activists "read" the political opportunity structure:

> That's when we increased the efforts, and in fact, we had lots of house meetings with legislators and their constituents who supported the second parent adoption bill...So, we just continued the same kind of grass roots organizing efforts once we moved to marriage.

Clearly, the political calculation was that the legislative arena was not only the appropriate arena for the goal but that it was the arena where significant movement toward that goal was possible. The calculation and the hard work paid off since in 2005 Connecticut became the second state in the nation to pass a civil unions law which extends all the state-level rights and benefits associated with marriage to registered same-sex couples. The organization that Ann represents was unable at that time to get the Connecticut General Assembly to follow Massachusetts' lead and pass a bona fide gay marriage bill thus giving some credence to the research pointing to the inevitability of policy compromise when progressive activists enter the legislative arena.[6]

These progressive activists do not fret too much about the tradeoffs involved when they decide to pursue an insider strategy. For some it is a no-brainer: if you want social recognition in the form of a law passed, changed, or repealed, a practice prevented, more money or services for your constituency, the normal electoral route using the normal electoral strategies makes the most sense. They insist that just because they are engaging in processes of lobbying, negotiating, compromising, and adhering to the conventions of normal politics does not mean that they are not pursuing progressive social change. Nor does it mean that an insider strategy is an easier alternative to other types of collective action strategies.

The best example of the difficulties and challenges associated with insider challenges of a progressive nature is the construction of a progressive electoral coalition and a political party that dominated Hartford politics briefly in the late 1980s and 1990s, called People for a Change (PFC). This example also illustrates the ways in which progressives push this second set of strategies away from efforts to effect policy on a piecemeal basis to a larger mobilization around changing the balance of political power in government. PFC involved the support of several sectors of the progressive community in the city who previously had little contact with one another: progressive elements of the African American community, progressive labor unions with sizable memberships in the city, progressive members of the lesbian and gay community organized in the Coalition for Lesbian and Gay Civil Rights, and the newly emerging Puerto Rican political community. Unlike the mainstream political parties that simply mobilized constituencies around platforms consistent with the broad policy proscriptions with principles of the Democratic or Republican parties, People for a Change had to bring together several constituencies which, although all marginalized in the political process, had different short-term political interests. PFC activists had to give these constituencies a reason to come together. They also had to negotiate a policy platform composed of specific initiatives that did not give everyone what they wanted but enough of what they wanted to remain in the coalition.

Several activists involved in this effort spoke of these challenges. One activist in particular addressed directly the social movement dilemma of progressives working on electoral campaigns. Steve, a union organizer for the service workers union in Hartford, one of the more militant unions both locally and nationally, quickly names the People for a Change experience as a major success both personally and for the progressive community in Hartford:

> Well, the first thing that jumped into my head actually wasn't labor stuff except in a coalition sense. It was the People for a Change first victory...a third party actually winning, not an independent candidate, but a third—we actually built an organization and then figured out who the people should be to run, which is the right way to do it...And winning two seats that time and then being able to continue that work for a good six–seven years, that to me was, I felt very good about that work....This was at a time when everyone had abandoned progressive work outside of the electoral arena. Everyone was being funneled into pretty straight electoral work. And I was really unhappy with that idea, and I resisted with all my might. I just thought it was a huge waste of time, and also really distasteful in the way it pandered to people's worst, you know, if crime was the issue you'd come up with the biggest crime brochure, anti-crime brochure. You'd pander to whatever you thought would get you a vote. And with People For Change we had to fight off that tendency too, but still we were fighting it from a perspective of, "This is wrong, how can we win without going to the lowest

common denominator?"...And within a year we had an organization and we had a party and we had some victories. I think that was, now that kind of success is sort of fleeting because that's just a blip on the electoral radar screen, but it showed that that kind of stuff was possible.

Another key participant in this progressive electoral effort, John, a gay rights activist at the time, gives a good idea of how this pandering to the lowest common denominator, definitely one of the dangers of electoral politics, was avoided through a strategy of deep coalition building:

> I think the coalition building was significant because it put on the agendas of labor unions and others, [the issue of gay rights]. They had not been as strongly supportive in the past, but throughout all of it, it was again those personal relationships that changed either homophobic progressives or indifferent progressives into advocates for gay rights. I mean it was a struggle to get the full agenda we wanted in the People for Change platform. [I]t was breaking [new] ground and they didn't know how to handle gay issues beyond basic civil rights. We wanted stuff in and around HIV/AIDS and a commission on gay and lesbian issues, a city commission. So that fight in People For Change, not a fight, but we had to advocate, had ripple effects because it raised their consciousness as progressives, that gay issues are a civil rights issue and needs to be on par with a lot of the other issues.

These recollections on the challenges and pitfalls of an electoral strategy for progressive social change reminds social movement scholars that the distinctions we make between different sets of strategies and tactics are porous and movements frequently rely on combinations of those strategies. One only needs to read "between the lines" of both Steve's and John's comments to see the importance of internal processes of education and consciousness raising as well as more direct action strategies of demonstration and confrontation for the successful application of this electoral strategy.

These more disruptive direct action strategies comprise the third type of strategies and tactics scholars identify as part of the repertoire of progressive social movements. These strategies entail the public demonstration of demands whether in the form of public rallies, marches, vigils, or civil disobedience. This repertoire of tactics depends on the state's legal system to authorize or prevent such collective displays and on the right to free assembly associated with the liberal democratic state. Some scholars see these tactics as more consonant with progressive demands in that they create spectacle, call attention to the issues, and are oftentimes used because the issues get no hearing inside the halls of power. The groups who voice these issues, moreover, have little institutional power and are on the bottom of the racial, ethnic, and class hierarchies.

If these tactics are not state sanctioned or if activists engage in civil disobedience these constitute a different form altogether, one characterized by disruptions of "business as usual." These tactics can serve several ends. They force everyone, elites in particular, to take notice thus making visible the progressive demands of the group. By disrupting business as usual, they may encourage immediate concessions if only to restore order. They also frequently invite conflict which can solidify the commitment of the members of the group and also increase support for the group especially if the nonviolent resistance is met with police violence, arrest, and imprisonment. Of course, there are dangers associated with this tactic, not only personal risks and dangers but also the possibility that disruption will alienate potential allies, invite repression from elites, and provide the media with an opportunity to vilify the movement.

Activists spend a great deal of time puzzling over this thicket of dilemmas associated with this high-risk strategy. These dilemmas are bluntly stated by Josh: "[In our work] we confront all the classic tensions: non-violence, pacifism, property destruction, do we get a permit, do we march in the street, [or do we] fuck the cops, fuck the permit?" Kevin, in his account from the introduction of the chapter describing an anti-war demonstration that resulted in several arrests and some bad publicity, insists on the continued importance of these disruptive tactics for building internal solidarity: "if nothing else ..., you're getting people together, getting them energized, and that's part of the thing."

Carmen, also cited in the introduction to the chapter, is a fierce advocate of these tactics, which is not surprising given her history of activism for low-income non-white women in the city. The short-lived grass roots organization she helped found, Warriors for Real Welfare Reform, was built using these outsider tactics and, as her account below suggests, was successful owing to the disruption caused by these tactics:

> One of our first victories was with Otis Elevator. We went to the Otis Elevator Company with about two or three busloads of people, and a TV crew. We went looking for jobs. And we filled out applications. And we went in their lobby and blocked all the process up, and all these kids are running around, it was wonderful. And then they sent us to the back, where the employees go—all the employees who were getting their paychecks were all black and Latino—so it gave it more impact, because they were like, "Yeah!" You know? And the TV's catching this. We wound up—they assigned a representative from their company who started working with us, and we got about four or five of our people earning $20 an hour...living wage jobs, with benefits.

Carmen is quick to point out the limits of this strategy: that the campaign generated jobs for only "four or five of our people." Perhaps understanding these limits, the organization frequently supplemented the disruptive strategies with other strategies that built connections across other grassroots organizations. These organizations then confronted various elites (e.g. state government, social service bureaucrats, employer organizations) with specific demands, once again illustrating the connections across social movement strategies.

As just mentioned, most progressive activists are not satisfied to simply "cause a ruckus" and leave it to elites to address activist demands without some sort of ongoing input on the part of activist groups. Several activists were deeply involved in a seventeen-year effort to pass a gay and lesbian civil rights bill in the state. For the most part, this was an effort of lobbying, constituent building, enlisting influential allies, and fundraising—a repertoire taken from that second type of strategies and tactics. Periodically, however, and particularly toward the end of the struggle, these strategies were paired with more disruptive strategies. As Carolyn tells it, these decisions were made in response to the slow pace of change and internal frustration with the insider tactics utilized:

> ...So, we all went up, it was greatly orchestrated, and we went up into the gallery [of the General Assembly], and the capitol police were really not that aware of people doing this type of action, so they were fairly relaxed, so at a certain moment we threw the banners down into the house—the hall of the house, and started chanting for gay rights, lesbian rights...and we got arrested and actually had to go to court...I think that strategy of direct action raised the ante, put more pressure, helped energize and sort of mobilize some people who really felt, "Are we ever going to get our rights?" Because some people were frustrated.

Soon after this, and due partly to the positive publicity the civil disobedience received in the press, the civil rights bill was passed.

Another aspect of this carefully calibrated use of both outsider and insider strategies used by activists is what resource mobilization scholars call the radical flank effect, discussed in Chapter 2. This dynamic involves two sectors or organizations in a campaign or a movement fighting for a similar goal: one group demands the goal using traditional interest-group tactics; the other group pursues a more disruptive set of strategies such as public demonstrations, civil disobedience, and radical rhetoric. The encounter with elites to meet the demands is made by those engaged in lobbying and education. They employ some version of: "we are the reasonable one, give us what we want or else you will have to engage the radicals." It is a strategy to deliver progressive goals by playing the radicals against the reformers in the movement's encounter with elites.

This strategy has a fairly long history first identified by scholars studying the civil rights movement. At several points during the 1960s the integrationist sector of the movement represented at this time by Martin Luther King and the Southern Christian leadership Conference juxtaposed their strategies and demands with the increasingly militant separatist wing of the movement represented by Malcolm X in the North and the Student Nonviolent Coordinating Committee in the South (Haines 1988). Most recently, this strategy has been used by the animal rights movement to get more humane treatment of animals in scientific research and food production (Jasper 1997: 246–8). They have done this by presenting the goal as the more reasonable goal compared to animal liberationists who demand the elimination of animal testing and the use of animal products for clothing and food. The success of this strategy depends on the implicit cooperation between the reformists and the radicals. After all, the radicals don't get all of what they want and even get cast as the extremists by the movement and by the public at large.

Some Hartford activists who employ radical flank strategies attempt to avoid these pitfalls by emphasizing the careful coordination between factions. Even neighborhood organizers in Hartford who have accumulated a fair amount of insider power and are quite hesitant to employ these strategies speak of the need for a radical flank. Alta states this bluntly:

> You've got to have somebody outside to attack. Any movement, I don't care if it's the PLO, the ANC, if you've got somebody outside, and that was the genius of Nelson Mandela, and he's probably the only person who could do this, and did this, to change from the rebel leader to the president. It's always a challenge.

In the case of the mobilization for the gay civil rights bill mentioned above, many of those who comprised the radical flank were longstanding members of the moderate faction and this feature of the strategy helped mitigate tensions that often characterize the radical flank approach to social change. Carolyn, a participant in both the moderate and radical factions of the campaign, assesses the pitfalls in this way: "you use all forms of strategy to win," and that timing is crucial:

> It wasn't just the direct action—all these other themes were also working, but to me it was the combination of many of those different things that were happening, sort of politically in the environment as well as our choices in some of our organizing.

The direct action happened alongside a variety of other strategies: lobbying, coalition building, organization building, and the highly publicized "coming out" of two influential state officials.

Conclusion

Listening to the strategies and tactics of Hartford's progressive activists using the typology developed from sociologists' theoretical frameworks yields several potentially useful insights for activists. One insight involves the concept of the radical flank and its usefulness for achieving progressive goals. In particular, research that identified the operation of this dynamic in previous mobilizations suggests several potential risks for the internal cohesion of the movement. This insight, as well as the experiences of several activists with this strategy, suggests that these tensions can be averted by close ties between factions and ongoing conversations about when to employ this strategy.

In addition, sociologists' concept of collective identity that highlights the internalization of progressive ideas, goals, and strategies into the social psychology of individual activists can assist in facilitating discussions within different sectors of the progressive community. This concept can help activists understand the depth and power of the commitment of individual activists to different kinds of progressive action. In turn, this understanding can inform discussions of collaboration and coalition across activists with different kinds of collective identity. As the preceding discussion emphasized, different kinds of collective identity are associated with different costs and benefits. This knowledge can serve as a starting point for these discussions.

Conversely, the stories that activists tell about their strategies can inform the theoretical frameworks sociologists use to understand the tactics and strategies of social movements. The immediate lesson we can learn is that tactics and strategies are not always easily distinguishable from the goals of social movements. The tactic of educating and raising consciousness, sometimes a means to an end, is also a goal of social movements. Direct action tactics may affect policy and institutional practices and in that way serve as intended: as a means to an end. But they can also have other consequences as well, such as creating media awareness or heightening solidarity among participants. These consequences are also seen by activists as equally worthy goals.

Additionally, activists would also want to complicate the scholarly concept of political opportunity structure in several ways. Again, these activists reinforce the importance of this concept since some activists do indeed devote considerable time to "reading" the opportunity structure and strategizing on the basis of that reading. They also reinforce the idea that activists are a part of that opportunity structure since activists develop strategies and tactics to change the nature of the political environment. But there are others, particularly those doing cultural activism or progressive social service delivery, whose "strategizing" takes place outside that structure. These activists respond to different contextual cues not captured by the political opportunity concept.

Chapter 5

What Activists Do: Gathering Resources, Forming Organizations

We knew that we were going to lose a lot of our funding through the Department of Public Health because the money comes in through the CDC [Center for Disease Control]. The CDC changed their criteria for HIV and AIDS stuff, and youth are no longer considered a high-risk population...Only about 3% of our total income right now is personal, private donors. But building a donor base is going to be our critical piece. And fee for services currently represent about 12% of our income...And we need to bring that up to 40 or 50% in order to keep up a little more. And then we also have private grants...You almost grow, I think it's called like the Peter Principle, growing just beyond your capabilities. Budgets and finances and stuff like that is not my strength. It's been a painful process of going from receipts in a sack to coming up with budgets for programs and stuff. It almost seems like in an ideal world there would be somebody whose job it would be to do organizing and visionary stuff, and somebody else who would be doing, like all successful men, the woman behind the man...And so, it's definitely challenging, and I get behind on grant work. And on the finances and stuff and trying to remember what reports are due when. (Robin, 47-year-old white working-class female)

It's hard [to keep the money flowing]. We write grants all over the place all the time. We get grants, we get state grants, city grants, corporate things, you know, foundations give us money, we write grants all the time. I mean, my attitude always had been, if we're doing the right thing the money would come, but damn, you really have to work for it, and nobody wants to fund ongoing programming expenses. So, once you get a good program everybody wants something new. That's crazy. We're not going to start a new thing, and get a new group going, and then tell those girls [in the Latina empowerment group], "Oh, sorry, your group ends this year, you're all into it, and you've just established a real strong support network among each other, but we're going to have to close you down." (Lisa, 39-year-old white middle-class female)

[My biggest challenge now] is doing real true grassroots organizing. Being able to just do grassroots organizing, not programming, not getting people to come together to give out turkeys, not that stuff, just plain good old-fashioned grassroots organizing. (Karen, 43-year-old West Indian middle-class female)

If you're not building organization, you're going to end up losing....So, one of the things that we learned even when we're doing issues and campaigns that might take a while is paying attention to the small things that are constantly helping to build the organization...And as we gradually started winning those smaller fights and winning and winning, it's to the point now where it is just basically understood and it is in fact the official policy of the city of Hartford that organized neighborhoods are a real asset. That neighborhood people should be setting a priority. So you don't have to put a group together to win that—even get respect, to get in the room, they invite you in saying, "Yeah, what do you want?" So that change in the power relationships changes what you do in Hartford. (Jack, 58-year-old white middle-class male)

Is building organization necessarily building the movement? When you're developing organizations, you inherently become focused on money, membership and growth. And is it so insular that we focus too much on the organization and not on the world around us and on what the organization is doing to support the movement?...I mean we're in the middle of it right now because there's a lot of recent talk of the 501 c(3) issue. Is it time for us to become one? Because becoming a 501 c(3) opens us up to so many financial opportunities in theory. And legitimacy within the liberal money circle. Thinking long-term, thinking having an organization last into the future, is it vital to become a 501 c(3) to move into the future and be more lasting? And the other idea, is that "selling out," being recognized by the IRS to feed back into the capitalist system that we're supposed to be rejecting, on paper you need to have a board of directors, you need to have a lawyer for the paperwork or whatever. Are we compromising if we do that? And then just as a basic idea, just because you become a 501 c(3) it doesn't mean money's going to fucking pour into you. You gotta work your ass off to get that money. You need someone who is very talented at writing grants and moves within those circles, and for us who've never done that, we're all volunteers. Is it even worth it? And in most foundations or whatever, most foundations will only give you money if others have given you money. They want a proven track record, and so for a start-up like us, there's no reason to believe we're going to get money anytime soon. So we're in discussions right now just evaluating different things. You know, some say all this is on paper, who gives a fuck, you know, Joe Schmo is our president, who gives a shit? It's only for the IRS. It doesn't mean we have to change how we operate, it's only for more opportunity. Just because that system operates like that doesn't mean we have to join that. (Josh, 28-year-old white working-class male)

I was one of two Latinos on a board of directors that were all white. And I knew nothing about leadership development, and they were deliberately talking over my head, and they would say things I had no clue what the hell it meant...to deliberately keep me in the dark. (Luz, 52-year-old Puerto Rican working-class female)

I'm used to being tokenized. But I felt like my thing is: once I start off I might be the only one but I am pulling in everyone I can. That's what happened. I would get in being the token but I would not behave like they wanted me to because I knew they expected certain things especially when you are disabled: that people kind of like want to take care of you and not listen to anything you have to say. So they were like patronizing and protective and say: "look, what can she do, she's blind you know, what's the deal." (Cheryl, 53-year-old African American middle-class female)

While Chapter 4 introduced and complicated our understanding of how activists think about strategies and goals, this chapter highlights the constraints on as well as the facilitating factors for implementing effective strategies and achieving desired goals. As the introductory excerpts illustrate, these factors are both external and internal to social movements, factors like money, bureaucracy, and internal conflicts. As we will see below, however, some of these factors are best understood as neither external nor internal but as constituted in the interaction between the two. Also, these excerpts resonate with many of the concepts and frameworks of social movement scholars introduced in Chapters 2 and 3, although not always in predictable ways.

Robin and Lisa run progressive service delivery and advocacy organizations for LGBT youth and young Latina mothers respectively. Both lament the pressures of finding funding but these common pressures have different effects on their organizing. Changing and declining resource streams affect Robin's ability to do the grass-roots organizing that she loves. As Lisa notes, appealing to funders' idiosyncratic requirements limits the effectiveness of the organization's long-term programs and perverts the planning necessary for the rational delivery of services.

Successful activism usually means pressure to institutionalize that activism. Jack insists on the vital importance of building formal organizations among the disadvantaged in order to, among other things, exert countervailing power in the corridors of power in the city. Karen, who is also a community organizer, would agree with Jack about the importance of building formal organizations among the poor, although she is keenly aware of the tradeoffs involved. Unlike Jack, Karen, and others who embrace formal organizations for progressive work, Josh is much more ambivalent and agonizes over the pros and cons of formal organizations as the most common route toward institutionalization. Whereas Josh cites the anxieties around "selling out" as a danger, Luz's and Cheryl's experiences in progressive organizations suggest a different kind of cost for activists of color. Luz experiences tokenism and marginalization in a neighborhood organization and, after much conflict, resigns from the organization to do her own independent organizing. Cheryl, however, remains in the gay and lesbian organization but uses her token status to bring more people of color into leadership positions in the organization.

These stories confirm the importance of the concepts of resources and formal organizations that scholars have utilized for many years to understand the emergence and development of social movements. The encounter between activists and scholarship suggests several complications to these concepts. When we listen closely to these stories, we hear about different kinds of resources besides material resources, a fundamentally different understanding of how resources emerge and are used, and different models of organization besides formal organizations that mitigate some of the pitfalls of these organizations for progressive activism.

Resources

Scholars working within the resource mobilization framework discussed in Chapter 2 identify the variety of resources that have assisted various social movements in both their long-term survival and their successful pursuit of goals.[1] Most of these resources are similar to what would be required of many collective endeavors regardless of their nature. These are things like money and steady resource streams, influential allies or supporters who lend both their money and political capital to the cause, and infrastructure in the form of meeting places, technology, office space, etc. These are particularly important for social movements that are almost by definition resource poor (Cress and Snow 1996). Resources also consist of human capital such as leadership skills and a pool of committed organizers who provide continuity, information, and labor (Morris 1984).

Scholars have documented the importance of these resources in a variety of social movements. The best and most intensely studied example is the southern civil rights movement (McAdam 1982; Morris 1984; Payne 1995). Recall the summary of the movement using a resource mobilization framework from Chapter 2. This summary called attention to the changes in the material conditions and physical location of the African American community in the South in the first half of the twentieth century: from sharecropping under serf-like conditions in the countryside to low-wage industrial labor in the city. Particularly important for this discussion of resources is the formation of a black working class and middle class in both southern and northern cities with their somewhat increased level of economic resources under conditions of racial segregation. In addition, these resources helped to reorganize and strengthen the black churches and colleges in the South. These resources and their aggregation within churches and colleges were important in providing money for organizations to pay staff, hire lawyers, defend those arrested of violating Jim Crow laws, and provide bail to get them out of jail. They were equally responsible in creating leaders and social networks that could be easily mobilized for any number of actions, campaigns, and meetings.

As Robin and Lisa mention, these resources are crucial and, in many cases, seem to be the unstated assumption of progressive organizing—that there is never enough money, never enough people, never enough time. A week after I observed John spend 15 minutes in front of a group of activists appealing for money, door knockers, phone bankers, and poll watchers to help elect two members of the Working

Families party to the City Council in 2007, he discussed with me the different constraints he confronts as a progressive activist. Surprisingly, he doesn't mention these appeals for money and manpower that I had just heard him make. When I remind him of this, he says:

> Well, raising money. Money is an ongoing issue. Volunteer recruitment, money, whether to get your members involved in elections or not: These are standard lists of things we always face. The others I talked about are in a different category.

These resource constraints are so obvious, so much a constant, that oftentimes they go unmentioned.

They go unmentioned until they dry up or when activists ruminate on how the constant need for material resources affects the actual content of their organizing. This bit of ruminating is obvious in Robin's and Lisa's comments about pressures to apply for grants and the effect of these pressures on their ability to organize rather than administrate and on the nature of their programming. With regard to this latter concern, Robin provides another example of just how profound this relationship between resources and the nature of the organization can be:

> One of the biggest issues we dealt with was whether or not we would accept funding from Borders, because at the time, the adults in the independent bookstore, feminist bookstore movements, where they had lived their coming out, those places were so important to them in supporting them with feminism. And the kids were like "whatever!" you know, "I can come out wherever." And that became a huge issue, and actually we lost a lot of adults in the organizing over that. And it led us into a whole conversation about who we will and won't take money from.

This decision was cast in terms of the mission of the organization, and since the mission was focused on queer youth, Robin could not afford to alienate them and thus recruited Borders as a corporate sponsor. In this case, the availability of this resource stream led to conflict between the older and more established lesbian and gay activists who were on the board and the younger activists who saw the mission of the organization differently from these board members.

The distribution of material resources across progressive organizations also has consequences for the quality of interactions and the potential for coalitions across those organizations. This was particularly the case for neighborhood organizations throughout the city. The neighborhood organization in the South End of Hartford has received the lion's share of foundation and government funds while those in the North End struggle for survival. While there are many reasons for these resource inequalities, they stem from the basic structural reality of separate organizations for separate neighborhoods all competing for finite resources. Important for this discussion is the consequence of these inequalities not only for the ability of these individual organizations to do progressive work but also for their capacity to do collaborative work throughout the city.

Janice, a community organizer who has worked in neighborhood organizations in both South and North Hartford, describes this dynamic but also captures the resentments and hostilities built up over at least three decades:

> I got to [the organization in North Hartford] and realized there was this huge gap in funding. A huge gap in moving forward as a community and that there were certain things put in place in South Hartford that weren't in place in North Hartford and so I had to learn this whole new system. But what I remember the most is that when I got there how resentful folks were to me for coming there. There was no "Oh here comes the black sister to save the day and we're glad she is here." It was, "Who the fuck are you? Why the fuck are you here? You know, you're from [the neighborhood organization in the south end], don't bring your black ass over here!"

Janice experiences not only the profound differences in resources between the organizations in the north and the south but also the framing of those differences in racialized ways.

As we can see, there are many reasons why scholars have focused on the importance of material resources for social movement emergence, development, and success. When we listen to how activists talk about resources we see precisely how resources matter. Of course, they are important for getting initiatives off the ground and keeping them running, as scholars note. But we also see how the obsession with gathering these resources, the idiosyncrasies and biases in funders' preferences, and the constant uncertainty and inequality of resource streams profoundly affect the nature of the organization, the motivations and commitments of the activists within the organization, and the relationships across organizations throughout the city.

There is perhaps another reason why material resources drift off and on the "radar screen" of activists when they talk about the important ingredients for successful organizing. When John says "the other [ingredients] I talked about [besides the material resources] are in a different category," he is referring to his discussion of "a community of activists....who identified common ground, common threads, common ways of looking at various oppressions and being able to work together on each other's issues." John echoes what I hear from several progressive activists about the importance of a whole range of non-material resources for building and sustaining progressive actions, campaigns, and organizations. These are not referred to in any scholarly account of resources. In John's view, the ideological commitment to progressive principles of social justice was the key resource that made the many victories of the progressive political party discussed earlier, People for a Change (PFC), possible.

These alternative resources referenced by several activists remind scholars that the instrumental and utilitarian focus of the resource mobilization framework is limited in helping us see what is unique to many progressive social movements. As suggested by John's discussion of his participation in the eight-year-long PFC movement, the outstanding ingredients for mobilization were of a qualitatively different character than money, meeting space, leadership, or politically connected allies, although at various points these were important as well. What activists mention just as frequently and speak of as far more important are the ideological, attitudinal, and communal resources available to progressive social movements. These can be best referred to as cultural resources since they involve the mobilization of common ideas, dispositions and understandings. These cultural resources, of course, do not somehow circulate freely but are embedded in various kinds of structures.[2]

In addition and again quite different from how material resources are conceptualized in the resource mobilization framework, activists describe these resources as not simply "sitting out there" waiting to be utilized. Instead, these resources are more dynamic, constructed and contingent. They rely on various kinds of social interaction and social contexts to emerge and develop. In many cases, these interactions and contexts are constructed by the already mobilized and motivated activists.

These cultural resources are also best understood as factors that simultaneously make possible collective action as well as individuals' participation in that action. While social movement scholars distinguish between the factors that lead to social movement emergence and those that lead to individuals' participation in social movements, these activists do not make these distinctions. They collapse this distinction insisting that empowered individuals can create their own momentum for social movements.

The most common cultural resource cited by these activists is the existence of a progressive community: a network of like-minded individuals that provides ideas, commitment, excitement, dialogue, and education to activists. These are in addition to other kinds of contributions from that community such as money, manpower, and the like. Chris references the importance of community for his work in the North End of Hartford through the Catholic Worker Party:

> This work, in my mind, is only possible through community. Community makes this possible. If my wife and I, if we're trying to do this as a private couple, logistically we couldn't do it, try and support ourselves. Spiritually we couldn't do it. We couldn't have kids we're working with be murdered and not lose our minds. We're able to continue because of the community. People sharing their resources, their physical resources, their human resources, their time and understanding, and that's an incredibly kind of subversive idea in twenty-first-century America.

In this passage, Chris states quite forcefully that the resources necessary for both him and his wife to do their activism are not simply material but human and spiritual in nature. His notion of community implies a common ideology that supports them in their work. Importantly, this ideology is situated within the social network of the Catholic Worker organization and points to the structural embeddedness of these cultural ideas.

Other activists talk about this "spirit of community" also organized in specific contexts as an important resource for the emergence of progressive activism and for these activists' participation in this activism. Some younger activists, for example, cite the progressive ideas and networks available at schools, particularly in student organizations and friendship networks. Beth and Kevin as recent college graduates discuss their social networks at school. In the first excerpt, Beth's changed social networks redefine her understanding of activism. In the second excerpt, Kevin's membership in the progressive student group melds socializing with political consciousness-raising:

> I started hanging out with a whole different group of people that did a lot of labor issues, that did animals rights stuff, that did protesting the war, and all of a sudden I just saw that it [activism] was so much bigger.

> The groups that I have been involved with have been so remarkable that getting together at meetings is like a social event...And some of the best ideas and some of the best brainstorming come about when you're sitting bullshitting, listening to music, and had a few drinks or whatever. So that's just as valuable, and maybe even more so, because it's healthy to get away and be more casual and relaxed, and complain about GW all the time. And recite Bushisms left and right. So, there's some of that melding, I think. But since, especially in the last year, I've had to say, there's been a real melding of the social and the political and all that stuff, which I think is great. Because it's almost like you're going to a party when you go to the meeting or something.

Schools and school organizations are, in some sense, material resources since they provide the setting and infrastructure for activism. However, as Beth's and Kevin's comments make clear, they only work as resources because they are filled with a particular cultural or ideological content. Additionally, this content was not "already there" or "completely formed" but constructed in the process of social interaction.

One of the best examples of this combination of ideology, context, and social interaction that becomes a cultural resource for progressive activism is the story of the founding of the Reader's Feast Café and Bookstore in the mid-1980s that lasted until 1996. The activist founder of the Café, Carolyn, describes its origins as an explicitly progressive political space in Hartford.

> I pulled together and got 28 different people who were willing to collectively come together and put money in to buy the store. And this was sort of the hey-day of community bookstores as being really the base of a lot of political activism, particularly women's bookstores. There was a network of women's bookstores throughout the country that were really like almost women's centers and very tied into a lot of the political feminist work. So anyway, we got 28 folks together, and we bought the store, and expanded it to include a café so that we could have all kinds of events and activities, and that was the Reader's Feast. And we did have the vision of saying we wanted to be, really, building communities together.

Reader's Feast Café and Bookstore became a place for dinner, reading, meeting friends or listening to music but, more importantly, a place where progressive people in the city "hung out," discussed ideas, held strategy sessions, and debriefed after meetings, demonstrations, and protest actions. Its existence depended on money, to be sure, but as Carolyn notes, it also depended on a "common vision" of the founders to "build community together."

Other activists also talk about this commitment to a progressive ideology as an important resource for successful activism and are even more explicit about its interactive and constructed nature. The dynamic nature of these cultural resources provides the spark that moves the individual from attitude to action and, at the same time, helps build a campaign, initiative, and perhaps even a movement. Adam mentions the conversations he has with friends and how they changed his progressive ideology:

> some of my friends were—about half of my friends were socialists, half of them were anarchists, and talking to both of them, and I think, maybe at first there was a little bit of, "Hey, this is cool, I'm more radical than I was minute ago." That was sort of enticing...some of it sort of made me realize even more what I believe.

This changed ideology had real consequences for his commitment to activism in that he moved out of a number of hierarchically structured organizations around community organizing and feminism and into more loosely structured, democratically based activities around anti-war and global justice issues.

In his job as an education director of a progressive union in Hartford, Steve provides a somewhat different example of this same process. In discussing "what one needs in order to do progressive organizing" he states that "You have to have politics" by which he means progressive politics. He then goes on to lament the absence of this politics among a generation of young people whom he encounters as novice organizers. He describes the interactive process he engages in to create both these politics and the passion necessary to act on these politics:

> I want to try to give them a sense of what it means to commit your life to, not necessarily this union or this project, although I would love that, I want them to stay around, but the idea that this is a life's work. It's not just, "Well, I'll go to Peru for six months and work in a school down there, and then I'll come and become an investment banker." The idea is that this is a commitment, this can be a lifetime commitment of being an activist and being in a struggle...I ask people to talk about individuals or actions or movements that they know of that are grounded in non-violence. And they'll talk about Gandhi and Martin Luther King, and maybe they'll go a little beyond that, and we'll tease more of it out so that they'll get a sense, without me saying it at first that there's this good history, this great body of history.

Engaging in this interactive process of education and action generates an ideology that is a crucial resource for progressive social movements. Implicit in Steve's account is a critique of sociologists' concept of resources: they are not only material in nature but composed of cultural scripts that are activated and mobilized in the course of collective action itself.

Conclusion

Both scholars and activists stress the importance of various kinds of external resources for the emergence, development, and success of social movements. Scholars have developed a fairly exhaustive accounting of the financial, physical, and human resources that have proven significant in past mobilizations. This accounting can provide a checklist of sorts for activists wanting to know "what it takes" to get movements "off the ground."

Activists, however, make their unique contribution to this discussion as they assert the importance of cultural resources interactively constructed in pre-existing organizations and through the many conversations and actions that take place in those organizations. In making this contribution, they also implicitly argue that the distinction that scholars make between the resources necessary to create movements and the resources necessary to build individual support and commitment to movements is overblown. They assert their ability to do both simultaneously.

Organizations

Closely related to the concept of resources about which both activists and scholars have a great deal to say is the concept of organization. Both groups see organizations as a necessary resource for successful mobilization: that is, as a social form that facilitates, shapes, and limits the activities these movements engage in. For these reasons, organizations are crucial to the study of social movements. Activists encourage us, however, to think more complexly about social movement organizations. They encourage us to "unpack" the precise nature of these organizations and, in so doing, reconceptualize them not only as social forms composed of rules, roles, and resources but also as cultural forms that promote values, norms, and ideals and that exert their own influence on what goes on in these organizations.[3]

For many years, social movement scholars studied social movements by concentrating on social movement organizations, effectively equating or conflating a movement with the organization or organizations that (imperfectly and partially) it comprised. This conflation was done for methodological, theoretical, and political reasons. First, organizations, with their records, their formalized procedures, rules, agendas, etc., were simply easy to investigate from the outside looking in. For the sociologist trained in positivism, quantification, and statistical procedures, organizations became an important way into the study of social movements. Second, social movement scholars in the 1970s were challenging strain theory discussed at length in Chapter 2. This theory collapsed movements into many other forms of collective action such as crowd behavior, fads, and panics and portrayed all of these as irrational, emotional, and evanescent. By directing attention to formal organizations—the quintessentially rational and weighty social form of the modern era—these scholars asserted the importance of social movements as sources of study in their own right. Finally, this attention to organizations came on the heels of the heightened period of activism in the United States beginning in the 1960s. As a way of asserting the political importance of this activism and derailing scholarly efforts to portray it as emotional outbursts of the disaffected (in the case of the civil rights movement) or as the unruly whining of spoiled white youth (in the case of the student and anti-war movements), the focus on organizations became very useful. Having said all that, we can also see why the standard way of conceptualizing social movement resources would be material in nature since all organizations need the basic infrastructure, staff, equipment and expertise provided by money.

By now, scholars have amended this narrow focus and unraveled the conflation of movement and organization in several ways. As suggested above, there is much more to social movements than the formal organizations that may or may not comprise them. Movements may entail informal networks of similarly thinking individuals who plan actions or sustain campaigns (Friedman and McAdam 1992). Recall the discussion of new social movements theory from Chapter 2 that insisted that movements be seen as essentially "submerged networks" of like-minded individuals (Melucci 1989). These networks may never morph or "evolve" into formal organizations. Similarly, there may be virtual networks of individuals organized via the internet through websites and blogs where strategizing and decision making over tactics, targets, and goals may be a more iterative process than is common in face-to-face collective encounters. In addition, the social change may occur more in cyberspace than in real space.[4] Finally, all these informal networks or fleeting associations can exist on their own or they can exist alongside and maintain a relationship with formal organizations.

Social movements are capacious enough to make room for a variety of social forms. My activists illustrate this capaciousness and diversity and thus challenge scholars to think more complexly about the relationship between movements and formal organizations. These activists also encourage scholars to see the unique set of challenges that accompany formal organizations in progressive movements. My activists tell me that progressive values, progressive people, progressive agendas sometimes do not mesh well with a hierarchically structured form for getting people recruited, agendas developed, work accomplished, and action taken.

Several activists give us a glimpse of a social movement landscape that cannot be described in strictly organizational terms. Although Adam is one of the younger activists in my sample, his involvements span several different activist forms and structures:

> For maybe about a year, year and a half that organization network, coalition, we never actually clearly defined it, existed and we did a lot of direct action and campaigns with labor, going to the mobilizations in different cities, stuff

like that. And that lasted for about a year, year and a half. After that I started working with United for a Fair Economy on a campaign against Fast Track, a coalition built around that campaign, and that's lasted up until now, and now we're trying to transfer that to a Free Trade Area of the Americas campaign, which is going to be another two-year campaign.

Adam describes his involvements as "direct action and campaigns...going to mobilizations in different cities" and building a "coalition around Fast Track." Some of these involvements "morph" into participation in organizations for Adam but some of them do not. This landscape allows Adam to participate in progressive activism even while he remains skeptical of the benefits of social movement organizations that oftentimes come to embody that activism. Adam's preference for grassroots campaigns over formal organizations is shared by other activists, some of whom are quite explicit about the evils of formal organizations. Luz, a longtime grassroots activist in the city, bluntly states: "People have to come first. When you worry about the organization, you're selling out the people."

One reason to form organizations is to extend activism into the future. This assumes, of course, that a goal of progressive activism is organizational longevity. Some progressive activists see their efforts as short-lived or as preludes to other more organized efforts. Oftentimes, these efforts take the form of cultural or social activities with goals of consciousness raising and empowerment. Cheryl's experiences with organizing youth of color point to the need for these types of activities.

We did a project at the community center where we had dances, gay youth dances. And really the gay youth dances brought the kids. I think when we added the social part of it, the fun part, that's when you got them to come in. They weren't going to come for political reasons even though they were harassed and troubled [at school and at home].

For many youth, that was all they needed or wanted. Another youth organizer, Robin, notes the support function of these activities: "they get in there, they meet a few other people and they're like, 'Oh, I'm okay? Good. Now, let's go to the movies.'" For progressive activists, the challenge of these cultural events is to turn them into opportunities for consciousness-raising. Cheryl talks about the next steps:

So we would incorporate into the dances...We would say "let's have a monthly meeting" and we would talk about HIV/AIDS issues. We would talk about political issues. We talk about whatever kids want to talk about. But we would also incorporate the political aspect so we could teach them there's a political part of all this that they might not be aware of. It was a lot of work; it was. It took a long time. It took quite a few years.

As Cheryl seems to suggest, these non-structured, somewhat casual attempts at consciousness-raising needed time, thus raising the question of just what kind of organization can best accomplish that. These activist stories tell scholars not to abandon a focus on organizations but to broaden that focus to include the myriad forms and structures that activists use to do progressive work.

Even as activists speak of the importance of formal organizations for sustained social movement activity, they complicate sociologists' understanding of these organizations and why these organizations are important. Of course, activists mention features of organizations you would expect any member of a formal organization to mention. Many activists echo the anxieties of Robin and Lisa expressed in the introduction to the chapter about how the ongoing need for funding can shape (and distort) the activities of the organization. Others echo the assessment of Jack, also from the introduction, that organizations of the underrepresented become vehicles for representation in the "corridors of power." As Jack bluntly states: "If you're not building organization, you're going to end up losing." But activist organizations with a progressive ideology have unique sets of challenges not fully accounted for in scholars' theories of social movements.

One of these challenges has to do with leadership development in formal organizations and the skills and resources needed to build an organization and interact successfully with other organizational actors. Jeremy, a labor organizer, and Alta, a community organizer, talk about different aspects of this same issue:

> It's really hard to get workers to take a whole series of steps that it takes to become an organizer. I mean, we had a guy who's very responsible...He's a cook at [college]. He was supposed to come meet reps on campus this morning and he didn't show. He just blew it off. Yeah, I mean there's just a whole series of steps that you're supposed to go through in development to be ready to come on staff. [Another worker] came out and did three day training and the ten day internship but because of reality reasons, because he has children by many different people, and he has lots of them—it wasn't possible. I think he now has a driver's license. I mean that was an actual impossible barrier for us, if you don't have a driver's license. He drives, but you couldn't be an organizer and risk being immobile. He's a great person, and he should be an organizer, he's so talented and so charismatic but, you know, he's not there yet.

> Organizations that operate in communities of color—when they seek leaders of those organizations—have to fall back on recruiting for a long, long period of time and then settling for the white guy from outside to come in and improve the leadership. Or, they may in fact find someone that they like but who is not capable of doing the job. And the result is mismanagement, not necessarily intentional, but mismanagement, lack of experience, people over their heads...What we decided to do was look at who's going to fill those positions and see if we can develop a group of people that want to move up into those positions and give them the skill so that when they start they're at least not behind. We found especially writing skills are a huge

glass ceiling. They have to write program evaluations, grant applications... It's a huge wall.

Organizations that are supposed to be composed of and represent poor and working-class people who, as a group, do not possess the variety of resources required for successful operation find themselves at a disadvantage. As Jeremy and Alta mention, these skills are both technical and social in nature; not only literacy skills but the time to work long hours and the "schmoozing" skills to interact with different constituencies. What then happens is that these organizations oftentimes become run by individuals outside the group which undercuts a progressive principle of democratic participation and creates the potential for class or racially inflected conflicts.

Left out of these accounts of the potential mismatch between poor and working-class people and the formal organizations that are touted as the models to represent and push their interests is the simple idea that these people have very busy and oftentimes chaotic lives. Formal organizations, with their seemingly endless meetings, agenda setting, periodic planning for congresses, resource acquisition, etc., do not mesh well with these lives. Labor activist, Abbey, who moved from a position as a chef at a college to a paid organizer's position in the food service workers' union of which she is a member describes this tension:

> It's a very stressful job. People's lives, sometimes, are in your hands, like, their future; whether or not they have a job. But, also, I mean, it's a job that takes a lot of time. I have three children. So, sometimes it's hard. Most of the people that work this job don't have children. And, those that do, like, there's this organizer out in New Haven that has one child, but he's married, right. I have three children and I'm a single parent, so it's really hard.... When I finished interning, and I had to make the decision of taking this job, I sat down with my kids and I explained to them about the job, and what I've been doing. And they've always known, like when I'm in a big fight...they know I'm going to work every Saturday for the next four weeks, so I'm only going to see them one day a week, then they have to know why that is. I explain to them what I'm doing. I am the only one [on staff in the union] that came up from the rank and file...There are a lot of people who would like to get involved in doing this, but the pay holds them back, and the fact that it's a lot of work....When I came on staff it was a challenge, and I almost wasn't able to do it [because of the money]. And our membership had to vote to change my salary, so that I could do it, because, just in child-care alone...it's ridiculous!

Of course, Abbey is one of those working-class activists that did manage to adjust to the demands of the organization but she gives voice to the pressures that prevent more rank-and-file workers from becoming staff members in this union organization. Part of the pressure that Abbey also acknowledges elaborated in more detail in Chapter 7 involves the culture of the organization. Quite ironically, the union's culture is virtually indistinguishable from that at many U.S. corporations where managers are expected to work more hours, more days, and always be "on call."

Managing intra-organizational conflict is another challenge that all organizations face but these conflicts can be more frequent due the unique features of progressive organizations. These are supposed to be organizations governed by principles of democracy and equality. The conflicts are quite familiar to scholars of social movements who have documented rifts in many progressive movements throughout the twentieth and into the twenty-first century. These rifts existed in the local progressive community in Hartford as noted in Chapter 3 and as activists tell us below. By listening closely to these local activists we can begin to find ways of addressing these rifts and minimizing their destructive impact.

Adam, whose activism spanned college-organizing, anti-racist organizing in the region, global justice, anti-war activism, and community organizing, expresses his frustration with these tensions and rifts that surfaced in every activist setting:

> We always talk about how we want to be a multi-racial, multi-cultural movement and organization, our coalition or whatever, and as much talk as we've had, in every organization I volunteer with, it never happens. Another frustration, I also consider myself a feminist and feminism is never included in the analyses of what actions we take and what positions we take, and that frustrates me to no end. [At a rally] against the leader of the World Church, the creator of a racist organization, there were two comments that were made, one was that when the Nazis screamed at us, "You're white trash," someone screamed out, "No, you're white trash," and so there was a hint of classism in what supposedly working-class activists and activists who are working for economic equality were saying, and also the other comment, it was a gay-bashing comment, someone called the Nazis "faggot."...And nobody would admit to homophobia. And since then I've been very cautious about coming out to a group because just because they're progressive doesn't mean that they're not homophobic. And that frustrates me.

Similarly, Luz and Regina experienced racism in two different progressive organizations: Luz in a neighborhood organization in the predominately Latino neighborhoods of Hartford and Regina in gay and lesbian organizations in the Hartford region:

> I was one of two Latinos on a board of directors that were all white. And I knew nothing about leadership development, and they were deliberately talking over my head, and they would say things I had no clue what the hell it meant....to deliberately keep me in the dark.

> The gay movement, when I tried to be in it, I felt tokenized. I didn't know where I was. It didn't smell like home and it didn't smell like the white people I knew and was comfortable with. It was more like the ones that I was bused out to and didn't want to hold my hand in gym or something. The ones that were like, "Eww! We're not going to talk to her!"

These exclusions and biases exist in many different kinds of groups and activities and not just in formal organizations but these stories (and others like them) tell us that part of what organizations do is construct cultures of exclusion or bias. These cultures in turn embed the contradiction between exclusion and equality even deeper in progressive organizations.

One response by activists is simply to break away from those "contradictory" organizations and create their own that better addresses their progressive interests. Regina, the activist who felt tokenized in the gay movement did precisely that and organized the Kwanza project, a support and advocacy group for lesbians of color. As she states, "it came out of the need to make a home rather than go one mile to be black and two miles to be queer and never the twain shall meet." In 2002, Regina helped found an organization called FACE, Featuring All Colors and Ethnicities, whose focus is urban youth. Of course, this strategy does not address the contradictions in organizational culture but as Regina implicitly acknowledges this "breaking away" is sometimes necessary to continue to pursue the activism instead of battling the organization.

The contradiction is not inevitable in progressive organizations. Some Hartford area activists struggle with the contradiction and develop strategies to prevent it or respond to it in productive ways. One strategy that activists mention is building coalitions among a broad variety of constituencies, interests, or organizations for specific goals. A good example of this is Cornel's campaigns against drug dealing and police violence in the North End of Hartford. Below he discusses framing the campaigns in such a way to appeal to a diverse set of progressives broadly interested in racial equality.

I think you have to put in different groups in order to help in the action. Some of the activists, you know, only work with Christians. And I say, "Hey, man, you know what?" I say "I am a Christian but that evangelical viewpoint is often parochial...There's more knowledge in the universe than the Bible, and there are other things that you can do in order to bring about certain results, so focusing on that narrow evangelical viewpoint just keeps taking everything back up to God, which needs to be turned around." You need to tell people, "God plus action works." So I said to some of the other activists, I said, "Now who wants to make this thing work? You can't just go out every day talking about 'praise God' and evoking God's name, because if you notice, we have more people in the community other than Christians, let's do this, let's go out and say, 'Oh creator of the universe, give us the strength to continue and keep it safe.' Everybody can deal with that. Let's have an ideal, a concept, the community must be made safe. That appeals to the lesbians, gays, Muslims, blacks, whites, and youths"...

I know that any movement needs a coalition of the people, and it's not always easy to hold people to their word, so I started, I had Muslims, Black Panthers, I had Puerto Rican Nationalists, I had Orthodox Jews, I had feminists....I held all these different groups together based on ideology. So, what I'm trying to say is, ideology, I realize is essential. You have to have a central theme...Once I said that, everybody else fell in line and they said, "Okay, we could go for that...."

Such a coalitional approach provides broad-based support for specific goals such as a community review board of police practices. In addition, it also provides a learning process for the different groups involved in the campaign in that it seeks to find points of commonality amongst difference and break down some of the reluctance to work together that may exist across the organizations. As Cornel concludes toward the end of his narration, "I think those things helped raise the consciousness of the people." Cornel's "solution" begs the question of how to sustain this coalitional structure over time.

Another solution to the contradiction between bias and equality that bedevils many progressive organizations also lies in coalitions and does address the question of a long-term structure. Rather than pulling in different groups each with their own specific interest or identity for isolated campaigns, some progressive organizations build cultures, agendas, and structures that are explicitly coalitional. Very self-consciously they frame their issues, recruit their membership and leadership, and decide on agendas, strategies, goals, etc., attentive to the racial, ethnic, class, gender, and sexuality-based hierarchies central to a progressive movement. Needless to say, these organizations are the exception rather than the rule in the recent history of Hartford progressive activism.

Carolyn helped found a state-wide coalition devoted to expanding democracy and participation in politics. Adamant that this organization not become another "good government" organization that supports uncritically the tenets of representative democracy, Carolyn describes both the structure and culture of the organization:

By March we incorporated and had formed a board, but with a real commitment to bringing a very strong diversity to our board and to the voice of what we were creating, really wanting to make sure that we had sort of that intersection of looking at institutionalized racism and sexism and economic justice issues, and having that very integral to the mission and the vision of the organization...Coalition building: that's the theme or the sort of strategy of our work is really to bring together and build coalitions around important issues. The work we've been able to do and be so effective in a short period of time is because we have that commitment and that credibility in different communities to bring folks together. And so, like this [one campaign on economic inequalities in the state] is now this 80 organizations and real combination of grassroots and labor based and faith based and human services and a really wonderful collaboration of different groups. And a couple—just might mention a couple of the other important coalitions so you can get a sense of the work we do, one of the most important things and successes that I think we've had was this issue of the increasing incarceration of particularly—disproportionately people of color due to the drug policies. And so as part of that, people who have been incarcerated and in Connecticut up until this last year lost their voting rights...And the growing number of people who are disenfranchised due to felony convictions is huge, and mainly because of changes in the last ten years in the drug policy. And so there are now over 4 million people in this country who are disenfranchised, and a lot of people see it as the parallel to the poll tax of past days where, you know, it's very clearly targeted at race and class issues. So what we did when we were first organizing is we took on that issue and we formed what we called the Rapid Voting Rights Restoration Coalition. We had about 40 different groups. We worked closely with Latino and African American communities to really look at this issue, and we were able to change Connecticut's law to now say that people on probation, which is 36,000 people in Connecticut, have the right to restore their voting rights, well, actually they wouldn't even lose their voting rights if they were just on probation without incarceration. So that was sort of a major victory.

This example illustrates the dedication to coalitional thinking at every point in the operation of the organization. It is not organizations per se that inevitably lead to bias and exclusion as some scholars seem to suggest; it is the culture of the organization that invites either equality or exclusion. Activist efforts to combat these tendencies are "points of entry" for social movement scholars to think more deeply about how progressive organizations develop different cultures.

Another set of challenges associated with progressive organizations also pivot around this idea that there are inevitable dangers in trying to pursue a progressive agenda and build a progressive movement using formal organizations. The challenges are invoked by several activists in the introduction to the chapter: Josh worries that forming a legitimate formal organization will make his media activism susceptible to elite cooptation. Karen recalls nostalgically her earlier days of grassroots organizing when she wasn't worried about maintaining the organization through service provision in order to maintain her funding and when she was freer to "raise a ruckus." These concerns are quite familiar to social movement scholars who, at least since the publication of Frances Fox Piven and Richard Cloward's important book, *Poor People's Movements: How they Succeed, Why they Fail* in 1979, have been preoccupied with the dangers of formal organization for the ability of social movements of the poor to gain significant advantage.

According to Piven and Cloward (1979), the only real power that disadvantaged groups possess is the power to disrupt the normal routines and social institutions that those in power rely on to maintain their legitimacy. When faced with the escalation of disruption by individuals only fitfully or sporadically organized, elites respond with concessions of various sorts. These "carrots" are typically offered with caveats of one sort or another, the most important one being to present their demands in an orderly and systematic way. Meanwhile, the initial successes of protest invite some members of the disadvantaged group to institutionalize these gains by forming protest organizations with the hope that these organizations will build on the momentum of these past gains and advocate for even more gains. Piven and Cloward (1979) state that this decision is the "death knell" of social movements in that it (perhaps unintentionally) vitiates the real source of the poor's disruptive power. Formal organizations dissipate the energy of the people who were drawn to the activity in the first place, provide opportunities for protest leaders to consolidate their power over others, and lend themselves to cooptation from elites since these organizations (more precisely, the leaders of these organizations) are drawn into negotiations with these elites where compromise is the name of the game. With the disruptive potential of the movement gone, these organizations lose a valuable leveraging tool in these negotiations. Hence, the movement loses ground and the initial gains are eroded.

At first glance, this critique resonates with several progressive activists. We have already read Josh's and Karen's critique of formal organizations based on their organizing experiences. Several other activists also give voice to other aspects of the Piven and Cloward critique of formal organizations. Lorenzo, an African American community organizer, describes the temptation of being "taken up" into the political establishment:

> As a black male I catch flack from black leadership to my face and behind my back for working at [the organization]. [They say]: "Lorenzo, hey look, you know, you're smart, you're this, you're that. You're a black male, you speak in complete sentences, you should run, we could put you on town committee. You can be a part of the political structure.

Regina mourns the loss of the spontaneity that comes with a more formalized movement sector:

> I'm glad that it's organized. But, I'm not glad that some of the spontaneity, and so much of the spontaneity and passion seems to have gone, and that people are kind of almost ashamed to just come right off the cuff with stuff. And I think it is sad in that it's discouraging to regular people becoming involved, you know, thinking that they need to get, I don't know, some degree or some stamp of approval before they're really qualified to do it....If I had followed the route of many of my colleagues, one step would have led to another and I would have accepted the invitation into corporate responsibility units of some private corporation or state administrative management kind of position. And I backed away from that.

Finally, Rich expresses his frustration with the loss of radical goals as the movement turns into a non-profit organization:

> [We are] supposed to fight the system...but we're actually built and designed after the system. We have a board of directors, we go through the 501 c3 process, and we do all the audits and everything else. To fight the system we

> need to conform to the system, and then it's funny because the fighters, now the warriors in the system, myself included, lose your focus. And it's true, because not only is it a fight and your passion and your gut but it's your paycheck, your house and your mortgage. How do you do that?

Taken together, these progressive activists provide ample evidence of the power of the Piven and Cloward critique.

These same activists, however, temper this critique in several ways. Although they recognize these dangers of organization building, they do not abandon this form but seek to reform the aspects of the organization that may sap creative energy or encourage accommodation with the powers that be. Lorenzo refused to be co-opted; Regina involved herself in explicitly grassroots organizing devoid of the trappings of formal organizations; and Rich grafted a more informally organized, youth focused, direct action group onto the 'non-profit' to which he was (somewhat ambivalently) affiliated. These examples as well as the previous examples of activists who experiment with models of organizations built on values of coalition and inclusion help us see some ways around the Piven and Cloward dilemma.

More to the point, what these activists teach us is that formal organizations are human creations and, once created, they take on a life of their own. But, they are nonetheless subject to change. These activists also contain an implicit critique of the Piven and Cloward view of formal organizations. When Piven and Cloward (1979) and others talk about organizations they are usually talking about particular kinds of organizations: ones that are bureaucratically organized with national, state, and local chapters or branches, a hierarchy of leaders, a committee structure, membership lists, charters, dues structures, and an election system of representation at each level of the organization. Not surprisingly, these organizations have the most constraints and thus pose the greatest danger to grassroots activism in the pursuit of progressive social change. Thus, it is not all organizations per se that produce detrimental effects but a particular kind of organization.

As if to provide evidence of this critique, Hartford activists inhabit a number of different kinds of organizations that attempt to be non-hierarchical, democratic, inclusive, and effective. Some of these efforts are self-consciously non-hierarchical and participatory such as Charlie's experiences in a coalition to protect undocumented immigrants in the Hartford area:

> We've been as democratic as we can possibly be, you know. But we have different people with different sort of agendas, also, that you have to take into account. And basically what we try to do is hear everyone out, like you saw at the meeting, we took votes. We don't say, this is what's going to happen so... that would be, like, absurd for us to do, you know. And we say, we want everybody's voices to be heard, we want everybody to say what their concerns are and then we take everything into account you know, always keeping in mind our own ideas, you know just like, just like the people that work for [other groups] have their own ideas, and they bring that in, and you know hopefully

we all come to a consensus you know, something that is going to be good for everybody. We want to build up a movement.

Charlie's final comment about building a movement seems part of the reason he is so adamant about participatory democracy. There is a vague awareness that organization building and movement building are not the same things.

Because the focus is on movement building, there is less of a concern with putting in place organizations that will be self-sustaining. This is another reason why different structures other than formal organizations are put into place to "get the work done." Kevin recounts the informal structures put into place by college students doing progressive activism both on campus and in the city:

> We always had weekly meetings, and more and more we started to follow the sort of principles of participatory democracy...if you agree with something you do this, things like this. It really facilitated the meetings a lot better; it made them pretty efficient....So we really got pretty good at that. You just had great people who were motivated...These were people who really believed in what they were doing. And then there was no leadership board...You didn't have to do that [have leaders] because people were there because they wanted to be there. If you're going to do something, do it, and then if people show up then they obviously support. So it unofficially worked that way.

This structure was quite successful in mobilizing support for several campaigns throughout a two-year period. For a time, it also provided a kind of excitement that recruited many other students to the group.

Perhaps more important than whether an organization is formally or informally organized, hierarchical or non-hierarchical, has elected or rotating leaders, etc., is the issue of the culture of the organization. We already saw this in Abbey's discussion of the culture of overwork in her union. Here is an example of how activists' knowledge and creativity dovetail with some emerging concerns of social movement scholars. These scholars have somewhat belatedly recognized the importance of both the form and the content of social movement organizations: that the ideas that animate the organization are as important as the structures that are put into place to communicate and perpetuate these ideas.

The best examples of the importance of culture come from activists involved in the labor movement. For the past 15 years, certain sectors of the labor movement have parted company with their more conservative counterparts and have adopted an explicitly progressive agenda that includes, among other things, an increased commitment to organizing the unorganized. Laura M., who at the time of the interview was an organizer for the hotel and restaurant workers union, now a part of a larger coalition of progressive unions, UniteHere, talks about the organizational and cultural transformation of her union:

> Up until 1998 the tension [in the national leadership] was about how much of the union was really on a sort of progressive organizing or a social union

program, and how much of it wasn't, and how we were trying to move forward onto a progressive agenda. From 1998 to now the tension has completely flipped around because now [the progressives] run the union, and so now the tension is about never having enough trained, qualified, competent lead-organizers to do all the stuff that suddenly it's within our reach to do.

So, even as the union remains bureaucratically organized, the leadership subscribes to a progressive ideology. Steve, the labor organizer for the service workers union, describes this culture of progressivism of his union:

> It's based on the idea that people can fight and win, and that is through organizing and using your collective power through strikes. That's not just theory, that's our history. And the other is, back in New York they used to call it "union power" and "soul power." It's the idea of social unionism, it's the idea that your union is also a force for social change. So we were one of the first but few organizations that came out against the Vietnam War, but before that [the union] was striking in Harlem to get black pharmacists to be able to work in Harlem drug stores in 1936, so there's this long civil rights history, long anti-war history and social justice history that we continue in our work in Connecticut.

Neither Steve nor Laura deny some of the oligarchical tendencies of formal organizations but insist that a progressive ethos institutionalized in the organization can counter these tendencies. In Steve's role as a trainer of staff, for example, he communicates this culture:

> At some part in the course of the training I always make a point of saying that now, just by them contemplating [civil disobedience], blocking the world bank office or whatever they're going to do, they're now part of that history that that's their history, that they own it just as much as anybody else does, and that in 30 years somebody will be doing a training talking about them. And I said: "I hope that you're very proud of that because I'm proud that I'm there with you."

Activists remind scholars that organizations are composed of both structures and cultures and those organizations that have institutionalized a progressive ethos are most likely to have mechanisms to combat the dangers of oligarchy.

Conclusion

Both scholars and activists are thinking about organizations in more complicated ways. Activists employ and scholars have observed a whole host of forms by which social change takes place outside normal political channels. Still, formal organizations continue to be a major social form for activism, and both scholars and activists understand the dangers of that social form for doing the work of progressive social change. We have seen Hartford activists experience several problems with these organizations and, on the basis of those problems, experiment with alternative forms. Some eschew formal organizations entirely; others work alongside them but proceed cautiously. Still others reconstruct those organizations according to progressive values of one sort or another and implicitly reject or at least temper the tendency of these organizations toward oligarchy, exclusivity, passivity, and cooptation. Together, they assert that organizations are not only structures but cultures and that changing one involves changing the other.

Chapter 6

What Makes Them Do It: Recruitment and Commitment to Social Movements

I was involved in the underground punk scene...And this was in the early mid-90s. So there were bands like *Earth Crisis*. They didn't drink, smoke, do anything, and they were vegan. All their songs were about anti-factory farming, killing drug dealers...all this crazy shit. But, so, there were bands like this. And not everyone took it to that degree. [But] I would say, because there were bands like that, people who were interested in animal rights got more and more involved in it. Every time you'd go to a show at the VFW hall or something like that, there'd be a table set up with a videotape playing and all kinds of literature...For me, this was part of what was so appealing is that you got music but also you got educated. So that was important. So, there'd be five tables set up, every band would have their "merch," their t-shirts, their CDs, you'd go down the line and then there'd be ADL (Animal Defense League). (Justin, 26-year-old white middle-class male)

[In the priesthood] I learned liberation theology, a theology that said that it's history: the Church is in history, religion is in history, you're responsible for history, and so you're responsible for building a new society, a new Jerusalem. You can put the theological sentences any way you want. I really loved that shit...And so I came home having been taught that and believing and said, "Shit, let me do this." And so my getting involved in this local community organizing effort as a priest and doing it seemed to me like this is what I was taught to do. This is putting my theology and my training into practice (Jack, 58-year-old white middle-class male)

I was raised in a classic traditional white middle-class family...I got married, traveled where my husband was, and we moved around the country—and you know this is the 60s, the early 60s, but I came out of the 50s, really. I was born in 1941. So, part of that was "What are expectations for women?"...and it was a very narrow vision for women. It was the classic sort of get educated but be a mother and a wife as your primary responsibility with community service... So the women's movement really was a major force, really, in politicizing me. (Carolyn, 61-year-old white middle-class female)

I grew up with six women in my family and going back, you know, the majority of meetings are all female, my Aunt El, who also came here after we did, she's passed now, but she was director of the Community Action Project...And my mother was always—she had a group called *Prayer for Children United to Stop Child Abuse*. I shouldn't just say direct services because they also included advocacy. So, I always grew up with like this thing, I never really knew what it was, but we were always in some community center, or in the basement of some church, or Saturday at some event, some march, and you never knew what it was, you just knew that it was always about a family meeting. You go there, the whole family would be there. (Lorenzo, 30-year-old African American working-class male)

My father was a really gung-ho leftist activist. He really, really believed in it. And he still does, but a lot of stuff happened back then...I remember being in these huge rallies in New York, and I have never seen the movement be as powerful as it was then. I remember huge avenues in New York being shut down by hundreds of thousands of people. And it was, I mean, even to the smallest child it was just, wow, you know? It was just energy, everything, it left an impression on me that that kind of power is the power people should have....So, when I went to a rally it was just like, "Oh, I remember this." And I started bringing my children to it. (Abbey, 27-year-old Latina working-class female)

It comes down the whole [college] thing again. As a student coming where I come from, you know, I'm a Uruguayan from Leominster, Mass. whose father is a baker but now I'm sitting at a university here, the other day I got to meet the dean at one of the faculties in Uruguay, and I got a chance to talk to lots of people. And I'm privileged to be here...[I am] like a border walker, walking between two different worlds. And we have a lot of kids like that in our group. (Charlie, 20-year-old Latino working-class male)

It takes years and years, and generations to change the consciousness of people. But sometimes it seems very immediate because of things like Seattle where it's like all of a sudden, but it's been building up for years. There's sort of that ember, which is good, because it can sort of be something that people can point to and say "It's working." Or "Things are happening."...Since the fall of 99, obviously the big huge thing that's been going on is anti-globalization stuff. And that's been a unifying thing in a lot of ways too because it's so multifaceted, right? Because you've got to think about labor issues, you've got to think about environment issues, you've got to think about all these things. Corporate power, what it means in a democracy. (Kevin, 25-year-old white working-class male)

Both activists and scholars are very interested in and love to talk about the subjects of the previous two chapters. Their interest is motivated from the same sets of questions. What factors are responsible for successful social movements? What conditions are most propitious for organizing? What are the tradeoffs and dilemmas associated with different strategies and goals and ways of organizing collective action? These questions are the "what" and the "how" of activism. A lesser-studied but equally important set of questions deals with the "who" and the "why" of activism: How and why do individuals come to participate in and get committed to collective action? How and why do they lose, change, or diminish that commitment? What kinds of identities are formed both prior to and in the process of collective action that are both cause and consequence of social movements? These are the questions that will occupy my attention in remaining chapters of the book. These questions again require a serious encounter between the stories activists tell and the concepts and frameworks scholars use to analyze these stories.

Both activists and scholars have been interested in issues of recruitment and commitment to collective action, the subject of this chapter.[1] Activists always need to recruit individuals into participating and staying involved in various forms of activism. In doing so, these activists also reflect back on how they became activists and use those reflections in their own recruitment work. Scholars want to better understand how and why individuals join groups which require various amounts of time, risk, and sacrifice (Gould 2002; McAdam 1988). This understanding enables insight not only into particular dynamics of social movements but also into the general nature of group formation, and how individuals balance individual needs and interests with their membership in social groups.[2]

At first glance, the above excerpts suggest that there are as many stories of "coming to activism" as there are activists. Justin connects his youth involvement in the straightedge music scene to his animal rights activism. Lorenzo refers further back to his childhood in Chicago and his family's tradition of service to the black community to construct his story. Carolyn foregrounds the influence of the feminist movement to explain her lifelong progressive politics and Abbey makes a cautious but important reference to her father's participation in radical Puerto Rican politics as a touchstone for her involvement in the labor movement. Jack tells the story of his time in the priesthood in the 1970s and the profound influence liberation theology had on his subsequent career in activism. Charlie constructs his story from the contradictions he experiences between his identity as a working-class Latino and a student in an elite liberal arts college. And finally Kevin doesn't speak directly about his past but about the profound impact that the mass protests in Seattle in 1999 against the World Trade Organization had on the intensity and direction of his activist involvements.

Despite this apparent diversity, we can, with the assistance of the concepts of social movement analysis, reveal the ways these stories are socially patterned. By listening closely to activists' stories of becoming activists and how activists convince others to become activists, we can also reveal some silences or limitations in these scholarly concepts. Simply stated, the sociological concepts do not sufficiently capture the interactive, sequential, and iterative nature of social movement participation and commitment. Coming to activism is not a monocausal or determinant process. Nor is it an "all or nothing" phenomenon as if a switch is flipped and people suddenly become activists. As the word "coming" implies, it is a process.

Scholars use three social movement concepts to understand questions of recruitment and commitment: biography, social networks, and critical events. Biography is a broad category used to refer to family socialization and the consequence of "coming of age" at a particular historical period (Jasper 1997). Some scholars who work with this concept focus on attitudes and try to distinguish predispositions toward social movement participation based on attitudes (Klandermans 1997). One notable example of this research comes from the study of the student movement of the 1960s that demonstrated that the young people most likely to join the student organization, Students for a Democratic Society (SDS), were those who grew up in liberal middle-class households and subscribed to ideas of individual freedom, equality of opportunity, and liberal democracy. These attitudes predisposed these young people to get involved in collective action when they perceived that these ideals were being violated by the universities they attended, state governments in the South, and the federal government in Vietnam (Whalen and Flacks 1989).

Other research using this concept of biography focuses not so much on individual attitudes but on the intersection between favorable attitudes and a historical period which may offer opportunities to turn those attitudes into collective action. Nancy Whittier (1995) provides such an analysis of the radical feminist movement from the 1960s to the early 1990s. Throughout this period, participation and commitment to the movement waxed and waned depending on the opportunities provided by the local and national political and cultural context for activism. Many women subscribed to attitudes supportive of equality for women but whether and how they chose to turn those attitudes into collective action depended on the resources available, the political possibility of making social change, and the support for feminist action in the culture. In this research, biography intersects with history to both produce collective action and encourage participation in it.

Social networks also figure prominently in the discussion of participation in progressive activism. This research does not necessarily deny the importance of favorable individual attitudes but focuses on the formal and informal settings that may encourage or discourage turning those attitudes into action. This concept is utilized by Doug McAdam (1988) to account for the differential participation of "attitudinally predisposed" college students in an important voter education and community organizing campaign of the civil rights movement in 1964 called Freedom Summer. McAdam finds that the students who were most likely to attend this summer-long campaign of working alongside the Student Nonviolent Coordinating Committee in Mississippi were not those who necessarily had the most favorable attitudes regarding civil rights principles but those students who were better connected. In other words, those students who were members of student networks and organizations were more likely to attend than those who were not. McAdam (1988: 50–3) argues that these networks provided avenues of information and influence. The student organizations supported the goals of Freedom

Summer and encouraged their members to apply to the project. The members of the organizations and networks provided further encouragement: friends and organizational members applied together and provided support for one another in the application, interview, and recruitment process. In this research, the nature of people's social networks—both the simple fact of affiliation and the culture of the social networks—is crucial in turning favorable attitudes into participation.

The concept of critical events is meant to capture the galvanizing impact that any number of somewhat unpredictable or unique historical events or actions can have on an individual's willingness to participate in collective action. This concept relies less on pre-existing attitudes or social networks as a precursor to collective action. Instead, it calls attention to the ways in which external shocks to the system can themselves motivate individuals to participate in collective action regardless of their attitudinal dispositions. The research of Edward Walsh (1986) on the Three Mile Island nuclear accident is a very good example of how "system accidents" and their attendant "target vulnerabilities" can compel people to act. Prior to the 1979 accident, the surrounding communities were not particularly organized and the area surrounding the accident was notable for its political conservatism. The accident and the subsequent political and technical failures of the utility shattered that conservatism by providing stark evidence that government and business do not always act in the best interests of citizens.

This idea that a critical event can promote both collective action and attitude change is also argued by Rick Fantasia (1988) in his book *Cultures of Solidarity*, although on a somewhat smaller scale than a regional or national "critical shock." Using a series of case studies of labor activism, Fantasia analyzes strikes and union organizing drives and demonstrates that it was confrontations with management which was anxious to derail workers' power that led to collective action and changes in workers' social and political view of the world. Critical events, in the form of walkouts, strikes, lockouts, and the like, occurring in interaction with potential activists, led individuals to participate in and commit to collective action. These are not events external to an individual's daily life. Instead, they are part and parcel of that life and occur in interaction with (and oftentimes in conflict with) others.

Biography

The activists' stories of how they got involved in progressive activism complicate the concepts of scholars in several ways. Most importantly, they give insight into *how* these concepts actually operate as pathways to participation. For example, several of the stories at the beginning of the chapter reference specific aspects of an individual's biography and describe how those aspects led the individual to participate in progressive activism. Abbey's and Lorenzo's stories excerpted above serve as good illustrations of how an ethos or a set of attitudes communicated in the family predisposed them to participate in activism. Abbey's reference to her father's radical past left an impression on her about the "power people should have." Lorenzo remembers growing up in a family with a strong service and advocacy ethic in the black community in Chicago. Neither account, however, reveals the process by which these biographical experiences became relevant for the decisions involved in becoming activists.

Another activist, Lisa, who also cites attitudes communicated by her family socialization as crucial to her participation, gives us a more detailed account of the connection, helping to trace the pathway to her activist participation and commitment:

> I grew up in [the affluent suburb] of Avon, but I used to come down into Hartford because [my father] is a pediatrician and he would do visits to the hospital, you know, and visit the babies. But my mom was always active with the church, and doing different things in church, and she told me one time, and I was really bored with religious ed. by that point, but I went with her, and we packed up clothes for some donation for somewhere, and it was just a mixture of adults and kids, and we were just having a good time and we were doing something good for other people, and I was like, "Gosh this is just really cool." So, I joined the social action committee actually when I was like 15 years old at St. Anne's in Avon. But also what happened at that same time was my Mom was on the parish council and they took on St. Michael's Church in the North End as the sister parish. And it's really, really cool because we started these bus trips, we would take a school bus that we would rent from St. Anne's into St. Michael's once a month for what they called unity masses, and we would bring food, so it would be a pot luck afterwards. So we'd have this, a mass, and then we'd go downstairs everyone. And it was awkward, I mean really as a 13, 14 year old kid it was very awkward. I didn't talk to any of the kids that were from St. Michael's....How are we the goody-two-shoes coming in from the suburbs, and how can we be nice without being condescending, and what exactly is this relationship that we're trying to make?

This excerpt illustrates that it is difficult to separate attitudes and behaviors as important in socialization to activism. Lisa and others who reference their "upbringing" as crucial, talk simultaneously about "ideas communicated" and "actions performed" as instrumental in their decisions to become an activist. Even with this important caveat that biographical influences on activism involve an interactive relationship between attitudes and action in Lisa's suburban church, we are still a distance from how this experience led to her longstanding involvement in progressive service delivery. That distance is closed somewhat when we begin to view the interaction between biography and experience, and attitudes and action, sequentially and iteratively.

Lisa does not passively internalize the liberal paternalism of her family and suburban church. Instead, it becomes one factor that interacts with subsequent factors in her life that leads her to commit to progressive activism. The critical questioning that Lisa began as a teenager continued as she entered the Jesuit Volunteer Corps where she pushed this organization to take a more social action orientation and less punitive relation to its work.

Well, I was really a thorn in their side. I technically wasn't fired because I was a volunteer, but they wouldn't let me come back. There were four women that wanted to come back. And I think later on, looking at the thing in retrospect, I think they knew they were going to close the mission, and I think they knew that we would have put up a stink about closing the mission, so they just cleaned house, basically, and got a whole bunch of new Jesuit volunteers who didn't have a clue about anything. I put up a stink because there had been this big thing the year before where there was this big drug bust they call it where some of these kids in the mission confessed that they've smoked once or smoked a few times, or whatever...I just thought it was a terribly stupid idiotic waste of resources and waste of talent and a misuse of an opportunity that really could have been a teaching opportunity, you know? Anyway, so because of my involvement in that I think they decided that they didn't want me back.

This incident is one of several life experiences Lisa recounts as her thinking about social change becomes formed and reformed in a kind of interactive and dynamic fashion. The process of "coming to activism" involves more than simply favorable attitudes or socialization. As Lisa's biography suggests, her pathway to activism was shaped by an ongoing interaction between and among her already existing attitudes and socialization, subsequent events, and her reactions to those events. This dynamic process somehow leads her to work that fosters social change. For social movement scholars, her story suggests that the social movement concepts should not be seen as monocausal or static explanations for social movement participation but must be studied in terms of how they interact with one another.

Some scholars do study biographical factors as they interact with other influences. Recall the "biographical" research which argues that certain historical moments provide more opportunities and resources than others for individual participation (Whittier 1995). In this view, participation is the result of an interaction between being attitudinally predisposed and having opportunities to transform those attitudes into action. Carolyn's story in the introduction to the chapter that narrates how her moderate republicanism came smack up against the politicizing force of the feminist movement provides a good illustration of this interaction between attitude and action. Similar to Lisa's story, this interaction, however, was not between an already formed favorable attitude and a static and monolithic feminism:

When I'd had my three children and I was beginning to think, well, what else do I want to be doing with my life, my real interest around reproductive rights and family planning...But I was coming at it actually out of more of family planning, and zero population growth. That was the big issue in those days, and a lot of sort of environmental perspective. It was a very different perspective than women's control over their bodies and their lives. But, then as the women's movement was gaining momentum, it was a course then that merged, for me, and took that issue and brought it with a whole new analysis to really be something that I felt very committed to. So I became very active in the women's movement.

Carolyn's story emphasizes the changes in her attitudes through the interaction between her inchoate attitudes around family planning and reproductive control and the women's movement's powerful critique of that discourse. Carolyn's attitude of service to women was a far cry from a feminist ethos of gender equality, and it was through a sequential and interactive process of involvement and rethinking that led to her deep, life-long commitment to feminism.

Biographical factors and social network factors interact in ways similar to the interaction between biography and historical moment that produced Carolyn's recruitment to and participation in the feminist movement in Connecticut. Several activists describe attitudes vaguely supportive of social justice which led them to pursue majors in college or post-college education that exposed them to activism. Liza, a young LGBT activist, describes this interaction:

> [As] a child, my mother was always saying, "You don't ever treat anyone differently because of who they are. Treat everyone with respect." Just seeing that there are so many things wrong in this world with the way people are treated just because of who they are...It's not like my mother was ever really exposing me to things, but when you saw something it was always, "That was wrong, don't do that." But you get exposed to it all in college. Not first hand, but at least through an education.

This vaguely liberal socialization interacted with a vaguely liberal college experience. It was not until she got turned down for law school and "chose" social work school that this liberal socialization interacted with the clearly progressive orientation of her social work program to produce a progressive activist:

> I wouldn't have considered myself [an activist] then. [That happened] really this year, in school, getting involved and being around all these like-minded people, and getting involved in stuff and having people to push me, and go do this...Yeah, the people that I met through school, through the community organizing major. It's just, these people think like me, and it's kind of cool to hang out with them. People like that who can always talk about politics with me, and talk about social issues.

Perhaps less dramatic than Carolyn's "feminist" encounter between biography and history, Liza's encounter nonetheless entailed a transformation of attitudes and associations as she subtly started to alter her self-understanding and to refer to herself as an activist. We see the iterative nature of the process as attitudes lead to actions, reactions to those actions lead to changes in attitudes, and then these attitudes in turn lead to further action. This entire process is facilitated by interactions within different social networks.

There are other dimensions of biography that can impact social movement participation besides socialization patterns and attitudes. And there are also less obvious and more circuitous interactions between biography and social networks that can lead to social movement participation. As illustrated below, Andrew's drug addiction led him to "the recovery industry" and then to political activism; Rich's anguished "coming out" led him to the gay and lesbian service sector and then to queer youth activism.

When asked what led him to his activism, Andrew quickly responds, "Fifteen years of drug addition":

> I've struggled majorly with drug addiction since the '70s, and in 1990 was the last time, August 18, 1990, was the last time that I used anything...I started working with one of the alcohol and drug recovery centers who was very helpful in my recovery. I had bounced in and out of treatment as well over the years prior to that—prior to it sticking. I tell my clients in substance abuse that this is an industry. I tell my adult clients that, when I meet with them, and folks in the street, that, "Hey, listen. The frustration that you're experiencing with human services, that sense that something's not right about this, because everybody's giving you the run around, it's real."...The only way to stop or slow down the roll of the industry is that you stop the very first person that you meet, particularly your counselor after you get in there, and say, "You know what? I'm not going to leave the office, or I'm going to keep coming back until I get exactly what I came in here to get. Otherwise you're going to keep pumping me out, and saying, 'Next?'." That's why it's much, much bigger. It's much, much, huger... And I said to myself, "You know what? I need an outlet." And the outlet came with working with youth to prevent them from falling into the river of alcoholism and drug addiction. That's when I started with youth groups and working with youth. And coming into schools...And then, that's when I started really taking a look. My eyes started getting wider and wider around the issues that human service organizations were faced with. And so, that's sort of where the link is at.

Somewhat similar to Lisa's experience of a critical engagement between family socialization and subsequent biographical experiences in the Jesuit Volunteer Corps, Andrew's ambivalent experience with the recovery industry leads him to youth activism, and then later to antiracist organizing. Each stage in this process, moreover, is informed by a mixture of personal and political motivations.

Personal and political motivations figure centrally in the iterative process Rich uses to lead to his activism with queer youth. In his case, it is an interaction between "coming out" as a teenager in a Portuguese family and his involvement in volunteering for a gay and lesbian health organization:

> I had a hard time coming out in general and actually went through my suicidal phase, and dropping out of high school. Actually I don't want to call that a

phase, but was suicidal at a point in my life. And then, probably six months after high school, started volunteering at the [AIDS organization]. I definitely think it [the volunteering] kept me alive because I was so miserable...They say volunteering is good for you and it helps people, and I mean, I believed it. I needed to get out of the house and that gave me an excuse to get out of the house.

Through this volunteering, Rich becomes involved with and subsequently disillusioned by many of the adult gay and lesbian social networks in town and, in response to that, fashions a particular kind of activist participation:

I think, and my frustration had always been that it was great that I was a young person and I was involved and people got to check that box off when they applied for grants. And people got to say, "We have young people on our board." Or "we have a young person on staff"...[Through my contacts], the base of young people I knew just expanded incredibly, and then I just started emailing. And I think I'd like to say I was one of the beginning people who started to organize over email, at least, locally because that's how young people communicated. And then in 1998, right around the time Matthew Shepard was killed, actually, right before, there was a small group of us who had decided that all this informal work we were doing and the conversations that we were having were great, but we wanted something bigger. And so we were talking about doing our own organization, or our own group that was more politically focused called Q&A, which was Queer and Active.

Like Andrew, Rich expands on this sociological concept of "biography" to go beyond attitudes or behavioral dispositions and illustrates how personal "events" can serve as a catalyst to collective action. Additionally, both Rich's and Andrew's stories show that these events interact with other social factors; in these cases, it was the social networks they were subsequently involved in as a consequence of their personal traumas.

Several activists suggest another dimension to the concept of biography that dovetails with the concepts of collective identity and oppositional consciousness discussed in Chapter 2. These activists narrate vague but powerful feelings of marginality at various stages in their lives prior to activism that imparted either an oppositional identity or that made them feel like an outsider. This identity or these feelings interacted with other factors to produce social movement participation. The marginality came out of social factors of class, ethnicity, and religion.[3]

We need only return to Charlie's quote at the beginning of the chapter to see this marginality at work. His notion of himself as a "border walker" nicely captures the uneasiness he feels as a working-class Latino in a predominately white elite college. This marginality is a motivation for his immigration rights activism. It also informs how the college-based group does its activism:

The most challenging aspect by far is being able to get in contact with immigrant communities. You know we've gotten a lot of support from students, from different activists, from labor unions but when it comes down to it that means nothing. You need to get the people to come out, and that's really been our biggest challenge...And a lot of it has to do with the fact that, you know, people are scared. Another thing is that they see us as [college] kids, and we have to break that barrier too.

Charlie's implicit understanding of the conflicts between the class and ethnic makeup of the group and the activist group on whose behalf it is operating comes from his biography as a "border walker."

Another example of a biography of marginality that drives social movement participation comes from Carmen. More than Charlie, Carmen's biography is defined by an oppositional consciousness. For Carmen, this was formed initially by being a light-skinned Latina and living on the physical border between races in a poor urban neighborhood in Connecticut:

[I grew up] getting my ass beat every day. I'm a white Puerto Rican. My skin color is white, and the fact that I was over here and I was Puerto Rican made it ten times worse for me, because it was the war between the blacks and the whites, and we happened to get caught up in the middle of that. And I had long, long hair, so I was a target, a walking target for everybody. So I got beat up by both different ends. The whites didn't like me because I was Latina, and the blacks couldn't stand me because I was white. And so, after being beat up a couple times by a bunch of different girls, I started retaliating. My cousin got a rock, a sock, he put some rocks in it, and they were all boys. I was the only girl. That's how I learned how to defend myself.

Of course, this marginality, in and of itself, did not lead to Carmen's early and lifelong participation in activism in multiple communities in the Hartford area. But, when combined with her later participation in Puerto Rican social networks in Hartford that facilitated her consciousness raising as Latina, that marginality became an important factor in how she became an activist:

That's when we [she and another Latina activist] partnered up. I went to some meetings, and I found out a lot of things about my culture. She couldn't tell me, because those things you don't speak about, she just pointed me in the right direction, and I went into a room, and I met some brothers and sisters from my country who explained to me what racism was and what I was going through....Once I learned my roots, and I started realizing what oppression was, and what—how our culture has been oppressed for so many—way beyond six hundred years, you know what I mean? That this began. And I had a hard time understanding why, if I had the same qualifications as this white woman, why was she getting the job and not me? I had a high school diploma. I was

> starting to go to college. I had more experience than she did, and why—what
> was the problem?

As this excerpt suggests, these many interactions and experiences not only led to her participation in progressive activism in Hartford but they also altered her oppositional consciousness enabling her to see the intersecting issues of class, ethnicity, and gender in her identity and her activism.

Social Networks

As the previous discussion illustrates, the concepts of biography and social networks are very important in the stories of coming to activism for Hartford progressives. It also illustrates that these concepts operate interactively to produce participation and commitment. By foregrounding the operation of social networks as recruiting devices as I do briefly here, I do not want to contradict this idea of an interaction among social movement concepts but to make a point about social networks that oftentimes gets lost. When activists tell stories about the importance of their social networks affecting their decisions to participate and commit, these stories are simultaneously about the interactions among the people, and the interactions around ideas. In other words, these social networks are simultaneously associational and cultural. The association with groups of similarly thinking people encourages participation; the ideas, meanings, and values embedded in these social networks are equally important in the recruitment process.

The introductory excerpts of Justin about his involvement in the straight edge scene and Jack about his life in the Catholic priesthood illustrate this two-fold nature of these social networks. About the straight edge music scene and its influence on him, Justin says: "what was so appealing is that: you got music but also you got educated." About the training he received in the priesthood, Jack says, "this was liberation theology....This is religion as I love it!" In these stories, the contents of the social networks are just as important as the close connections they made with people in those networks who provided additional encouragement to participate in activism.

Similar to the stories of activists that foreground biographical factors as important in how these activists got involved in progressive activism, the activists who say that social networks are key to their involvement also talk about these networks in interaction with other factors. Again, Justin and Jack illustrate this interaction nicely. For Justin, the reason the straight edge music scene resonated so strongly and had such an impact is because of a feeling of marginality he experienced in his community and high school.

> We lived in a very upper middle-class, white, Jewish area on Long Island, and
> we were like the odd family out. We didn't have very much money...When
> you're really young it's not an issue, but when you become a teenager, like,
> right around that teenager time...In Long Island, everyone's having Bar Mitz-

vahs: some Bar Mitzvahs are insane, insanely expensive and gaudy and some are more modest, so mine was more modest...And everyone got their permits and got a brand new imported car and I had a 1980...The people I started hanging out with as a result of this, as a result of being economically unable to hang out with the other ones. So we'd hang out at their houses or the train station and skate, and stuff, stuff that you didn't need money to do. And everyone was involved in hardcore and punk, and I got into [activism] because I was really into the music and I was an angry teenager. Because I didn't want to go [to the concerts] by myself, that's how my brother got involved too. I didn't know anyone in the scene. I didn't know anyone in the hardcore scene involved in it, so we would go ourselves...There was these kids at school who were into the same things, and economically we were on par. So I started running in a group—circle of friends who—and then people start calling you a faggot and a freak because you're dressing—you start dressing differently, and all the jocks abuse you and stuff because you look different or because I bleached my hair.

This social network had tremendous importance for Justin because it served as a place that made him feel less marginal. In this case, his unique biography interacted with this social network to produce a progressive animal rights activist.

Jack's experience in the social networks of the Catholic priesthood in the 1970s reveals that sometimes these social networks and their associated culture can operate in contradictory ways to produce participation in social movements. Even though the social networks were supportive of an activist ethos that Jack clearly embraced, the institutional hierarchy of the church wanted to "put the brakes on" the practice of that ethos. Part of Jack's reaction to those interactions was a deepened commitment to community organizing:

We did a demonstration at city hall one time and I got a little carried away. Of course that was part of the plan for me to get up there and really make a scene, so the cops come in and they pulled me out. The reason we were causing the scene is because it was a Democratic mayor, and I'm representing and living in and doing ministry in the poorest neighborhood in that town and the politics of the town were pretty much not to put any of the town's resources back into that neighborhood. I mean, we were considered to be the shit-hole, and they were going to leave it that way. And so we were saying, "No, you can't do that. Let's get some more resources back in here." ...And so the [television] tape in the morning of course is about this priest who gets pulled out of city hall. And so I get a call from the bishop, he says, "I want you to come down and see me?" So, I go and see the bishop and he starts it with "What the hell are you doing you jerk, you're causing trouble here." So I just said, "Bishop, when I get a call from you in the morning like that to come and see you, I really don't expect to hear you're disappointed in what's going on. I'd rather hear you say, 'I understand you have a fight, how can I help you?' But I expected you were

> going to be on my side, not on the mayor's side." And that kind of epitomized why I had to leave because he said, "I don't want you doing that." And I'm saying, "No, no, no, bishop, you got it wrong, this is what we all should be doing." And he said, "No, no, no, no, I don't really want you doing anymore." And I said, "Well, that's really what I'm supposed to be doing. You're the one who's wrong." But seeing as he was the bishop and I wasn't, that meant that in order for me to keep doing it, I had to leave. So I did. I called [the community organizer] and I said, "Look I want to do this full time."

Clearly, Jack's experience in the priesthood at a particular moment in the history of the Catholic Church was instrumental in recruiting him to a life of activism. By disentangling the various components of social networks—in this case, the culture that was communicating one thing and the hierarchy that was communicating another—we can see how recruitment to activism is a dynamic process where individuals retain their ability to interpret and reconfigure the meanings inherent in those social networks.

Critical Events

Although several activists say that they were motivated to get involved by any number of critical events—the election of Ronald Reagan in 1980; the massive anti-globalization demonstrations of the International Monetary Fund meetings in Seattle in 1999; the decision of the Bush administration to go to war in Iraq in 2003; the shooting of a young black boy by the police in Hartford in 1999—very rarely are these events portrayed as the only factor responsible for their participation. More typically, these events are part of a larger narrative that combines aspects of biography, social networks, and important events in a dynamic and interactive way to construct a pathway to participation and commitment.

In his excerpt at the start of the chapter, Kevin recognizes the galvanizing impact that the Seattle protests of 1999 had on his willingness to participate in collective action. As he says, it was the "ember...that people can point to and say...things are happening." But for Kevin and other younger progressive activists for whom "the battle of Seattle" holds symbolic value, it did not take them from inaction to action. Nor did it galvanize them because it posed an immediate threat to their neighborhood, their livelihoods, or safety, as was the case for the residents surrounding Three Mile Island. These activists were already somewhat involved, and "Seattle" served not only to increase it but to shape their activism in new ways. As Kevin states, "Seattle" did not necessarily make him an anti-globalization activist—he was involved in the Connecticut Global Action Network prior to December of 1999—but it did make him think about the interconnections between labor, the environment, corporate power and "what it means in a democracy." In other words, he learned from the Seattle protests the potential power of this vast coalition. This critical event did more than simply provide one more step in his pathway to activism. It also provided an important lesson about the nature of his progressive vision:

Part of the globalization stuff is understanding how we should be connected and the kinds of power relationships [that exist]. What does that person have to do with me over there? Well that's your brother or your sister or your daughter or whatever.

Kevin's observations and analysis of the critical event of "Seattle," combined with his vaguely liberal socialization in a suburban Catholic family and his college involvements in progressive social networks led him to both an increased commitment to activism and to a slightly different understanding of that activism.

Another global justice activist, Adam narrates his activist biography prior to Seattle:

In high school I started out very liberal environmentalist, recycling, that kind of stuff. Stuff that I—I didn't consider myself an activist, and now that I look back, I don't know what I was thinking. But when I got to college I was still involved a little bit with environmentalism, and I happened to go to a conference in Philadelphia, and I don't remember what it was called, but at that conference they were talking about some big protest in Seattle, and this was in '99, and so it piqued my interest. Unfortunately I didn't have the money or the time to go, but I had a friend who was going. She came back, I heard the stories, and that sort of turned me on to the anti-globalization movement. And from then on I've been working on economic justice issues mostly around globalization, but also labor and other issues. And then since September 11th, I've tried to include peace activism into my globalization activism, trying to meld the two, but it's been sort of difficult to do both at the same time.

Clearly, Adam's activism was encouraged not only by the critical event of "Seattle" but also by the political fallout of the terrorist attacks of September 11, 2001. But it occurred in the context of pre-existing biographical factors (i.e. his liberal upbringing) and his social networks (i.e. conference contacts and friendship networks).

Adam's and Kevin's accounts of their coming to activism suggest another way in which critical events lead to greater participation and deepened commitment. Similar to the dynamic described in Rick Fantasia's book, *Cultures of Solidarity* (1988), Kevin's description of the anti-globalization protest that introduced Chapter 4 not only illustrates the importance of collective action as a consciousness-raising activity but also points to its impact on participation and commitment:

We ended up blocking Main Street...We had a rally from the park that went downtown and then basically stopped [at Main Street]. And this was rush hour. And everyone just sat down in this intersection, which is a very busy intersection downtown, and it ended up freezing about three blocks on each side. It had a huge, huge effect. It was all over the papers. I think about 18 or 24 people got arrested ... But they couldn't ignore it, and it had a chain reaction with a lot of things. Because then there was some stuff that happened in New Haven with the janitors down there not getting benefits, not getting living wages, and a similar thing happened where they occupied an office and it led to a victory for the janitors in both instances. So it was really just a motivating event.

This critical event in the form of a highly visible, conflict-producing protest probably did not take many individuals from non-participation to participation but, according to Kevin, it heightened existing members' commitment and provided an example for other activists of what was possible through highly visible protest tactics. Moments of solidarity among similarly situated individuals engaged in conflict with "the powers that be" oftentimes strengthen solidarity as individuals learn powerful lessons about the nature of power. And, it can increase an activist's commitment to the cause. As Kevin says, "it was really just a motivating event."

Finally, in the context of discussing the importance of critical events as a route to social movement participation, some activists understand that these events are only important if they are actively utilized to bring otherwise non-involved folks into the orbit of the movement. Chris, a peace activist and member of the Catholic Worker community in the North End of Hartford, speaks about this challenge and his decision not to take it up:

We've got enough to do that we don't get involved in partisan bickering. You know, if we're going to do a national action there's folks we can call upon to be a part of the affinity group that we're simpatico with. In terms of our work here, it's just way too time consuming and energy consuming to go to meetings where this group and that group are arguing about: do we hold this sign or that sign at a demonstration. Who gives a flying fuck? We just don't have the energy for that. To tell you the truth and this is awful, but in some ways, before all these people came out of the woodwork because of the war, it was much easier because it was just a handful of us, we could call each other and just show up and do something. And now there are all these folks that, and this is cynical of me, but in a few years, they're all going to be gone.

Other activists who are more interested in building a movement would disagree with Chris's decision to sidestep the challenge, and I discuss some of these disagreements over strategy and goals in Chapter 4. Suffice to say that Chris's goal of giving moral witness trumps any interest in building widespread support for a peace movement.

Conclusion

The concepts that scholars use to make sense of why individuals participate in collective action are present in many of the activists' stories of how they came to progressive activism. These stories cannot be rendered in monocausal, static, or structurally determined terms. Nor can they be told in terms of an all-or-none understanding of participation. No factor or factors serve as the "magic switch" that flips an individual from a non-activist to an activist condition. The accounts of "coming to activism" reveal multiple influences and interactions across influences. They reveal participation in fits and starts and in several directions at once. The stories show how activists create their participation and commitment through an active dialogue across the concepts of biography, social networks, and critical events. In this way, activists encourage scholars to abandon or at least hold in abeyance the search for definitive explanations of "why people participate and why people commit." Instead, scholars should listen to these activists' stories in dialogue with the concepts of social movement analysis. When we do, we observe a more dynamic model of "pathways to participation" whereby activists actively combine aspects of biography, social networks, and critical events. This process results not only in progressive activism but in an always evolving progressive activism.

Chapter 7

What Makes Them Tired: Activist Burnout and Managing an Activist Life

Unfortunately [activism] has its toll. It takes its toll on the family. It takes its toll on myself, physical well-being, emotional, and mental health-wise. It takes its toll in a lot of ways, financially and so forth...But currently at the time, the more that I discover what's wrong, the more that it seems that I dig in. (Andrew, 44-year-old African American working-class male)

I know that oppressive forces will do everything they can to stop you even include getting at your loved ones. They [gang members] know that I am not afraid...and I can handle myself because I am a third degree black belt in jujitsu and hand-to-hand combat. He [gang leader] sent a man at me once to attack me and it wasn't a contest even though he had a two by four I took the two by four and put him down on the ground. They don't try that anymore. So they know they can't intimidate me but they might try to do it with my wife so I don't have her get involved. (Cornel, 44-year-old African American middle-class male)

It's kind of hard to say "I'm going to get out of the fight," I mean...the mother fuckers are still running the show! (Jack, 58-year-old white middle-class male)

I had a meltdown this weekend. I work to balance it. I am at least two people. But I have often said that if there weren't so much injustice in the world, just blatant injustices—it just makes me itch, and I have to do something to scratch it—I would be home making biscuits. I love to cook. I love kids. I love to act silly. I love to tell stories. I write; I'm a poet...That's what I would do all the time. I would be my maternal grandmother. I would be Mama Lula. You know? I would make a homemade pie every day and put it on the table and gather people around it. But it is that same, like, big mama spirit that won't let, you know, won't let shit just go on. (Regina, 51-year-old African American working-class female)

In terms of a social life, I didn't know how to have one. [The activism in town felt] like I was in a glass box. I was center stage—it's how I felt. So, could I go to a bar and go home with somebody and never call them again?...I didn't know how to date. I didn't know how to have sex. I didn't know how to have a life. (Rich, 25-year-old Portuguese American working-class male)

This work is only possible through community. If my wife and I we're trying to do this as a private couple, logistically we couldn't do it, try and support ourselves. Spiritually we couldn't do it. We couldn't have kids we're working with be murdered and not lose our minds. We're able to continue because of the community: people sharing their resources, their physical resources, their human resources, their time, their understanding. That's an incredibly kind of countercultural idea in twenty-first-century America...We're in this for the long haul. And, we need to support each other and care for each other. If things really get overwhelming, then we can cover for when someone goes away on retreat...or goes for a walk in the woods, or what not. We have each other's back in a way that would not be possible if we weren't living in community... if there was nobody to cover for us. Community is essential. (Chris, 38-year-old white working-class male)

Sometimes the internal politics [makes you burnout], and, you know, when we fight within our own communities and with our own organizations, that can be so much more frustrating and draining than fighting with the perceived enemy. (Ann, 43-year-old white middle-class female)

When I told you I was a lethal weapon, that's probably what burnout was. When I told this city council guy that "I wanted to rip the shit out of you" (laughs)... definitely burned out...It got to a point that it was too much. It really got to me. I had neglected my personal life. I have a child. Too many stuff that I had to do. It's not like I had therapy. I had no idea what it was. It was kind of cold turkey. Dealing with all the frustration so it affected me emotionally....Everything went down...I got a job....Took a training in accounting from the Data Institute again, those rip-off people. They fucked up my life because of the student loans...Never had a steady job after I left [the community organization]. I think it affected me. I was on welfare and did volunteer stuff...getting involved with [citizens' action group] and work with the lead safe house, and got involved in the coalition with Cuba. I was on welfare that's my pay. (Luz, 52-year-old Latina working-class female)

As far as my friends now, the activism came first, and then eventually, my social life and my work life melded together. I mean, it was like seven days a week job. (Adam, 22-year-old white working-class male)

The first six years, everybody was a volunteer, and then we got a grant that paid me, and then fundamentally things started to change. And part of that is my own internal "stuff" about no longer being willing to ask people to do scut work since they weren't getting paid for...I know that I'm a workaholic, I'm doing what I love doing in lots of ways, and in order to do what I love, I have to do all this other stuff that takes a lot of time, so I end up working late a lot of nights and stuff, or working weekends. (Robin, 47-year-old white middle-class female)

I was in a unique position in that I had some financial resources that allow me to do this. I have such great respect for people where [activism] is their only income, and they're choosing to have a lot less flexibility in their life, and, you know, a lot of comforts and things that people who make more money have and they're not going to have. (Ann, 43-year-old white middle-class female)

We get the impression from reading the scholarship that activists sustain almost heroic levels of commitment to social movements, experience little conflict between this commitment and other aspects of their lives or do not have any other lives outside their activism. If and when activism wanes, it is caused by external events such as a shift in political opportunities and a decline in resources which takes the social movement into the "doldrums." As the movement ebbs, activist enthusiasm, commitment, and participation also ebbs.[1]

The activists quoted above tell a very different story: tensions between activism and other aspects of their lives abound; some progressive organizations do better jobs than others in helping activists manage these tensions; some activists are better positioned economically and socially to devote time and energy to their activism. Despite all this, most activists speak of a passion or a commitment that keeps them involved. In the words of Andrew, quoted above: "the more that I discover what's wrong, the more...I dig in." Also in another introductory excerpt, Jack makes explicit the progressive nature of this commitment by telling me that he can't exit activism because "the mother fuckers are still running the show." The strength of his commitment is tied to a critique of power. And Regina attributes her commitment not only to a critique of power but also to her attachment to family and community. It is from her maternal grandmother (Mama Lulu) that she gets her passion for kids and cooking and her anger at injustice.

This deep commitment is a constant theme among most activists as they struggle to fashion a life around progressive activism.[2] Indeed, expressions of this intense commitment came up most frequently and somewhat surprisingly during the point in the interviews when we were discussing how activists balance activism with other aspects of their lives. Many of them felt guilty complaining about such seemingly mundane matters as laundry and relationships when there was such important work to be done! In addition to Andrew's and Jack's comments in the introduction to the chapter which were spoken in that context, Lorenzo recounts a conversation he had with his wife that puts these two aspects of activists' stories in bold relief:

I said to my wife about a month ago...she was talking about leaving her job and going back to school. And in that conversation she said to me, "How strongly do you feel about organizing?" And not that she wanted me to stop doing it but just to say, "We are talking about making some serious changes. Are you going to stick with this while I go to school?" and I said "I feel this strongly about it: If you told me today that unless you stop being an organizer, I'm going to pack the kids up and I'm going to leave, my response would be to help you pack." If I go with you and I'm not being an organizer then you're not going to be with me, you're with something else.

In some respects, these expressions of commitment amidst the cross-pressures of daily life are not surprising since my activists are, by definition, the ones who have "stuck it out" and the ones whose sense of self is heavily invested in their activism. This is not the group for whom these cross-pressures required that they withdraw from activism. It stands to reason then that this group of individuals would elicit a high level of commitment even as they detailed the difficulties of maintaining it.

We have seen from Chapter 6 that social networks play an important role in generating commitment to social movements. Many activists report a high degree of overlap between friendship and activist networks, and this overlap helps solidify that commitment. Adam communicates the totalizing nature of this overlap in his introductory excerpt, when he says that "my social life and my work life meld together." As he and others note however, this "melding" has contradictory consequences.

Sometimes, for example, these overlaps also contribute to burnout. After spending several minutes discussing her struggles with burnout, Ann insists on the importance of "taking a break" and finding friends outside activism.

> I think about people who don't have someone in their life, be it their partner or a child or a network of friends, who pulls them out of that life, so that would be hard to put the brakes on yourself and find the balance...Just to be able to have something outside of the activism world, even if that's what some of your conversations are about when you're not doing the work. For me personally that's really important, to get a break from it. I need that break to just recharge the batteries ... It is important to have that group of friends, those were, again, to give balance to the friends who, whenever I would see them, we would start out talking about "How was your vacation?" but very quickly move into "Could you believe what happened at that meeting?" and "What do you think, what's good strategy to talk to this legislator?" or whatever it is.

Implicit in Ann's comments is an irony of activism: that the intensity of the work leads to a high degree of merging of friendship and activist networks but this same merging contributes to an activist overload that leads to burnout. In Ann's words, "you feel overwhelmed. At some level, you don't care anymore and, of course, you do care. You're just too burned out to feel it....It feels terrible." She precisely captures the conundrum: that the reason you feel so bad is because you care so much.

Scholars and Burnout

Until recently, scholars have focused on activist burnout or declining participation only indirectly in the context of analyzing the life cycle of various social movements. The analysis typically uses metaphors such as waves, ebbs and flows, heyday and doldrums, to describe these cycles. The patterns or rhythms they are describing are primarily at the level of social movements: the number of activities, the amount of participation in these activities, the rate at which these activities increase or decrease, and the size and nature of the response to these activities by targets, bystanders, and allies.

In an influential essay on the long history of the U.S. women's movement, for example, Verta Taylor (1989) analyzes the ebbs and flows of activity from the suffrage campaigns of the early twentieth century through the denouement of the movement in the immediate post-World War II period to the renaissance of the movement with women's liberation in the late 1960s. She uses the experiences of the National Women's Party that was formed during the suffrage debates in the early twentieth century to document and analyze the changing fortunes of the women's movement. Taylor explains the flows and ebbs in activism in terms of the degree of material, political, and cultural support for women's equality across time. With the "flow," the movement gained members; with the "ebb," it lost them.

Most interestingly, she focuses on the small cadre of women in the National Women's Party who sustained their commitment to the movement in its 30-odd-year lull—the doldrums she calls it—by creating a close-knit, centralized organization with a charismatic leader who doggedly and unsuccessfully pursued the singular goal of an equal rights amendment. There was something about that intense organization, which Taylor describes as an "abeyance structure"—a holding pattern for feminism until the times became more hospitable—that kept these women highly committed despite the lack of policy progress or support for women's rights in the larger society. When a new wave of activism emerged with the women's liberation movement in the late 1960s, the ideas, people, and social networks cultivated in this abeyance structure facilitated that resurgence.

Although this concept of abeyance structure is employed to help us understand the ebb and flow of social movements, it can also aid in our understanding of how activists manage burnout and fatigue. The concept invites us to ask about the strategies that movements or organizations use to bolster commitment, the resources they provide to enable the many hours of activist work, and the supports they put in place to nourish members' emotional and political lives. In the case of the National Women's Party, Taylor alludes to features such as a shared history, residence, identification, and rituals that enabled this small cadre of women to remain committed even as others fell by the wayside (Taylor 1989: 770).

Another sociologist, Sharon Erickson Nepstad (2004), reworks this concept of abeyance to make it more useful for addressing directly issues of fatigue and burnout. She studies the Plowshares movement, a pacifist organization formed in the 1950s by the Catholic Worker movement that engages in various forms of high-risk civil disobedience such as damaging military equipment, blocking the movement of equipment and troops, and "sitting in" at combat locations. Rather than abeyance structures, Nepstad uses the concept of plausibility structures to convey a set of practices, networks, and relations that provide material, cognitive, and emotional supports for activists doing demanding work. The term "plausibility" connotes the sense that what these people are doing—engaging in high-risk action which demands many sacrifices and offers few material rewards—requires a structure and culture that makes these ostensibly irrational actions understandable.

Nepstad shows that the Plowshares movement held retreats to re-energize activists' spirits and provided assistance with child care and housing for activists who needed it. In these ways, the movement provided support structures to counter the biographical pressures to leave the movement. The biographical pressures of activists are not the focus of the analysis. Nepstad sees these pressures as always present and thus always a potential reason for exiting the movement. The crucial question is what social factors can mitigate the potential effects of activism on people's lives.

Activists and Burnout

While scholars may be reluctant to talk about the fullness or complexity of these lives, the activists themselves are only too willing. To be sure, progressive activists in Hartford talk about the aspects of the activism that keep them committed and enable them to manage activist burnout and fatigue. We only need recall activists' comments from previous chapters that mention the many satisfactions associated with different aspects of their work: the intense friendships and solidarities among different groups of individuals, the peak experience of working for something meaningful beyond one's narrow self-interest, the enjoyment of a good fight, to name a few. One result of those satisfactions is the high level of commitment you hear in several of the comments that introduce this chapter. But, also in those introductory comments, you hear about the cross-pressures of managing a life with the demands of organizing: the financial pressures experienced by Luz while doing organizing in Latina neighborhoods, the physical dangers expressed with some bravado by Cornel as he confronted drug dealers in an embattled African American neighborhood, and the emotional dangers of "living in a glass box" by Rich while he was doing queer youth activism. Ann and Luz talked about the tensions and fierce conflicts that led them to shift their activist energies or even temporarily abandon their work, despite their deep and abiding commitment to progressive social change. With all of them, a complicated connection exists between the intensity of their commitment and the personal costs associated with the activism.

These stories serve as reminders to social movement scholars that studying the lives of activists in all their complexity is as important as studying the activism itself. As the stories above suggest, we cannot understand features of activism such as strategies, goals, allies, etc., without understanding the social situation of the activists who engage in this activism. For a discussion of "why activists get tired," this means we need to examine both the plausibility structures (and support structures more generally) of movements as well as the informal strategies individuals use to manage the cross-pressures between activism and demands in other areas of their lives.

Activists were only too willing to talk about their experiences with "burnout" and the strategies they construct to balance their activism with work, friends, family, lovers, relationships, and children. The strategies they devise are best viewed as creative and diverse techniques for remaining committed to an activist identity. Sometimes the support structures of an organization or campaign aid this process; other times, these structures are nonexistent. In all cases, the commitment to a progressive sense of self leads activists to change their personal lives to adjust to their activist lives or, conversely, to change the specific nature of their activist activity to adjust to their personal lives. Taken together, these stories encourage activists to see their struggles around "balance" and "burnout" not as a personal problem or a manifestation of "activist guilt." Activists need to spend as much time fashioning plausibility structures and other forms of internal support for themselves and others as they do engaging in the more externally directed battles for social change.

Support Structures

One of the few activists who talked about a structure and culture of support for their work was Chris, whose comments about "community" as an important cultural resource of organizations are discussed in Chapter 5. Not surprisingly, he works with the Catholic Worker movement in Hartford, a local branch of the same movement that Sharon Erickson Nepstad studied when she developed the concept of plausibility structures. After describing the kinds of activities that take place at the safe house located in one of Hartford's most impoverished and neglected neighborhoods, Chris echoes Nepstad's observations saying, "We have each other's back in a way that would not be possible if we weren't living in community." His brief quote mentions several aspects of support captured in the concept of a plausibility structure, especially the material and emotional components. In addition, Chris stresses the non-normative aspect of the concept of community which gives activists succor and strength:

> It's the way the first Christians lived, and they were forced to live that way because they were hunted and persecuted, and if they didn't have each other then they wouldn't have made it. Community, sharing, what they had with each other so that nobody went hungry. It's not a new idea, it's pretty old. But it's hitting up against the grain of American individualism.

I did not hear that sentiment and the importance of support structures in general expressed as strongly or unambiguously for any other activist.

Although not as definitively, another set of activists, labor progressives, also discussed the support structures just developing in their unions to handle the stresses of activism. Since the mid-1990s, several unions have dramatically increased the amount of resources devoted to organizing the unorganized and, more generally, to reviving the radical ethos of the labor movement (Clawson 2003). In concrete terms, this has meant hiring more organizers and recruiting new members in new sectors of the labor force, especially young people, women, and racial and ethnic minorities. These efforts also involve innovative tactics of community-wide alliances and new goals such as community-wide living wage standards to pressure businesses during organizing drives and contract negotiations. This approach has brought thousands of new organizers into unions, ratcheted up the demands on these organizers, and infused their work with missionary zeal. Not surprisingly, an unintended consequence of this approach has been organizer burnout, rapid organizer turnover, and high levels of stress, exhaustion, and anxiety.

Steve, a veteran labor organizer who welcomed this new progressive push by the union leadership, recognizes the pressure and incorporates "stress-reduction" strategies into his training:

> I take new organizers aside and I say, "You know what? Nobody is going to take care of you in this organization except you. So, if you're at that point where you're just about to jump off the 10th story of a 10-story building, you've got to figure out a way to find some time and space for yourself. And that's in spite of the fact that you know you've got to work six or seven days a week, 10 hours a day, or more. You go to that movie in the afternoon, or go do your laundry, or whatever, or just chill out." And so, and I followed that advice, right? I work all the time, I'm always working, but I'm also always taking a break whenever I need to, and I find the quiet times.

Although he recognizes the stress that accompanies the nature of the position, the training still exists at an informal level and has yet to be institutionalized into the rules and practices of the organization.

Other unions are further along. Abbey, a fairly new organizer for the hotel and restaurant workers at the time of the interview, talks about how more formalized structures are being put into place in her union:

> It's a very stressful job. People's lives, sometimes, are in your hands. But, also, I mean, it's a job that takes a lot of time. I have three children. Most of the people that work in this job don't have children. And, those that do are married. I have three children and I'm a single parent, so it's really hard...I don't know how our union was before I started working here, but I've been told that ever since [I started] we started really looking at the fact that organizers have to have lives outside of organizing, I don't know too many unions that say, "Listen, you know, take this day off." Now we don't work on Sundays...me coming on staff has helped that idea.

Abbey is one of those new organizers drawn from the rank and file in food service work. She is also a single mother who must balance childcare and domestic work with her organizing work. Somewhat reluctantly, the union is grappling with these changed life circumstances of its organizers. To the extent that Hartford's progressive organizations are establishing support structures for their members, Abbey's comments illustrate that they are doing it in response to pressure from their own members.

While the concept of plausibility structure stresses the social and emotional supports that movements provide to sustain commitment and deter burnout, many Hartford activists point to other more tangible economic supports that enable them to do activism and balance it with the other demands of their lives. Scholars tend to downplay this aspect of activism and thus romanticize the notion of the altruistic activist tirelessly pursing social change unselfishly and without reward. Activists know this is not true. Quoted at the beginning of the chapter, Robin appreciates how the success of her queer youth advocacy and support organization enabled her to draw a salary, even as she recognizes the challenges of this shift. Also quoted at the beginning of the chapter, Ann has an independent source of income that makes possible her volunteer activism. She does appreciate her "unique position," and marvels at those who "have a lot less flexibility in their [lives]." Luz, also quoted above, is one of those people who does not have that flexibility. Her excerpt makes explicit the connection between the tensions and conflicts inherent in activism ("It got to a point where it was too much") and the precariousness of her economic and family circumstances ("I was on welfare, that's my pay"). Her narration of "burnout" moves effortlessly from a series of conflicts in an especially difficult campaign to the profound economic deprivation she experienced during that time.

Even activists like Jack who downplay the importance of social support structures stress this economic component of support:

> I'm never as worried about burnout. I think people adjust. The longevity of people in organizing has much more to do with, can you keep them connected to the vision. And if they can, then they make the adjustments in their lifestyle to keep them at it. But it also has to do with just being realistic: people got to make a living doing it. As committed as some of the people that we had, we lost good people simply because whatever organization they were working for couldn't afford to pay them more than minimum wage, and people got to move on from that. I mean the organizers want to raise families too. They want to go off and whether it's with a family or with their friends or whatever, they want to have some kind of a quality of life that they can enjoy also and they don't want to always have nothing.

Even as Jack implicitly acknowledges that activist organizations have some responsibility for helping individuals stay "connected to the vision," he asserts that the more important responsibility of these organizations is paying activists "more than minimum wage."

As described earlier in Chapter 5, resource constraints constantly bedevil progressive organizations. Here we see how these constraints operate in activists' personal lives and affect their ability to do activism. Further, my interviews suggest that this ability interacts with the class position of activists. Better-off activists in better-off organizations are less susceptible to burnout than activists with fewer economic resources and more demanding family lives who do their activism in more precarious grassroots organizations.

Being Burned by the Movement

As seen above, Hartford progressive activists talk about not having time, money, or the flexibility to manage many different aspects of their lives. They do not talk as much about the social support structures available in organizations or campaigns that would assist them with these "troubles." Activists point to experiences in their activism that create stress, exhaustion, and disappointment and, in many cases, lead to "cutting back," withdrawing, or shifting the nature of their progressive work. For them, it is less about being "*burned out*" and more about being "*burned by*" their work in the movement. Again, the comments of Luz and Ann at the beginning of the chapter are apropos of this experience. Ann refers to it as the "internal politics" of the movement and says that it can be more "draining than fighting with the perceived enemy."

Of course, conflicts are inevitable in all organizations and perhaps even more so in organizations so deeply committed to doing social change work that is, by definition, slow, frustrating, and "against the grain." We have seen several examples of these conflicts in previous chapters especially with activists who experience racism, classism, and homophobia in organizations and campaigns and, because of these experiences, become disillusioned and subsequently withdraw, cutback, or reimagine their activist work.

Another kind of negative experience speaks directly to this absence of support structures in social movement work. When John, the activist involved for over a decade in a host of progressive causes in the city, reflects on that experience he speaks of the inability of the movement to deal with the "feelings" dimension of this work:

> That kind of heady period fostered personal deep, wonderful friendships but, as a group setting, sometimes it was alienating. Even with the friendships and the intense dynamics that were created, you had all these strong personalities. And the bantering and the stuff didn't always feel great. But, this political arena doesn't really deal with the personal and it's not personal enough, it's more about the system and ideas and not about feelings at all, really, although feelings were driving it, it doesn't know how to deal with the feelings fully... So, it takes a toll on the individual.

John holds up the organization and the people in the organization to a higher standard because of their commitment to a progressive ideology. The betrayal he experienced is doubly painful because of this standard:

> If you were burned in this process, like when I felt betrayed, some people would say it's a game anyway. But we resisted that view. Is it healthier to go into it saying it is a game and whoever can out-organize the other wins? But if you believe in certain things so strongly it's hard.

When you combine this sense of betrayal with the fact that, for many of these activists, their friendship and activist circles are one and the same, the betrayal feels intensely personal. Based on these experiences, John speaks directly and eloquently to a need for support structures that focus explicitly on these complicated dynamics:

> In the midst of all this wonderful work, I feel that we have neglected a very basic element of living and growing together as a community—catering to the details of the soul and spirit of the movement and its individual members.

Once again, Hartford activists point out the importance of devoting as much energy to the internal processes of community building and conflict resolution as to the externally directed processes of strategizing, goal setting, coalition formation, etc.

Activist Strategies to Manage Burnout

This reluctance or inability of the movement to foster support structures leads activists who, by definition, do not completely disengage from participation to construct their own solutions to balance activism with other aspects of their lives. We have already seen some of these strategies with Ann's attempts to create some separation between her activist self and other aspects of her life. Regardless of the particular strategy or how important these strategies are in the lives of activists, the starting point for this discussion is the high degree of commitment that these activists have to their work and the values and vision guiding their work. Like Ann, other Hartford activists also attempt separation between their activist role and other roles, thus resisting the totalizing experience that progressive activism oftentimes becomes. Others attempt to do just the opposite and give in to the totalizing experience, and subordinate or refashion their personal lives more in line with their activist role. Each of these strategies comes with its own risks and rewards.

When activists adopt this first pattern, it is oftentimes in response to a personal crisis of some sort. In the first quote of the chapter, Andrew gives an exhaustive list of these crises: physical, emotional, financial, family. Queer activist, Beth, experiences only one of these crises which is enough to trigger a strategy of separation:

> I just recently ended a relationship. But when I was in that relationship for three years, that was constantly a tension for us because I wanted to be out doing all this stuff and I was supposed to be at home being with my partner as opposed to out in the world....I've gotten a little bit better about that. But it

never feels like you can do that because it feels like that [the activism] is so much more important than me going home and, I don't know, doing laundry or something.

As we can see for Beth, this re-prioritizing is tentative at best since she struggles with the tensions between this totalizing commitment to progressive social change and what she sees as the humdrum aspects of everyday life.

Others respond to the tensions between activism and other aspects of life in more creative ways, turning time pressures or conflicts in activism into opportunities for positive change. Cheryl uses the exhaustion that came not only from her activism in many different areas but also from the tokenism she felt as a bisexual, disabled, African American woman to reevaluate and refashion the nature of her commitment to progressive activism:

Unless you get with some big organization you really don't make a lot of money at organizing. That's what I found out. But that's what I love to do. So I had to balance making a living and doing my organizing work, so what I decided was to go into consulting business. It would free me up from going to a 9 to 5 job. And at the same time do my volunteer work and the other things I want to do and make a connection between my consulting work and my volunteer work...So I can kind of control my destiny a little bit more because I wasn't able to, and to make the choices that I wanted to make in my life around what was I going to do in the next 3, 5, 10 years. And I wanted to do anti-racism organizing, and what made me decide that this is the time for it is that everywhere I went, when I organized in the disability community, which is the first place that I cut my teeth, and then I went to the gay, lesbian, bi, transgender community, what happened was that I always would face racism in each one of those endeavors, you know? I always kind of felt that people didn't get it. So I said, "Instead of me trying to keep talking and keep trying to pressure people to see racism as an important focus," I said, "You know what? Let me take my issues to where people are—where they're at." So instead of being part of the disability community and then the gay-lesbian, I wanted to go into the people of color community and bring my issues there, because I'm my whole person everywhere I go, so everywhere I go I talk about my disability, my bisexuality, and then of course, racism stuff. So it comes from me wanting to go full circle....I wanted to make a connection between my consulting work and my volunteer work which is what I do. I am trainer. I am a grant writer. I've had a little bit of everything. I organize. I am a conference planner, an events planner, a fund raiser. So what I did was I tried to get my networks, my connections of people who do antiracism organizing and that is my pool of people who I reach out to, and also people who have known me over the years from doing organizing. These are the people who usually call me and say, "Cheryl can you do this?" "Cheryl can you do that?" So it's the network that I made along the way for my organizing work.

Cheryl needed to make a living as well as continue her activism. That constraint as well as the frustration of people "not getting it" about racism encouraged her to refocus her activism and refashion how she would balance her activist role with her work role. Interestingly, she created a job that emerged directly from her activist role thus allowing her to pay her bills and continue doing the work she loves. Cheryl's creative solution to the tension between activism and "making a living" led her to reshape her activist work as well as her work in the paid labor market.

Another creative solution to the overwhelming demands of activist work and its effects on activists' other roles was in the area of personal relationships. As Beth mentions, many times these competing demands are a part of the reason relationships dissolve and marriages end.[3] There are other times when the crisis in a personal relationship does not result in failure but in redefinition. In the case of Robin who works with queer youth, she utilizes some of the insights of this activist work to inform her "work" in her personal relationship:

> I would [tell my girlfriend] "I will just get to the end of this project and then I would have time." Then what happened is that she actually met somebody that she's developed a real emotional connection with and she wants to be able to explore that piece, and that situation put us into a crisis of such proportions that we're actually resolving all of this stuff around it. That we made the commitment that we're going to stay together, and that until we're going to figure out how to do this, and that crisis has created the opportunity for us to look at my work, to look at her relationship, to look at us as individuals differentiating from each other.

Robin's creative strategy of reimagining the relationship involves utilizing some of the insights of queer relationships that she learned in her activist work. The crisis in the relationship due to the time demands of her activist work led her to re-evaluate her understanding of the definition of a "good" relationship and the costs and benefits of the couple form of traditional relationships.

Some activists reject the idea of a separation of spheres between activism and other roles and, like Robin, use the ideas or the networks of activism to effect a more complete merging of the different areas of their life. Again, this strategy takes place in the absence of supports from progressive organizations to sustain energy levels and balance multiple roles. Lisa's passionate commitment to the Latina women and children in her organization leads her to readjust her personal desires to accommodate her activism:

> I am thinking that someday I'm going to get married and have kids; I always wanted a ton of kids. In a way I guess I have had a ton of kids, because I've known a ton and loved a ton of kids [through my activism] but I kind of gave up on the idea, that I was going to wait to buy a house until I was married. Then I thought, "Yeah, right. What the hell am I waiting for?" So, I bought my house on Bonner Street, and I loved living there, and I loved having my

garden and letting the kids from the neighborhood come in and play. That was balance to me.

Even though Lisa subordinates her traditional view of marriage and family to the realities of her activist work, she uses the activist knowledge she has gained about love, home, and community to rework that view and reconstruct an alternative understanding that in effect merges her activist and her personal lives.

Laura M.'s story about her career in the labor movement illustrates many features of these two strategies for managing the tensions between a personal life and an activist life. It also shows how her efforts to carve out more time for herself led to a changed activist life, an even greater commitment to activism, and an erosion of the distinction between a life outside and inside the movement.

Laura M. experienced a series of personal crises that brought the tensions between her activist commitments and her personal life into sharp relief:

> The union wanted to move me to Palm Springs, and I said, "Absolutely not. I will not go. My sister has cancer, I am 34. I have lived my life at this point entirely for the union. My personal life needs to be more important now, and I don't want to leave the union, but I want both...As my 30s went on, I started getting increasingly sad about not having more of an intimate, emotional relationship with people. I think I wanted a lover and a husband. But the most significant factor was my sister getting cancer. So, when [she] got cancer, and—you know I was dating—when she got cancer I sort of said to the guy I was dating, "You know what? My sister has cancer. I'm going to be in Boston every weekend. See ya." And so that process of the cancer diagnosis and the chemotherapy and spending all the time with her, and thinking about death, and her death particularly, which of course leads one to think about, "How does one live? And what are the choices we make?."...And so it was, part of my thinking about going to work in Boston was that there was just a larger pool of possibilities [for relationships], you know, more people in the labor movement. Because I have always had this dream: it's two people who in the early part of their life made a commitment to social change, lived together, got married, and spent their whole life working for social change.

Laura's story is interesting and complicated for several reasons. At first glance, her sister's health crisis forced her to subordinate her activist role to her role as sister and family member, adamantly refusing to move to Palm Springs as desired by the union. This family crisis and the personal crisis that followed, however, did not lead Laura to cut back her commitment to the union and to activist work in general. Instead, she crafted a strategy by which she could pursue both her activism and her desire for a romantic relationship by moving to a new location with greater possibilities for meeting (and merging) these two goals within the labor movement. This strategy did not necessarily subordinate her personal desires to her progressive activism but instead served as a way for her to make the activism a truly totalizing experience. As Laura speculates, she would meet someone and they would both make a "commitment to social change, live together, get married, and spend their whole life working for social change." Laura's story also indicates that these two patterns of responding to activist stress, overwork, cross-pressures, and burnout are not mutually exclusive and can co-occur within the same activist across her/his biography of activism.

Conclusion

We hear little about these creative strategies to avert burnout in the scholarship on social movements. These creative strategies described above can be used to develop concepts that exist alongside those of abeyance and plausibility structures to aid scholars in thinking about how activists sustain commitment and manage stress. They can also be used to inform our understanding of strategies, goals, and allies since, as we have seen, decisions around these are made in ways to alleviate the tensions, stresses and cross-pressures that may exist among activists as they balance activism and other aspects of their lives. Related to this latter lesson, scholars can also use these stories of burnout to explore the possibility that part of the ideological diversity we observe in progressive movements is related to managing these tensions. In any case, scholars may need to supplement the concepts of abeyance and plausibility structures with ones that capture the support structures created by activists themselves outside the movements in which they participate. The two sets of concepts—ones that capture the nature of the support and resources made available by movements and ones that capture the support and resources actively created by activists themselves—nicely capture the dynamic interplay of individual and structural factors that operates in this process of sustaining commitment and avoiding burnout.

In these stories from this chapter, activists also seem to be sending messages to the organizations, the campaigns, and progressive initiatives they participate in to better address the interpersonal and emotional lives of themselves and other activists. Quite ironically, these activists and by extension the organizations they participate in are so focused on externally oriented social change that they fail to turn their progressive values onto themselves and ask themselves how communities of activists should take care of one another.

Chapter 8

Who They Are: Collective Identity and Oppositional Consciousness

I know I was just born to do this kind of stuff. I can't help it. But, the older I get, the more clues I think I have as to why I do it. I was born in 1953 in rural Kentucky...bathroom outside, all that stuff. I saw people who looked like me all the time...you know, were crazy about me, loved me to death. We moved when I was an infant to New Jersey to a blue-collar neighborhood where my parents were the most well-off. They both were college educated. The neighborhood we moved into at the time was pretty much mixed in being Black, Italian and Polish...And I was bused K through 12 to lily-white upper middle-class suburbs. That's where I first learned about classism...Because all of a sudden I realize them Poles that lived on that street where I did were not really white people, you know? Their white card wasn't stamped. My neighbors were first generation born in America and we were all being bused together. And I started seeing. Even though my father had a degree in biology, I learned later, due to racial discrimination, he managed a bar most of his life. And it was there that I learned things about how what your father did for a living made a big difference in your so-called status...(Regina, 51-year-old African American working-class female)

Once I learned my roots and I started realizing what oppression was and how our culture has been oppressed for so many years...And what racism was, and how internalized racism begins, that this [my organizing] began...I met some brothers and sisters from my country who explained to me what racism was. And I had a hard time understanding why if I had the same qualifications as this white woman, why was she getting the job and not me...I took all that anger, and all that energy, and I went into meetings...I remember how pretty they were going to do Park Street, and how they were planning on doing this, and how they were planning on doing that...I said "What's happening to the people?" If they're fixing this up, I didn't see no housing. There was no housing there. And that was the beginning...So I took all that negative energy and I started going to meetings, and I started to voice my opinion. And being heard! (Carmen, 42-year-old Latina working-class female)

I came out to my family, and throughout that year coming out was really a great weight off my shoulders. And because they were so positive, I felt, well, I've been blessed so I need to go out and advocate for those who it wasn't so positive...I want to stick with queer youth work. I'd like to get more involved here at [the organization]...to come on [staff] full time or possibly working for the state, children and families, being active with them. (Nick, 23-year-old white working-class male)

High school was where I started [my activism]...graduated high school in '69. I was working on a newspaper...I did a little underground newspaper when I was a junior. When I was a senior I became editor. We did stuff mostly around civil rights, Vietnam War, and especially student rights. That's where I learned about power relationships: as a student, having grown-ups because at seventeen that's the only power you know, being angry at you or calling you into the office or undermining you or whatever...I went to UConn, the University of Connecticut...and I was becoming more and more active...full-time political work: a student strike in 1970; we did a moratorium in '68, '69; the strike in 1970. Politics was like full time! And May Day in New Haven in 1970 where Richard Nixon said that the revolution was going to happen that day. And we did too. There was just so much... The contradictions were just so great between what was supposed to be and what was actually going on all over the world and right here. (Steve, 52-year-old white middle-class male)

[My union] has an image that's grounded in history. It's based on two things: one is that you can fight and win, and that is through organizing and using your collective power through strikes. The other is...social unionism, it's the idea that your union is also a force for social change. We were one of the first but few organizations that came out against the Vietnam War, but before that, [the union] was striking in Harlem to get black pharmacists to be able to work in Harlem drug stores in 1936, so there's this long civil rights history, long antiwar history and social justice history that we continue in our work in Connecticut. (Steve, 52-year-old white middle-class male)

It was through the women's movement that I actually became a lesbian. It was very much tied to an analysis about sexism in our culture...So that was really the merging for me of taking and moving from reproductive rights and a strong relationship in the women's movement through reproductive rights and abortion rights and then connecting that with the personal is political, and personal relationships. And so that's when I hooked up with [my partner] because [she] was also a political activist-feminist activist at that point. So she and I have been together for 22 years. (Carolyn, 60-year-old white middle-class female)

As we have seen in the past two chapters, activists tell many different stories about their initiation into, continued participation in, and occasional weariness of progressive activism. I have shown how these stories are patterned using concepts from social movement scholarship. I have also shown how these concepts can be further clarified by listening closely to the nuance and complexity in activists' accounts. In the case of activists' initiation into and continued participation in activism, the concepts of biography, social networks, and critical events are useful but only when used in an interactive and iterative way which better captures individuals' creative capacities for innovation. Similarly, in discussing activists' experiences with burnout and disengagement from activism, the concepts of abeyance and plausibility structures were also useful if only to point to their relative absence in progressive activism in Hartford. I have shown that, in the absence of these structures, individuals create their own strategies to maintain their commitments while also seeking balance across the many social roles they perform.

One area in which activists' stories dovetail quite closely with social movement scholarship is in the area of activist identity: the notion that the processes of recruitment, participation, and commitment have profound consequences on an activist's sense of self. Activists rarely use the words "identity" or "sense of self" but all their conversations in one way or another are about "who they are." This idea of identity lurks behind all previously discussed aspects of activism. What they do and how they do it derive in part from who they are. How they define themselves, how they communicate to other people about themselves, how they make decisions and prioritize the roles they perform in life, and how they understand the world—in a word, their identities—are profoundly affected by their progressive activism. Although identity is never an explicit topic of activists' conversations with me, I see it everywhere in those conversations.

We see examples of activist identities in the above excerpts. Regina and Carmen talk about how their early biographical experiences of marginality led them to their participation in progressive activism. Nick references his "coming out" story as the impetus for his organizing. Steve talks about his "growing up in the 1960s " as the prelude to his work in the labor movement. Biography, memory, attitudes, and values are woven together into a (somewhat) coherent activist identity.

These excerpts are rich in detail and suggest a complexity to the concept of activist identity. These identities are more than simply products of collective action. When activists tell stories of "who they are," they include features of their lives prior to and independent of their initiation into progressive activism. When they do that, they create their identities in the process of telling their activist story. In other words, activist identities are constructed stories in the sense that memories of the past are refracted through their present activism, and the accounts of their present activism are told to give legitimacy to these memories of the past. In Regina's, Carmen's, and Nick's cases these are memories of marginalization; in Steve's case it is a memory of political awakening. This construction does not diminish their power. As a matter of fact, the repeated act of their telling continues to give power to their activist identities.

This idea of the constructed nature of activist identity has been captured by the concept of identity talk introduced by David Snow and Leon Anderson (1987). They define identity talk as the discursive presentation of an individual's identity in light of her/his relationship to collective action. This talk is constructed as a dialogue between the meaning systems from an individual's life experiences prior to and during her/his activism and the meaning systems of the various movements in which the individual participates. As the introductory excerpts suggest and illustrated in more detail below, this identity talk is not necessarily an empirically "obvious" or a "true" account of activists' lives. It is a creative accomplishment: bringing together personal biography and activist history to say something about the ideas, ideologies, and activities activists see as important; the emotions, interests, and desires that move them; and the galvanizing or inspirational moments that mark their commitments...in a word, their identities.

In addition to this concept of identity talk meant to capture the individual component of an activist's identity, scholars of social movements have advanced another related concept—collective identity—to emphasize the groups from which individuals draw their self-concepts. This concept was introduced in Chapter 2. Recall from that discussion that collective identity comprises three important components: the incorporation of the ideas of the movement into the social psychology of the individual; the sense of group membership that exists among these similarly thinking individuals; and an in-group/out-group dynamic whereby the in-group pursues interests and understandings in opposition to other groups. An often-quoted definition of the concept of collective identity comes from Verta Taylor's and Nancy Whittier's (1992: 172) influential essay on the subject and precisely captures the group-based nature of this concept: "the shared definition of a group derived from members' common interests, experiences, and solidarities." The definition assumes a close correspondence between the identity of the group and the identity of the individual who is a member of the group.

Activists would find this concept quite useful to help them understand many aspects of themselves and the work they do. First, it explains the almost unconscious sense of duty or compulsion they feel, and their tendency to conflate who they are with what they do. Recall the discussion of activist guilt in the previous chapter where activists discuss how difficult it is for them to curtail their participation in collective action in the face of internal conflicts or changes in other aspects of their lives. We see this conflation quite clearly when Steve, the labor activist quoted repeatedly throughout the book, states, "One thing I know, in terms of who I am, I could never not be an activist." Second, the concept also explains activists' tendencies to see themselves as connected to other similarly thinking people. This is part of the "pronoun problem" I encountered throughout my interviews as activists would move back and forth between talking about themselves as individual actors and as an "us" collectively acting, thinking, and feeling. Third, related to this, they frequently mentioned the same set of people when I asked them who they thought was doing interesting progressive work in the area and who they were likely to ally with when doing their work. These networks also speak to the collective aspects of their activist identities.

Within this concept of collective identity, scholars have made various distinctions to capture different types of groups or collectivities that activists feel a part of or to signal the group allegiances that activists hold. In one frequently cited typology, William Gamson (1992) distinguishes movement-based, organization-based, and solidary-derived collective identities based on the source of the "we-ness" of an activist's identification (Polletta and Jasper 2001: 293). Movement-based collective identity refers to an identification with an established social movement and its frames, repertoires of contention, and goals. Organization-based collective identity is a set of identifications and subjective understandings that derive from a specific organization situated in a broader social movement sector. Solidary-derived collective identity refers to membership in and identification with a broad social category such as race, ethnic group, gender, or sexual orientation. These distinctions complicate the concept of collective identity by calling attention to different kinds of groups that constitute the "we" that moves activists to participate, commit, and lead.

While no typology can completely capture the broad array of individual and collective experiences that lead people to become and live their lives as activists, I have found Gamson's typology particularly useful for understanding the identities of Hartford's progressive activists. Steve's identity talk in the introduction to the chapter is all about his progressive union, a discourse informed by a specific organization but also by his participation in the social movements of the 1960s: both a movement-based and organization-based identity. Regina's and Carmen's identity talk stems from their membership in multiple marginal social groups, and their experiences in activism make sense only in terms of these multiple group memberships, a solidary-derived collective identity. Carolyn's identity talk gets its power from her participation in the feminist movement, particularly one of its defining ideologies: the notion that the personal is political and the political is personal. She has organized her activist life in terms of these and other feminist ideals. Using Gamson's framework, she clearly possesses a movement-based collective identity. This conceptual framework helps us see that Hartford progressive activists, while frequently operating side-by-side, oftentimes in the same organizations or campaigns, do not draw on the same set of ideas and ideologies and do not necessarily hold the same set of priorities and commitments. This insight can prove useful to activists who must work to find common purpose in setting goals and deciding strategy.

As we have seen repeatedly throughout this book, there is always a distance between the concepts used to analyze the social world and the social world itself. This distance is evident here as well since the conceptual distinctions that identify activists on the basis of a singular group (or combination of groups) cannot possibly capture the complexity of activists' identities. For social movement scholars, the challenge is not to reject the relevance of concepts as devices for organizing and explaining the empirical world but to use the inevitable gap between these concepts and that world to build better concepts. For social movement activists, the challenge is to use the concepts, themselves constructed by observing commonalities in the empirical world, to engage in more meaningful and purposeful action.

This challenge is especially important for the concept of identity. Many sociologists tend to view identities as relatively fixed and stable. After all, the concept is useful in bundling a whole host of attributes—behavioral, cognitive, emotional, and attitudinal—to convey a coherent sense of who a person "truly" is. Social movement scholars think of activist identity as the sum total of these attributes with specific reference to their activist life: the ideas and ideologies that guide their actions, the interests and issues that occupy their attention, the particular techniques or organizing philosophy to which they are wedded, and the galvanizing moments or inspirations that mark their commitments. This is a lot to pack into any one concept and, although I do find notable patterns across Hartford activists in terms of how they describe themselves, I do find contradiction and inconsistency as well. This refusal to act as a coherent social subject should remind us that the concept is a heuristic device. Identities are socially and culturally constructed in a deep way by social scientists and activists alike both struggling to find coherence among the whole host of attributes commonly referred to as "the self."[1]

Jeremy, an especially self-reflective labor activist, reminds us of the dangers of stabilizing the concept of activist identity. In response to a question about why he does what he does, he responds somewhat flippantly: "What lie do you want me to tell?"

> And I still don't know if I can explain why. Just, kind of talking about, you know, for lack of a better word, deconstructing various identities and what some people call ideology and all those kinds of things seemed to be very relevant to, not in a direct way, to organizing workers, but in terms of how you view the world. One answer I have given when people say "Why did you do this?" I think a real and honest answer is, I hated middle school and high school. I was a geek in middle school, and wasn't a geek in high school by design, that changed. I went to a public middle school and went to a private high school and was able to reinvent myself...I was just really angry all the time about people around me, and how they treated me and other people. And so, I probably was just really angry. I mean, I know I was really angry. So, I don't know maybe it kind of planted a seed....[At an orientation] an organizer from Washington DC, who comes from a similar background and [in response to a question:] "Why are you here?" said, "I hate the boss. I hate the boss. I hate the boss. I hate the boss." You know, and maybe that's it. Maybe the bosses are the people I grew up with. I don't know.

Jeremy's insistent uncertainty and cynicism captures one aspect of the "problem of identity": that one must have a well-worked-out "story" that explains one's activism. His next comments immediately recognize this problem.

> But you can't really be cynical. It's a useful front and tactic, but it's not really manageable...You got to have something to go on. I don't know exactly what

it is that I go on. I don't look into my inner self, because I don't believe I have one. But I don't have some set of core values...I really do like organizing. I definitely believe that workers have to organize and take power. I'm not going to call myself a communist or a socialist....It's a really hard question to answer. I guess people believe their answer like when they say there's this defining moment, and I guess that's good. I just don't have such a moment.

These comments capture perfectly both the usefulness and constructed nature of activist identity. It is a discursive construction created by individuals themselves in a culture that demands "inner selves." Once constructed, these identities take on a power that does indeed define who they are and influences what they do.

With these important caveats in mind, the identity talk of Hartford progressive activists requires that we revise our conceptual categories of activist identity to make them more sensitive to the dynamic and interactive relationship between individual biography and social movement contexts. As the introductory excerpts illustrate and elaborate on further below, activists' identities can only be characterized as movement-based, organization-based, or solidary-based in nature if we do not see these identities as mutually exclusive but interactive, if we recognize the somewhat unique biographical features that provide their own cultural material to the dynamic construction of activists' collective identities, and if we see the construction of these activist identities as creative discursive accomplishments.

Movement-Based Collective Identity

The social movement context of the 1960s forms a central identity trope for several progressive activists. We have seen that trope in Steve's and Carolyn's comments in the introduction to the chapter. The existence of this discourse is not surprising since many sociologists have noted the enduring importance of this social movement context as providing the cultural language for movement activism (McAdam 1988; Taylor 1996; Whittier 1995). These movements of the late 1960s circulated the language of civil rights, feminism, and student empowerment throughout the culture which then became incorporated into the identity talk of activists who came of age during this period. Steve's insistence that "[t]hat's where I learned about power relationships, as a student," and Carolyn's acknowledgment that "[i]t was through the women's movement that I actually became a lesbian" illustrate the importance of the 1960s social movement context for their activist identities. In their cases, the 1960s movement "moment" is so central to their identities that all their subsequent activism is explained in reference to ideologies of that moment.

To see the power of this trope, we need only revisit how Carolyn describes both her coming to activism and the priorities that inform her current activism.

I was born in 1941. So, part of that [time] was "What are expectations for women?" I was very much pre-feminist when I was growing up...it was a very narrow vision for women. I mean, that was really the vision of what my parents gave to me to get educated but be a mother and a wife as your primary responsibility but with a strong sense of community participation and commitment... certainly not social change. So the women's movement really was a major force, really, in politicizing me. And I was living in Florida, we lived in Florida but we moved a lot, in fact we moved 9 times in two and a half years, I mean, we did a lot of moving so that's why my choice of having children at that time made sense...You're a woman, you follow your husband, you have your children. But when I'd had my three children and I was beginning to think, well, what else do I want to be doing with my life, my real interest around reproductive rights and family planning were sort of one that I thought was a really important area that then merges and is a natural fit, obviously, with what happened in the women's movement. I was coming at it actually out of more of family planning, and zero population growth was the big issue in those days. It was a very different perspective than women's control over their bodies and their lives. But, as you can see, as you're coming in from that, and then as the women's movement was gaining momentum, it was a course then that merged, for me, and took that issue and brought to it a whole new analysis to be something that I felt very committed to. So I became very active in the women's movement.

Her identity talk is divided into a pre-feminist life, a life she describes as typical for middle-class women of her era, and her feminist life, a time when the issues she saw as important became redefined in terms of "women's control over their bodies and their lives." The feminist movement is the lens through which she sees her past.

The feminist movement is also the lens through which she sees her present and future activism. The core ideas of that feminism, moreover, are no longer rooted in the middle-class issues of reproductive rights but in a more expansive intersectional analysis of women where women of color, working-class women, and queer women are the touchstones of her activist identity talk. This shift came as a result of ultimately productive tensions and conflicts within feminism throughout the 1980s and 1990s. During that time, feminists of color and working-class women challenged some of the fundamental positions of second-wave feminism around equal access to jobs and abortion which were framed in ways that denied the historical experiences of these women and reflected the interests of white middle-class women. As the ideas that animated the movement changed, the cultural material available to Carolyn—a white middle-class woman—to reconstruct her identity also changed.

If you take where I was when I grew up to my analysis and commitment now, it's a huge change. I certainly have been empowered in a way around my own growth and my own understanding and my own ability to have an analysis that sees the connections about my experience as a white woman, and then as a lesbian, and how that links in my commitment to issues of racism. And working with folks and seeing how the agenda for different communities, how they link in a broader sense, but that we each sometimes out of our experience do define different issues. I mean a classic example in [my current work in] the pro-democracy movement has been the white male commitment to campaign finance reform. It's a very important issue, but it has never been a priority for people of color communities, and in fact, the key issues that have been there have been more around this felony disenfranchisement issue. And then also redistricting, which is a key sort of democracy-related issue about empowerment and voice and where you can't even have the potential for having power.

Captured here is a dynamic relation between Carolyn's involvement in the women's movement, the changes that took place in the movement, and Carolyn's continued commitment to a now-altered feminist identity. William Gamson's concept of movement-based identity is operative here but Carolyn's identity talk reveals that this identity is much more dynamic than the concept allows. This dynamism is apparent in her over 30-year history of involvements in progressive activism in Hartford. This history is not limited to feminist or lesbian and gay activism but has spanned labor and peace work, and now, pro-democracy, anti-racism work.

Steve's identity talk is also structured by the social movement context of the 1960s and in that way he can also be characterized as inhabiting a movement-based collective identity. Unlike Carolyn's activist identity that concentrates on a set of ideas or an ideological framework guiding her activist commitments, Steve's movement-inspired identity led him to a commitment to a specific organization, and that commitment is also a significant element of his activist identity. This connection between the movement and the organization is made explicit in his assertion from the introductory excerpt that what makes his union unique is that "there's this long civil rights history, long antiwar history and social justice history that we continue in our work in Connecticut." This discursive connection between the movement and the organization is crucial for how he talks about his organization-based identity:

> I'm impatient with other unions that don't rise to the occasion for either fear of losing or because it's just too hard. And we have to fight that tendency in our own organization too, because there's this union law of inertia that objects that are in motion tend to stay in motion, and the rest stay in rest. So, we always have to keep moving to make sure we're ready for whatever's gonna—for either the next new attack on us, or our ability to make real gains in people's lives, to make sure the jobs they have really have some dignity and pay a living wage. So, we do that, and other unions do that sometimes but we're very lucky to have that tradition to draw on.

For Steve, the ideals of the 1960s social movements for social justice led him to his job as a union organizer, and the job only has value to the extent that it continues to embrace those ideals. Here we see the dynamic interaction between two types of collective identity—movement-based and organization-based—with the latter getting its power from the importance of the former. In other words, his specific involvements in the union and the directions in which he pushes the priorities of the union stem from his movement-based identity. In addition, his political commitments extend far beyond the labor movement. Among other things, he has worked on Irish Northern Aid, anti-nuclear power, the peace movement, and on building a coalition between labor, the progressive Puerto Rican community, and the gay community in city politics.

While not always recognized by scholars of social movements, the 1960s social movement context was actually (at least) two contexts. One was the chronologically earlier context of the civil rights movement, feminism, and student empowerment in which many white activists "cut their teeth" and learned the ideas of "the beloved community," "the personal is political," and "letting the people decide." This is the one both Carolyn and Steve use to construct their collective identity. The other context, the one typically telegraphed into the earlier context or seen as the unfortunate unraveling of the earlier context, was the black power context whose heyday started in the late 1960s and lasted until around 1974.

This social movement context also affected the identity discourse of several progressive activists in Hartford. As the civil rights movement of the 1960s turned its attention to the North and confronted entrenched resistance and racism, it rejected the integrationist ideology of the earlier era and adopted a more separatist and nationalist discourse (Allen 1992). This discourse built on long-standing traditions of self-help, racial pride, and collective resistance to racism (Allen 1992; Dawson 2001; Shelby 2005) and empowered many people of color to engage in community activism. Many black men and women were drawn into activism through organizations and campaigns utilizing this discourse (Gilkes 1988; Naples 1998). As discussed in Chapter 3, Hartford participated in this black power phase of the "1960s movement," producing community activists from the Black Panther Party, and reproducing locally the internal conflicts between radical and moderate factions of the national civil rights coalition.

Several black progressive activists in Hartford come out of this black power tradition. Like the activists whose collective identities are movement-based, these activists also subscribe to a set of ideas—an ideological framework of sorts—from which they derive their activist priorities, commitments, and worldviews. Also like the other movement-based activists they engage in this dynamic interpretation process of their biographies in light of their activism, and their activism in light of their biographies.

Larry, who at the time of the interview was a community organizer in the predominately black North End of Hartford, illustrates these features of this movement-based collective identity. Larry participated in black power politics while a student at his college in the early 1970s and provides an eloquent statement of this politics made practical for community activism:

> Let's move towards a thinking in our community where we take ownership of our own children and our own community...To the extent that we are success-

ful to get more people to buy into that thinking we do much more than any amount of money, any amount of cops, any amount of jails could ever do in transforming our neighborhood. When you look at the tons of dollars thrown *at* distressed communities and not much sticks in terms of breaking the poverty cycle, a lot is aimed at perpetuating that cycle and helping people endure the predicaments they face. Controlling the resources that are aimed at helping is a key principle for us. So we actually believe that the institutions that are dedicated towards helping the poor ought to be controlled by the poor. That doesn't mean input, it doesn't mean influence, it means control!...It's all about changing the thinking of people in the community in order to affect individual behavior, and therefore bring about a higher quality of living. We believe that folks have finally come to realize that the answers for our community do not lie in the think tanks or the governmental or the foundations and all that stuff. There actually is no help on the way!...And that the only hope that we have is to unleash the power of people who have endured for so long and therefore who understand the pressure that they're under, and who are more motivated than anybody to get the problem solved, and to fix it in a way that it stays fixed.

As if to emphasize exactly what community he is talking about and why that community does not have access to resources, Larry moves quickly to the topic of racial inequality and racism in the city:

You go to downtown Hartford, and you see almost everybody downtown is white and don't live in the city, walking around. By that view you think that Hartford is a majority white population and affluent population. But you would never know that...Hartford is the poorest city in the United States of America with a population of over 100,000 and we're not in Mississippi or Alabama. We're in the capital city of the richest state in this nation. So, you see poverty is one thing, but poverty in the face of such prosperity is something very different, very dehumanizing as well....Some people call that racism. I agree wholeheartedly that it is an issue of color.

The trope of community control, black self-organization, and racism are all elements of a movement-based collective identity derived from the black power tradition of the civil rights movement.

This trope, however, is inflected with an additional cultural discourse that also characterizes Larry's identity talk. Woven throughout Larry's interview and his assertions of black self-determination is a discourse of the power of faith:

First of all, you got to know that you're talking to a person of total faith. Then you'll understand not only why I am here but why things go so well. Even in small things. Stuff is made so clear even at the start, through complicated processes it's made so clear as to what to do and even what to say....Because of my faith. No thanks to me, and no credit to me or anybody else. They just fall in place. I don't know how else you can explain it as to how things always work out as we started working...So it ends up being confirmed and then faith ends up being increased dramatically. And I think God has a wonderful sense of humor and how things that seem totally disjointed are brought back together in a perfect form.

This assertion of the power of faith and its "behind-the-scenes" ability to make "things also work out" serve as a counter-discourse for Larry's assertions of black self-determination, ownership, and racial uplift. In some sense, these assertions of the sacred help firmly root both his life and collective identity in a community where ministers and the black church still wield significant influence. It is not conscious or calculated. It is an element of his biography that he uses to construct his collective identity.

Cornel, another North End activist, grew up poor and troubled in Detroit where he had a religious conversion experience that led him to the ministry:

After the sermon, the minister said, "Who wants to accept God?" so I throw my hand up. I said, "I am kinda lost." He said, "I'll tell you what: Why don't you pray to God?" I said, "God I don't believe in you; I only believe in things that appeal to the five senses. But I will make you a deal. If you prove that you're real, you got yourself a man but you gotta prove it." And then at that point I was praying and it was like I felt something moving in my body and then I got all tensed up and then I got scared. The only time in my life I've ever really been afraid. He said that's God talking to you....I was confronting something that my puny brain couldn't even fathom...And now I am like Paul on the road to Damascus, man, I saw something and heard something I can't even understand and now my whole mind is someplace I never been before.

His identity talk combines rich and diverse religious and political imagery with a black power politics which places him at odds with the entrenched black religious leadership in the city. In the passage below, Cornel "reads" the Bible differently from these leaders and creatively constructs an ideological framework that incorporates the secular language of the black power movement with the sacred language of black theological traditions.

Faith without action is dead. Lenin said you got to have praxis. You got to do something. You can't just be running your mouth...Some of the activists, you know, only work with Christians. And I say, "Hey man I say I am a Christian but that evangelical viewpoint is often parochial if it keeps centering on God." And I said, "You know what, there's more knowledge in the universe than the Bible, and there are other things that you can do in order to bring about certain results, so focusing on that narrow evangelical viewpoint just keeps taking everything back up to God, which needs to be turned around."

The complexity of Charles's or Cornel's collective identity cannot be completely captured through the concept of movement-based collective identity. Clearly, a religious cultural discourse is also an important component derived from their unique biographical experience and from their membership in a racial group where important elements of its culture are derived from deep religious traditions (Harris 1999). Both Larry and Cornel combine this diverse cultural material in creative ways to produce activist identities than can be only imperfectly characterized as movement-based collective identities.

This racially-inflected movement-based identity does shape the nature of their involvements in progressive activism. Like the other activists with movement-based collective identities, both Larry and Cornel tend to move across campaigns and organizations. Larry's biography reveals participation in the black student movement in the south and in housing and anti-violence initiatives in Hartford's North End. Cornel's involvements are also focused in the North End around police brutality, drugs, and poverty. He has organized campaigns throughout Connecticut against racist practices of various business and government organizations. Perhaps the best known of these campaigns targeted suburban drug users by marching in affluent suburban neighborhoods to call attention to the racial and class components of the drug trade.

Organization-Based Collective Identity

We have already seen how some activists can possess both an organization-based and movement-based collective identity. Steve's commitment to his union—an organization-based identity—derives in large part from his subscription to a broader set of political values and goals from the 1960s social movements that he frequently references in his identity talk—a movement-based identity. Indeed, the distinctions that William Gamson makes in his typology of collective identities allow for this overlap. Recall his definition of organization-based collective identity: a set of identifications and subjective understandings that derive from a specific organization situated in a broader social movement sector. The identity talk of Hartford progressive activists suggests that sometimes the "broader social movement sector" contributes the dominant frames, repertoires of contention, and goals from which the organization-based identity gets its power (e.g. Steve's collective identity). By listening closely to activist identity talk, we can observe not only the relationship between types of identity within any one individual but also the nature of that relationship. For Steve and others, the movement-based commitment is temporally and conceptually prior to the organization-based commitment. That knowledge makes a difference for understanding how activists operate within organizations and how they move in and out of organizations. For others, however, the organization itself is the main collective action context from which they discuss the ideas, priorities, activities of their work and who they are as activists.

Sociologists of social movements have paid a great deal of attention to organizations as the source of collective identity. In Chapter 5, I discussed how and why scholars restricted their attention to the organizations that precede or emerge from protest, collective action, or other types of organized discontent directed to social change. Although we know that organizations are not the only form in which social movements manifest themselves, organizations have been a major way in which they do manifest themselves. These organizations provide sets of meanings and cultural scripts that activists use to construct their activist identities. To take just one notable example, Josh Gamson's (1996) research on the organizing that took place for two different gay film festivals illustrates how the organizations' relationships to two different sets of sponsors and audiences affected the kinds of films that were screened and the sets of priorities used to evaluate which films were selected for inclusion. Among other things, Gamson observes that activists' participation in these two different organizations led to two different kinds of collective identity by the end of the experience: a narrowly gay identity oriented around the concerns and interests of mainly white middle-class gays and lesbians, and a broader queer identity oriented around a broader understanding of gender and sexual non-normativity and the perspectives of queers of color. We see here how the structure of a social movement organization (e.g. where it gets its resources and who it perceives as its audience) interacts with the kinds of ideas it wants to promote in its collective action (e.g. film series).

I observe a similar pattern with several of Hartford's progressive activists. The identity talk of these organization-based activists reveals a commitment to a specific issue or organizational mission and a personal world view corresponding to this mission. Karen, who has been a community organizer in two of Hartford's many neighborhoods, represents this identity and echoes the sentiments of other organizers who have been trained in the philosophy of Saul Alinsky (1972). Alinsky-style organizers, who focus on uncovering the self-interests of neighborhood residents and conducting power analyses to determine the decision makers in the neighborhood, came to town in the early 1970s and within 15 years became a significant force in city politics. Karen was trained in that tradition:

> I think [community organizing] makes a huge difference. Just the fact of letting people know that you can come together with your neighbor and with other people on your street and change whatever it is you want to change....My mantra is "What have you got to lose?" What have we got to lose? We have nothing to lose, it's not like we have politicians knocking on our door, what have you got to lose? And once you say that to people and they understand it, it's like yeah, what do we have to lose?

Since this community organizing tradition begins from the notion of self interest, it is not surprising that Karen's introduction to activism stemmed from her "self-interest" in protecting the value of her property:

> My parents owned two properties and we were actually turning into absentee landlords...And I said you know what, "I'm going to move into one of the

apartments down there." All my friends thought I was crazy, this was in the late '80s, early '90s, where moving [out of the city] is what you did. You don't move to Hartford, are you crazy?

As she got more involved in the neighborhood, first as a resident and then as an organizer, her sense of self changed somewhat from a self-interested property owner to a group-oriented neighbor:

I love the fact that there are kids playing double-dutch in the middle of the street; I love the fact that my neighbors know me. I love the fact that the lady next door leaves on the light if I go clubbing at night...There's a connection with the parents, there's a connection with the kids, there's a connection overall. And again that goes back to building relationships.

These comments suggest an interactive relationship between her organization-based identity and her individual identity. As her self-interest in property preservation led her to participate in the community organization in her neighborhood, that participation changed her relationship to the neighborhood, essentially replacing self-interest with community-based values. Karen also indicates that these experiences may also be changing the nature of her racial identity:

My parents are West Indian...and we moved out of Hartford when I was 12, so...it was kind of hard for me to relate to some of the issues that people were having...Now, I have heated discussions at family get-togethers in regards to an inappropriate comment, trying to explain to someone in my family who thinks that they understand how things work. Again, being West Indian [they say]: "Hey, we came to this country, we made it! Hey, nothing was handed to us." And I say, "Well you know what, they're not begging either. We were able to struggle and make it, yeah by working five jobs! Well you know what, if they had an opportunity to work just one, that would be a start."

In this passage, Karen moves from an identification as West Indian to one as Black, indicating that her activist identity may be incorporating elements of a solidary-based collective identity as race takes on a larger importance in her world view. Even with these altered understandings, Karen is wedded to the philosophy of neighborhood organization. In her five-year history of activism she has worked only in community organizations going from a volunteer activist in one to a paid staff member in another.

Defining activists solely on the basis of this organization-based collective identity, however, ignores some of the unique biographical experiences which led these activists to a particular organization. It also ignores how that organizational commitment, in turn, reinforces a sense of activists rooted in those biographical experiences. In several cases, activists narrate their pre-movement experiences through the lens of their religious background and then assert the importance of their organization-based identity in terms of their religious values. Throughout this process, change occurs in both their individual identities and in the nature of their organizational involvements.

Lisa is a good example of this interaction between a biography marked by religion and her subsequent involvement in and commitment to a social service and advocacy organization for Latina teen mothers throughout the city. We have seen part of her story earlier in Chapter 6:

> My mom was always active with the church, and doing different things in church. One time, and I was really bored with religious ed. by that point, I went with her, and we packed up clothes for some donation for somewhere, and it was just a mixture of adults and kids, and we were just having a good time and we were doing something good for other people, and I was like, "Gosh this is just really cool." So, I joined the social action committee actually when I was like 15 years old at [church]...And then I was a Jesuit volunteer in Alaska for three years living with Eskimos. I did fundraising and volunteer organizing in Fairbanks, but the only native people you saw there were drunk and on the street, kind of homeless. I wanted to have an experience where it wasn't a white city, where I was in a village, where I was a minority, so I went to St. Mary's in the Woods which was an Eskimo village for two years....When I came back here I really missed living in community, because there had been in those two years at St. Mary's there had been 24 and 25 of us in each of those two years running the mission, so it was really exciting and invigorating and fun, and everything. So I really missed community, so a priest at the diocese sent me to Immaculate [Conception Church], he said, "Go, go to Immaculate." Because there's a lot of stuff going on there, and I did volunteer work actually for about a year before...Then the position [with teen mothers] came up.

As Lisa's comments reveal, her current organizing with teen mothers is simply an extension of her religious commitments and religiously based experiences. What leads her to this organization-based identity and to the organization that serves low-income women with very vulnerable life circumstances are, in Lisa's words, "the gospel values."

This relationship between her individual identity (as revealed through her biography) and her collective identity (her lifelong work in the organization of teen mothers) is interactive in nature. First, the gospel values (and her network and organizational affiliation to the activist arm of the Catholic Church) led her to her activism and informed her activist identity. Second, her work in the organization led her to alter that religiously based individual identity. She remains deeply religious but subscribes to a much more critical or cynical religiosity in light of her experiences with the women she serves and the battles she has fought gaining resources for the organization:

As I said, I think a big motivator for me was the Gospels, and listening to what Jesus is saying we ought to be doing and looking what in fact we are doing, and looking at the kids that I work with and thinking, Okay, so Jesus is—we've been listening to this message for 2,000 years, and we don't get it. And we still don't get it, and if Jesus came today he'd be crucified just like before. And he is, many times over!

As if to drive home her disappointment in the power of faith to bring about social change, she moves quickly to a heart-wrenching story that points out the distress and violence in the lives of poor women in Hartford, the glimpses of humanity of these women despite these realities and, most importantly, the compromised nature of Lisa's own faith.

We took [the young women in the group] on retreat down to [the inner city church] to the old convent down there. One of the women expressed concern, she was concerned that her daughter might be being sexually abused, and so we said, "We'll take you home right away." And she said, "No, they're all right, they're all right." And talked about things that had happened to her when she was young and stuff. And what ended up happening that night was that her 17-year-old cousin sexually assaulted and then murdered her four-year-old daughter whose name was Lydia which is part of the reason why [my daughter's name] is Lydia...Now, [the killer] was her first cousin. This was her mother's sister's son. We left that court room, and we were out in that hallway there with people around us, and she said, "Excuse me, I have to go and talk to my aunt because we both lost a child today." And I was just, like, I couldn't believe it, that this young mom who so many people would look at her and have so much judgment against her and about her and everything, because she went on to have two more kids, being on welfare, and losing her temper with her kids and stuff. And I know there were so many reasons why people would judge her negatively and I thought, "This is one of the best people that I've ever seen in my life, that she should be so generous of spirit and heart." And she did, she went over to her aunt and hugged her and talked to her, and I thought, "My God, you're a better woman than me."

Lisa told this story with both a profound admiration of the forgiveness shown by this mother whose daughter was murdered and a quiet sadness about the loss of this capacity in herself. Naming her daughter after the murdered girl is perhaps Lisa's attempt to restore her faith that has been tested many times over by, in her words, "human systems that have been designed in a moral vacuum." To fully appreciate the specific nature of her organization-based identity, we need to grasp the interactive and dynamic link between her faith-driven biography and her continuous attempts to enact that faith in her activism. That faith brought her to that organization, and the experiences in that organization changed the nature of that faith. Needless to say, she has spent her entire activist life in this organization.

As with other activists who possess an organization-based collective identity, Lisa's and Karen's own identities are consequences of those particular organizations: their philosophies, tactical repertoires, and goals. The collective identity typology is useful in calling attention to that correspondence. However, the stories of Karen and Lisa also show that their identities cannot be reduced to their collective identity, and that the relationship between the two is much more dynamic than can be captured by this typology. More important, the stories also suggest the possibility that this dynamic relationship affects the nature of the organization that these activists are committed to. As Karen and Lisa change as a consequence of their activist experiences in the organization, it is very likely that they will press their organizations to also change.

Solidary-Based Collective Identity

Several of the introductory excerpts for this chapter represent another type of collective identity: a sense of "we-ness" stemming from membership in and identification with a broad social category such as race, ethnic group, gender, or sexual orientation; what William Gamson refers to as a solidary-based collective identity. We see several examples of this collective identity in the introductory excerpts to the chapter. In the telling of her activist story, Regina attaches a great deal of importance to her memories of marginalization as a black working-class woman. Similarly, Carmen also tells a story of marginalization as a Puerto Rican women as a necessary prelude to her activist anger. Nick tells a fairly conventional "coming out" story to make an almost automatic connection between his membership in a social group and his responsibility to engage in activism on behalf of that group. Again, these solidary-based collective identities may coexist with other collective identities, and these identities are best seen as coexisting within any one individual. For example, Carolyn's identity talk is constructed interactively between the language supplied by the social movements of the 1960s and her understanding of herself as a member of a marginalized group.

There are several points of overlap between this concept of a solidary-based identity and another concept more frequently used by sociologists to refer to this sense of "we-ness" based on marginal group membership. The oppositional consciousness framework introduced in Chapter 2 and discussed further in Chapter 6 extends the in-group/out-group component of collective identity and elaborates the ways that such a consciousness may pre-exist collective action and may be key in understanding how social movement participation, in turn, influences an activist's collective identity. It also effectively synthesizes the structural and cultural approaches to social movements also described in Chapter 2. Briefly summarized, this framework asserts that there are structural systems of inequality that generate unequal power relations and encourage the creation of oppositional cultures by subordinate groups to resist those structures of power. These cultures provide the symbolic and discursive resources that can be harnessed by a social movement. This concept of oppositional consciousness differs somewhat from the concept of solidary-based collective identity in that oppositional consciousness calls attention to the structures of power that bring these groups into existence and place them in subordinate positions along racial, ethnic, gender, and sexuality hierarchies. In addition, group identifications can be singular or multiple in nature. An individual can see her/his membership in a racial or gender group as the most salient element of identity or she/he can articulate an intersectional understanding of identity in that multiple marginal group identifications intersect to produce an oppositional consciousness. Referring back once again to the introductory excerpts, Nick clearly articulates a singular group identity (gay) and Regina represents a multiple group identity (queer working-class women of color).

By listening closely to the talk of activists who possess a solidary-based collective identity, we see the need to make this concept more sensitive to a similar set of interactions between individual biography and collective action that we witnessed with both movement-based and organization-based activists. This activist talk about their marginal group membership sometimes combines with organization-based or movement-based talk. In addition, this solidary-based collective identity is interactive or iterative in nature as an individual's understanding of their group membership is formed and changes in relation to their collective action experiences. Once again, these activists remind scholars that identity is a dynamic concept: it is provisional, changeable, and constructed in highly creative but nonetheless patterned ways from a diverse set of cultural material.

This dynamic nature is best seen with the activists who occupy an intersectional identity. Regina's understanding of herself as a working-class, African American lesbian provides the lens through which she tells her activist story and the criterion she uses to participate in activist campaigns. Her astute and moving account of her multiple marginalizations was undoubtedly shaped by the movement context of her coming to activism. Consider her solidary-based identity talk in conjunction with other aspects of her biography. Regina weaves her narrative of oppositional consciousness with the movement context in which she came to that consciousness:

> We would go south every summer. So we went back to Kentucky every summer. And I became aware that when we changed trains in Cincinnati, we really changed trains! And we went into an all colored car. I mean, I was 11 before that was over. So, people talk about like what was a long time ago. And I had a good time in that car. I mean, the big difference I noticed was that everybody had a shoebox with food in it, and I didn't realize this is because you couldn't go to the dining car, but you know, we're little kids, and that meant every old lady was giving you something to eat. So, it was like, yeah, I can get into this. But it really incensed me so that by the time I was a teenager, actually the first kind of movement or activism stuff I did was with workers who were working for Cesar Chavez around farm worker stuff when they came through New Jersey as a teenager I started supporting that and working in that. And it went from there.

> Oh! It was a great time to be a teenager. I was a baby boomer. But it was, because there was everything to read, everything to think, and everybody was right there. And Trenton, New Jersey, which is no great metropolis, but right in Trenton, I saw and was able to meet Maya Angelou up close. I saw Mohammed Ali in a park real close. He was sparring with my brother. I saw Angela Davis speak, I don't know how many times. I sold the Black Panther newspaper.

Here we see the interaction between her primary solidary-based identity and her secondary movement-based identity. As this excerpt illustrates, her life in the movement nourished this multi-dimensional oppositional consciousness.

Regina's identity talk also illustrates the opposite dynamic: how her oppositional consciousness affected her experiences in activism. This is most clear in her discussion of history in the gay and lesbian movement. Recall this description from Chapter 4:

> ...The gay movement, when I tried to be in it, I felt tokenized. I didn't know where I was. It didn't smell like home and it didn't smell like the white people I knew and was comfortable with. It was more like the ones that I was bused out to and didn't want to hold my hand in gym or something. The ones that were like, "Eww! We're not going to talk to her!"

Regina's comment references the feeling of marginalization as a black working-class child bused to the white middle-class suburbs. This dynamic simultaneously informs her oppositional consciousness—now including a queer consciousness—and her evaluation of gay activism as being class and racially biased.

This "re-formed" multidimensional oppositional consciousness further informs her activism. Not able to separate the different subordinate groups to which she belongs when doing her activism, she organizes at the intersections of these groups:

> I think a lot of queer color activism comes out of having to create a home. I first did that in Hartford with [two other queer activists]. We formed a group called LOCK, Lesbians of Color in Kinship, which was really more social and support to encourage more black dykes to come out. And M. and I did the Kwanza Project which was advocacy and education kind of stuff. But it all came out of the need to make a home rather than go one mile to be black and two miles to be queer and never the twain shall meet.

In 2002 Regina helped found an organization called FACE, Featuring All Colors and Ethnicities, whose focus is urban youth. As Regina describes, it focuses on "queer students who are also ethnic and racial minorities and low income and live in cities and deal with a kind of homophobia that is affected by racism that makes the population more vulnerable and also makes those who are supposed to work on their behalf more resistant." Thus, to understand fully Regina's activist identity we need to appreciate the interactive nature of collective identity: that it is an interpretive and dynamic process as social group membership interacts with collective action which in turn changes the activists' understanding of their group membership and also the kinds of collective action these activists participate in or help create.

This tendency to move across organizations or campaigns in response to the changing nature of an activists' oppositional consciousness and/or the realization that a particular organization cannot accommodate the multidimensional nature of that consciousness is shared by other activists with a solidary-based collective identity. The introductory excerpts from Carmen, the low-income Latina who had a keen understanding of her multiple marginalities, illustrate the interactive nature of her oppositional consciousness. She captures this connection perfectly: "Once I learned my roots and I started realizing what oppression was and how our culture has been oppressed for so many years...And what racism was, and how internalized racism begins, that this [my organizing] began." As she stated in an earlier passage, her oppositional consciousness was constructed from both her biographical experiences as a light-skinned Latina in public housing occupied by African Americans in interaction with her participation in a white-led neighborhood organization trying to organize a Puerto Rican neighborhood. Her early experiences with marginality "taught" her one kind of oppositional consciousness. That led her to community organizing which in turn nurtured and changed that oppositional consciousness.

Just as important, Carmen's experiences in community organizing affected the kind of activism that she now sees as important (e.g. minority-led coalitions). This new approach arose from a dynamic typical of activists with solidary-based collective identities operating within formal organizations:

> We had a difference of ideas and a different way of organizing...that we as Latinos needed to call our own agenda, and we needed our own ideas. We were saying that, "They're getting money on our backs—off of our backs, and they're not representing our needs. And they're representing themselves, not us, and they're claiming that they're representing us, but why do we need a white man to come do our job when we're perfectly capable of doing it ourselves? And why are we outnumbered in that board of directors?" I was one of two Latinos on a board of directors that were all white. And I knew nothing about leadership development, and they were deliberately talking over my head, and they would say things I had no clue what the hell it meant...to deliberately keep me in the dark.

Although an extreme example, this "encounter" does illustrate the conflict that oftentimes resulted when an organization's mission cannot accommodate the needs of activists with a multidimensional oppositional consciousness. This is one reason many activists with solidary-based collective identities work in, through, and around many organizations throughout their activist careers. As Luz, another activist with a solidary-based identity who also experienced similar conflicts as Carmen, states: "My philosophy is I put people before the organization. People have to come first. When you worry about the organization you are selling out the people."

Conclusion

Why should activists care about the concept of collective identity and the distinctions among the different types that scholars see as so important? How can activists benefit from this concept and these distinctions? Regina's story provides a clue in that knowing "who she is" tells us what kinds of organizing she feels are important. As we have seen throughout this chapter, activists who possess different types of collective identity have different experiences in and different pathways through progressive organizations in Hartford. Those with movement-based collective identities tend to participate in a broad range of organizations and campaigns since they are more concerned with moving forward a broad social change agenda with ideological roots in the 1960s and 1970s. Those with organization-based collective identities are more loyal to a particular organization or a narrow range of organizations that subscribe to a specific organizing philosophy or cater to a specific constituency. Like movement-based activists, activists with solidary-based collective identities are more organizationally promiscuous than organization-based activists since these "solidary" activists participate in progressive activism to nourish an oppositional consciousness that is multidimensional in nature. This knowledge can assist in many areas of organizing from recruitment, issue framing, managing internal conflict and forming coalitions.

Activists more committed to a movement-based collective identity may tend to think through issues such as recruitment, goals, strategy, and allies differently from someone whose primary commitment is to a specific social movement organization. Movement-based activists may begin from a set of broad values rather than from a specific approach or constituency. They may also be somewhat flexible in terms of the specific strategies to realize those values. Those who see their identity in organizational terms tend to define the problem that needs attention in narrow or circumscribed terms such as the passage of a law or the implementation of a program. Those who are less committed to an organizational agenda may indeed acknowledge the importance of the law or the program but may view it as part of a larger agenda and may therefore suggest a different understanding of the problem, different tactics to address the problem, and different sets of allies to assist with solving the problem. Those who are more committed to a solidary-based identity may be more concerned with internal processes of education and consciousness-raising as important kinds of social change than those activists with other kinds of collective identities. In addition, activists frequently occupy combinations of collective identities of varying importance. Being attentive to differences in activist identities—seeing them as both fixed *and* changeable as I have described them in this chapter—can help activists build on the existing priorities of different kinds of progressive activists and think of ways to make connections between progressive activists with these different priorities. In this way, activists can more self-consciously participate in changing the collective identities of both themselves and their fellow activists.

Chapter 9

Rethinking Activists' Questions and Scholars' Answers

Most of the previous chapters give center stage to the stories of activists. The "what," "how," "who," and "why" of activism is how I have structured the presentation of these stories. Activists discussed their goals and strategies. They revealed what issues they considered important, how they made those issues the object of their activism, the strategies they used to pursue the issues, and the challenges, problems, frustrations, and satisfactions they experienced in this activist work. This "reporting" was usually done in the form of stories of memorable campaigns or as lessons they have learned throughout their years of activism. Activists spoke of specific bills or concrete neighborhood services they were fighting for but they also spoke about "larger" and sometimes more ephemeral goals as well: radical restructuring, changing individual consciousness, and changing culture.

Coupled with this discussion of goals, and sometimes indistinguishable from that discussion, were stories of how activists pursue those goals—their strategies for achieving social change. They spoke of the importance of building coalitions across different constituencies, building bridges across individuals with different specific interests but similar general interests. These coalitions and bridges varied in their structure: sometimes these were constructed by specific leaders and sometimes they were built into the very nature of the campaign or organization. These activists also spoke of the importance of consciousness-raising work as another way to seriously engage individuals across their differences. Sometimes this consciousness raising was itself a goal of progressive activism. Activists changed individuals' understandings of their situation, changed the way individuals viewed the world and their connection to others in the world or changed the way they viewed their privilege or marginality in that world. Other activists saw this consciousness-raising as a necessary prelude to other goals: changing laws, confronting policy makers, employers or government officials, for example.

Activists also described the resources they used to conduct their activism. Material resources loomed large in their activist stories that highlighted the anxieties around procuring them, the consequences of not having them, and the dangers of the strings attached to some of those resources. But, activists saw another type of resource as perhaps more important than material resources. When activists spoke of the "things that make their activism possible" their stories of resources were more about the cultural aspects of activism. These resources consisted of ideas, communities of like-minded people, and organizations or networks where progressive people and ideas circulated. These were the resources that did not depend on funding, donors, or government largesse. These were constructed, nurtured, and created by activists themselves in the process of doing their work.

Discussions about resources frequently occurred in conjunction with the places, settings or locations where activists mobilized these resources and conducted their activism. Sometimes these were formal organizations; other times they were informally structured as isolated campaigns or ongoing initiatives guided by norms other than rigid hierarchy, formalized divisions of labor, or by assumptions about the importance of longevity or organizational maintenance. Not surprisingly, the diversity of goals and strategies and the flexibility and creativity in the nature of resources utilized almost required a similar capaciousness in terms of organizational structure. Importantly, these stories of social movement organizations were, first and foremost, stories of activists' specific experiences in those organizations; in these stories, activists reflected on the advantages and disadvantages of different sorts of structures for doing progressive work. Tensions and conflicts within these structures resulted in experimentation with new organizational forms.

Activists also told more personal stories of how they came to participate in and become committed to activism. There were a few "aha" moments when activists remembered a pivotal event that "made them activists." More often than not however, they told less dramatic stories about their families, the values they learned from their families or from their churches or synagogues, or the conflicts they experienced between their religious values and the religious establishment. Others situated their stories in pivotal historical moments or events such as "the 1960s," Reaganism of the 1980s or the "battle of Seattle" in 1999. Still others told stories of racial, ethnic, class or sexual marginality. Participation and commitment were developed over time as different activists combined different influences in different ways. Conversely, stories of getting tired, changing directions or pulling back from their work also had this cumulative or iterative quality. In this case, activists expressed this "retrenchment" as a series of frustrations with the nature of the organization or as an increasing inability or unwillingness to make the necessary sacrifices in their personal lives to remain in the organization.

All activists had constructed an identity or a sense of self around their activism. As I listened closely and probed their political commitments and solidarities I got a sense of the nature of these identities. While none of us are consistent in how we represent ourselves, activists constructed more or less coherent stories of "who they were." Some spoke in grandiloquent terms about radical restructuring or a beloved community; others stressed the importance of the specific work they did with specific individuals around specific issues. Still the identity talk of other activists proceeded from the inside out as they talked about themselves along the social dimensions of racial, ethnic, class, gender or sexuality and how those dimensions were the touchstones of their activist identities. They were black activists, gay activists, Latina activists; and some were combinations of these dimensions.

What does all this mean? When faced with this dramatic diversity of responses, scholars are anxious to make sense of them, to apply theory, find patterns, evaluate theory in light of the patterns, and make new theory. This book engages in a different sociological project. I started with a simple question. What can scholars and activists learn from each other? I thought the best way to answer that question would be actual encounters between activists with varying amounts of experience in various kinds of organizing and a scholar who could bring to the conversation a familiarity with the theory and research in social movements. As we discussed the "what," "how," "who," and "why" of progressive activism, I quickly saw points of resonance and dissonance between the processes activists described and the concepts and frameworks scholars use to represent those processes. As I have argued in many of the previous chapters, activists' stories urge scholars to make their theories much less rigid and their concepts much more interactive and dynamic. These chapters also urge scholars to relax the distinctions we so often make between structure and culture and to see that relationship as interactive and dynamic as well. This is not theory critique and knowledge production in a political vacuum. It is knowledge for practical use.

These "innovative rifts" on social movement theory and concepts are evident when activists talk about what they do and how they do it. We can discern some patterns in the stories I summarized above. Progressive activists oftentimes combine restructuring and reformist goals, pursue cultural as well as political goals, and engage in strategies that run the gamut from service delivery, education and consciousness-raising on the one hand to highly visible forms of disruption on the other. Acknowledging this diversity allows scholars to see how activists resolve some of the thorny dilemmas, problems, and conundrums of social movement activism, everything from how to move beyond identity politics to how to change culture and institutions at the same time. Alliances, coalitions, and community building are crucial components to solving these problems. Progressive activists also complicate scholars' understandings of social movement organizations and resources. Activists don't simply "find" material resources. They also construct resources that are more cultural than material in nature, resources like "progressive ideas" embedded in communities and social networks.

The experiences of activists in formal organizations resonate with much of the research that finds these organizations good at getting things done but not so good at generating excitement or fostering solidarity and community. Activists, however, report inhabiting or creating a wide variety of forms for their social movement work beyond the bureaucratically organized form. And, they also display a creativity and facility in their use of organizations and other social forms, sometimes combining participation in formal organizations and loosely structured and temporary campaigns and other times committing to an organization but working to change its culture or shake up its bureaucracy. For the most part, it is the "quality" of the culture rather than the structure of the organization within which their activities occur that is so important for activists' satisfactions and continued participation. Does the organization foster participation and debate? Does it value friendship and human connection? These are some of the questions activists use to evaluate the value of the organization in meeting social movement goals.

Activists also complicate the concepts and frameworks scholars use to understand social movement participation, commitment, and identity—the "who" and "why" of social movements. Concepts such as biography, social networks, critical events, plausibility structures, and collective identities are useful but only when used in interactive and dynamic ways. Activists construct pathways into and out of participation and commitment using combinations of these concepts. These pathways are best understood as a series of interactions in which activists develop shared meanings, belief systems, and ideas about social change with each interaction yielding different degrees and types of participation. These meanings, belief systems and ideas are embedded in families, time periods, social networks, and social identities and they change as activists use them to participate in different types of social movement activity each with its own culture and structure. Reimagining the process in this more interactive way and in a way that highlights the role of culture can also assist activists in reimagining the process of recruitment and commitment to social movements. As activists' own stories suggest, there are many points of entry whereby individuals join social movements and there are many developmental experiences whereby individuals forge significant commitments to social movements. For activists interested in expanding their ranks, these different sites of meaning reconstruction provide some new recruitment opportunities.

New opportunities also arise for activists who take seriously the sociological concepts of collective identity and oppositional consciousness. From my many interviews with activists, I realize that it is difficult to disentangle what they do from who they are. That is, the many tensions, dilemmas, and conundrums of organizing were resolved at least in part on the basis of the philosophical and ideological commitments of the activists themselves. Decisions around goals, strategies and tactics, allies, resources, and organizational forms stemmed not only from careful consideration of the particular political opportunity structure or resource environment confronted but also from the shared commitments and understandings of who they were as particular kinds of progressive activists. Knowing the kinds of collective identities possessed by both themselves and others can help activists forge coalitions, resolve conflicts, and combine strategies and goals in ways that appeal to the broadest constituency. Collective identity is both an important analytical concept as well as a useful organizing tool.

The progressive activists featured here are not disembodied, decontextualized actors. Activists are embedded in time and space and this embeddedness affects what they do and how they do it. Hartford, Connecticut, shares many features with other post-industrial cities in the U.S. and elsewhere. Similar to other cities, it has lost its higher-wage manufacturing base only to be partially and incompletely replaced by a lower-wage service sector. Also similar to other cities, lower-income racial and ethnic minorities are concentrated in the city while better-off whites are still the statistical majority in most of the suburbs. While people of color have made tremendous strides in political power in the city, the ability to turn this power into tangible benefits for city residents is limited by the lack of control over economic resources, a long-standing neglect by the federal government of urban populations and community development, a state government that favors down-town development over neighborhood revitalization, and infighting and power grabs amongst different constituencies in the city. The grievances that emerge from this context, everything from lack of living wage jobs, street violence, neighbor-hood deterioration, and racism, are familiar to other progressive activists in similar urban settings.

Not surprisingly, this context affects progressive activism. What is surprising however, are the historical antecedents to this contemporary context and the impact of this history on the content and culture of progressive activism. By inte-grating theory and history, by distilling the concepts derived from the several theoretical traditions in social movement scholarship and applying them to the historical treatments of local activism, I identified several aspects of this unique historical legacy. In general, the theoretical traditions of sociology identify struc-tures and cultures of power, control, marginality, and powerlessness as important guideposts. These theoretical sensitivities help identify important historical and contemporary features of the city that encourage, shape, and limit the impact of social movements in Hartford.

The history of Hartford is not simply a story of a long-gone industrial past. Nor is it simply a history of unresponsive elites and oppositional masses. Due in part to the early establishment of a large insurance and banking sector and its close asso-ciation with the benevolent paternalism of Congregationalism, a diverse set of elites were more accommodating to social change than those in other cities domi-nated by more resistant and monolithic manufacturing elites. This proved to be a double-edged sword for progressive activism and activists. On the one hand, benevolence delivered resources, albeit with the strings of paternalism attached to them. On the other hand, individuals who were privy to those resources could sometimes use them to challenge that paternalism and loosen those strings. In other words, the institutions of benevolence and service delivery—the churches, the charities, the community organizations—sometimes yielded individuals who saw the limits of those organizations and developed more "activist-oriented" under-standings and dispositions. This creates a social movement environment that is contradictory in nature. It simultaneously encourages activism and produces activists even as it places subtle limits on the kind of activity that takes place. As some of the activists encountered here realize, the challenge is to accept the "encouragement" while pushing the boundaries of acceptable activity.

This analysis of the local context is one example of how scholars can inform the work of activists and flows directly from the mandate C. Wright Mills gave U.S. sociologists in the late 1950s to focus on the intersections of biography and history in studying human action. Not surprisingly, most activists do not place themselves in history. They remain focused on "the here and now" and do not give much thought to the culture or context that may shape the nature of the work they do.

Alta, the long-time community organizer whose words appear throughout the book, insists on the importance of a "power analysis" as a prelude to and context for any discussion of neighborhood problems. But, she also admits that the material resources, expertise, and time of organizers are limited to accomplish this analysis. This principle of community organizing entails an investigation of the stakeholders involved in a particular issue area and the nature of their interests, resources, and access to decision making in that area. This serves as a prelude to a discussion of how to exercise leverage and gain advantage for the challenging group. With the advantages of time and resources that scholars typically have, we can expand that version of an issue-specific, piecemeal approach to power analysis and provide an economic, political, and cultural roadmap for a whole host of progressive activists.

In addition to this important role that scholars can play in informing activist work, activists ask other more pressing questions that can also be addressed through scholarly research. Throughout the book I have tried to present that research not in a top-down way heavily laden with theory that does not connect with the people, activities, and experiences "on the ground." Instead, that research has been constituted in collaboration with the many activists I have interviewed for this project. Our discussions of goals, strategies and political opportunities, resources and organizations, participation, commitment, conflicts, and identities enabled a dialogue between scholars' theories and concepts and activists' concerns and dilemmas. The dialogue yielded many questions and some new ideas about where to look for answers.

As noted throughout, activists' questions are practical and immediate: How do you continue to organize with dwindling material resources? How do you manage increased participation in the aftermath of a dramatic event or a shift in political opportunities favorable for activism? How do you manage the tensions that arise between old and new members in this aftermath? Can you put together an agenda that works simultaneously on reform and radical restructuring? How do you decide what to fight for and how to fight for it? These constitute a few of the pressing questions I heard repeatedly throughout my conversations.

While some of the answers to these and other questions are fully fleshed out in the previous chapters, the most important work of the book revolves around rethinking some of the usual concepts and approaches to answering these activist questions. Thinking about reform and restructuring as a continuum rather than a dichotomy in order to do specific work without losing sight of a progressive vision; thinking about strategies as goals and goals as strategies in order to expand the meaning of progressive social change; thinking about the absolute centrality of coalitions at every stage of the mobilization process in order to recast "what we want" in dynamic and expansive ways; thinking about resources as cultural and constructed in order to build on pre-existing communities and social networks; thinking about the organizational forms of activism in more capacious and creative ways in order not only to win a campaign or obtain a service but to acknowledge internal differences and manage tensions that may accompany these differences. Chapters 4 and 5 introduced those questions and argued for these kinds of "rethinkings."

A second set of questions emerges from Chapters 6 through 8 which dealt with participation, commitment, collective identity, and oppositional consciousness. What are the different paths to activism? What are effective recruitment strategies into activism? How does one manage activist burnout? How can we manage the conflicts that exist between the personal identities of these activists and the demands and commitments of the movements they work for? Does one need to be rooted in an oppressed community to be a social change activist? How can activists communicate, cooperate, and act together in the midst of differences and disagreements? Although these questions were more about activists' biographies and identities than the "nuts and bolts" of organizing, the motivations, beliefs, and personal issues they discuss are intimately connected to the strategies, goals, resources, and organizations of social movements. This point is stressed repeatedly throughout the book.

Again, I argue for using an activist-informed theoretical thinking for addressing these questions. Thinking about recruitment and participation as consequences of education and action embedded in pre-existing communities and social networks enables an incremental approach to activist commitment. Thinking about activist burnout in terms of both formal and informal support structures encourages movements to include these structures as explicit goals of social movement activity. Thinking about identity differences across activists opens up opportunities for dialogue around strategies, goals, and short-term and long-term visions of progressive social change. Finally, rethinking personal identities as intersections of various types of penalty and privilege not only facilitates self-knowledge but also leads to productive conversations about various kinds of oppositional consciousness and which forms of organizing can accommodate and nurture these oppositional approaches to the cultural, social, political and economic status quo.

All these progressive activists stand outside this status quo to some degree and in some way, shape or form. As they describe it, this life "outside" is exhilarating and frustrating, mundane and extraordinary, familiar and scary. Their willingness to live and work in that liminal space is a testament to their multiple commitments to, passions for, and visions of social change. Their willingness to live and work in that liminal space is the reason I believe that progressive politics as it is practiced in many communities throughout the United States will continue to thrive.

Appendix: Interview Guide

Name:

Date of Birth:

Family Background Information:

1 Describe the kinds of activist work you do. (Give me an idea of activities you are or have been involved with.)
2 Starting from your most recent involvements, describe the activism and/or social justice work you have been involved in. (Give me an idea of "how" you were involved in them. In what capacity?)
3 Describe the methods you use to make change, to change people's minds, to work in your organization or activity. (Did you adhere to a set of strategies or tactics? Do these vary? How and why do they vary?)
4 Describe the goals of the work. What do you hope to accomplish? (Discuss short-term and long-term goals.)
5 What are your greatest challenges of doing this kind of work? (the work itself; the people or organizations involved in the work; your own personal challenges)
6 How do you know or do you know that you have accomplished something?
7 What are your greatest frustrations doing this kind of work? (the work itself; the people or organizations involved in the work; your own personal frustrations)
8 Describe the decision-making processes followed in the work you do. (Are these determined by a set of principles or do they vary?)
9 What was the most exciting period, campaign, or experience of your activism thus far? Why this one?
10 What has been your greatest satisfaction as an activist?
11 How has the work you do changed over the years? (Reflections on both the particular work you do and the larger field of activism.)
12 Describe the people and organizations you interact with doing this work.
13 What is the nature of your relationship with them? How have the types of people changed over your years of involvement? (Discuss differences in generation, race, ethnicity, class background, gender.)

14 Do you recruit/educate others to be activists? How do you do this? What do you tell them about this work?

15 What's it like doing this kind of work in Hartford?

16 Who do you find yourself working with and working against in doing this work? (What kinds of cooperative relationships have you forged with people or organizations in the area? With whom have you oftentimes done battle?)

17 Have you ever considered not engaging in this work? Describe when that happened and what it was like. How did you manage that?

18 How did you come to do this kind of work? (What was your initial involvement? What were your subsequent involvements?)

19 If you had to tell the story of "how you came to be an activist," what would it be?

20 How is the activism incorporated into your life? Is it your paying job? Your non-paying work? Describe a typical week for you when you are in the middle of a campaign.

21 Why do you do this? (What motivates you?)

22 In your opinion what are the most important things to work for? (long term and short term; for you personally; for the progressive activists)

23 How easy or difficult is it to connect what you are doing to your ideals or understanding of social change?

24 How has your work changed you?

25 How has it changed who you are? How you deal with other people? What you think is important? How you view the world?

26 How do you or do you balance your activism with other areas of your life? (Do you separate the two or try to keep them closely connected?)

27 What about friends, family, and relationships...do they share an interest in your activism, come from your activist work, or separate from your activism?

28 What are the sources of tensions or conflicts with family, friends, relationships, or work as a result of your activism?

29 Can you give me the names of other activists you know in the area who you think are doing important work?

30 In what areas are they working and what is your relationship with them?

* As the heading suggests, these questions served as the guide for the interview. My goal was to create a structured conversation where my narrators could describe what they do, how they do it, who they do it with, why they do it, and how they have been affected by their activism. More important, my goal was also to elicit "the stories" associated with their activism and the emotions and feelings associated with the work and their lives in terms of their activism since I was very interested in their identities as activists. For these reasons, the questions served as guides not as requirements. The bracketed questions or phrases were either alternative questions or follow-up questions to the more general open-ended questions. This style of interviewing is informed by the tradition of oral history (Grele 1991; Yow 1994), qualitative interviewing (Blee and Taylor 2002), and narrative analysis (Riessman 1993).

Table 1 Activist by Age, Race, Class, Years in Activism, and Areas of Activism

Activist	Age	Race/Eth	Social Class	Years in Activism	Areas of Activism
Abbey	27	Puerto Rican	Working class	3	Labor
Adam	22	White	Working class	4	Student, anti-war
Alta	53	White	Middle class	27	Community organizing
Andrew	44	Afr. Amer.	Working class	8	Antiracist, youth, antiviolence
Ann	43	White	Middle class	21	LGBT
Beth	25	White	Working class	6	Feminist, queer
Carmen	41	Puerto Rican	Working class	24	Community organizing, welfare rights
Carolyn	60	White	Middle class	31	Feminist, LGBT, economic justice
Charlie	21	Uruguayan	Working class	2	Immigrant rights
Cheryl	53	Afr. Amer.	Middle class	17	Disability, HIV, LGBT, antiracist
Chris	38	White	Working class	17	Peace, anti-war, anti-racist
Cornel	44	Afr. Amer.	Middle class	14	Community, antiviolence, antiracist
David	26	Afr. Amer., Barbadian	Working class	10	HIV, Queer youth of color
Jack	58	White	Middle class	31	Community organizing
Janice	35	Afr. Amer.	Working class	10	Community organizing/ anti-racist
Jeremy	24	White	Working class	3	Labor
John	39	White	Middle class	20	LGBT, HIV, community
Joshua	28	White	Working class	8	Student, anti-war, anti-racist
Julia	34	White	Middle class	13	Peace, globalization, theater
Karen	43	West Indian	Middle class	14	Community organizing
Kevin	25	White	Working class	4	Student, anti-war
Larry	47	Afr. Amer.	Middle class	9	Community organizing, anti-racism

Activist	Age	Race/Eth	Social Class	Years in Activism	Areas of Activism
Laura L.	42	White	Middle class	19	Community organizing, feminist, antiracist
Laura M.	34	White	Middle class	13	Labor
Lisa	39	White	Middle class	15	Latina women
Liza	25	White	Working class	1	LGBT/Queer youth
Lorenzo	30	Afr. Amer.	Working class	10	Community organizing, anti-racist
Luz	52	Puerto Rican	Working class	26	Community organizing, welfare rights
Nick	22	White	Working class	3	LGBT/Queer youth
Steve	52	White	Middle class	33	Labor, environment, IRA, Community, economic justice
Regina	51	Afr. Amer.	Working class	34	LGBT, Queer youth of color, anti-racism
Rich	25	White	Working class	6	LGBT/Queer youth
Robin	47	White	Middle class	10	LGBT/Queer youth

Notes

Notes to Chapter 1

1 A couple of recent books have begun to address this disjuncture in social movement scholarship. An edited volume by Croteau *et al.* (2005) bridges this divide using concepts of framing (cf. Snow *et al.* 1986) for the United States. An analysis of Australian progressive activists by Maddison and Scalmer (2006) highlights the many political tensions surrounding activism and demonstrates their connection to theory and the production of new knowledge about social movements.

2 There is now a voluminous literature on this concept of collective identity. For an account of its origins from developments in Europe, see Buechler (1995). For overviews of the research utilizing this concept, see Snow (2001), Polletta and Jasper (2001), and Bernstein (2005).

3 I do not want to disparage the social movement scholarship that appears in academic journals such as *Mobilization, Social Problems, American Journal of Sociology, American Sociological Review*, among others. The requirement that the essays that appear in these journals adhere to the scientific methods of positivistic social science sometimes makes the work inaccessible to students of social movements as well as activists.

4 In the U.S. context, these debates have a long history stemming initially from the troubled relationship between the Old and New Lefts (Isserman 1987; Gitlin 1987) and subsequent analyses of the rise of identity politics in the 1980s and 1990s (Gitlin 1995). These recent analyses continue to see class oppression as the only "real" source of oppression and dismiss discontents based on narrowly conceived status attributes such as gender, sexuality, race, ethnicity, etc. as ignoring their "root causes" in class and diverting our attention from the important issues of redistribution to the symbolic and less important issues of cultural recognition. For a theoretical critique of this approach, see Bernstein (2005). For a historical critique, see Duberman (1999).

5 The early work that articulated the intersectionality of multiple types of power and powerlessness and demonstrated the connections between struggles surrounding recognition and distribution was accomplished by Black and Latina feminists in the late 1970s. The classic statement is by the Combahee River Collective (1981) as well as the other essays, poems, and art assembled in the volume edited by Moraga and Anzaldua (1981). Social scientists such as Collins (1991), Crenshaw (1995), and King (1988) built on these initial formulations historically, theoretically, and politically.

6 These different approaches to service delivery are laid out by Fisher (1994) and Valocchi (1996).

Notes to Chapter 2

1 Most introductions to sociology stress the importance of theory, concepts, and method in order to decide what aspects of social reality to focus on and what patterns are the most meaningful. For two particularly lively and sophisticated introductions to these issues, see Abbott (2004) and Lemert (2005).

2 There are many different ways to "carve up" the theoretical frameworks in the area of social movements and collective action. The typology I use starts with a genealogical method and identifies the frameworks as they developed in the discipline over the past several decades. Because I am particularly interested in the relationship between structure and culture and between external and internal processes in the development of social movements, I refine the typology to more explicitly consider these relationships. Somewhat different from most standard typologies, I describe a general cultural approach which calls attention to the meaning-making components to social movements. I further refine that approach however by identifying an oppositional consciousness and a new social movements approach. These approaches identify structural processes of inequality and the meaning systems associated with these processes. This admixture of culture and structure is at the forefront of social movement theorizing. It is also a useful admixture for understanding what activists do and who activists are.

3 This summary is highly schematic and does not do justice to the nuance and variety in this framework that stresses strain, anomie due to the rise of a "mass society," or to the dynamics of relative deprivation in defining and reacting to social strain. McAdam *et al.* (1988) captures this nuance and variety while situating their strain within the broader history of social movement theory at that time.

4 This historical understanding of strain theory is based on the sociology of knowledge approach to social movement theory by Buechler (2000: Chapter 2). While not focusing on social movement theory in particular, Feagin and Vera (2001: Chapter 3) describe the interconnections between U.S. hegemony, the development of a scientific sociology, and the emergence of functional theory as the dominant paradigm from the 1930s to the 1970s.

5 As with most of the theoretical frameworks, there is a voluminous research literature of empirical research utilizing, refining and criticizing this approach to social movements. For a recent review of this literature see Edwards and McCarthy (2005). The classic statement of the framework and its necessity because of the limitations of strain theories is by McCarthy and Zald (1977).

6 This connection between resource mobilization theory with its emphasis on organizational resources and political opportunity theory with its emphasis on political resources was first made explicit in an analysis of the farm workers' movement by Jenkins and Perrow (1977). A more recent "state of the theory" overview can be found in Kriesi (2005).

7 Haines (1984: 32) describes two types of radical flank effects. In the first situation, dubbed the negative radical flank effect, radicals threaten to discredit the goals and activists of movement moderates and discourage the channeling of external resources into the movement. In the second situation, the positive radical flank effect, radicals provide a "radical foil" against which the moderates present themselves and are represented by outsiders, thus bringing resources and support to the moderates' political positions.

8 The singular focus on rationality, self-interest, and selective incentives as motivations for social movement participation is only one of the many criticisms of the resource mobilization and political opportunity approaches. For a critical analysis of these perspectives which includes the problem of participation in a larger critique of the absence of meaning structures and culture in general see Jasper and Goodwin (1999).

9 Unlike the previous three frameworks, the cultural approach, as I am using it, is not so much a formally constituted set of propositions but more an amalgam of sensitizing concepts: meanings, belief structures, and normative understandings that are both constitutive of the structures stressed by strain, resource mobilization, and political opportunity theories as well as structures that cannot be reduced to politics, economics, or societal strain. For a similar approach to these theories see Reed (2005: Chapter 10).

10 The most influential European social scientist who coined the term "new social movements theory" and made it accessible to English-speaking audiences is Alberto Melucci in his many books and essays (1980; 1985; 1989; 1996).

Notes to Chapter 3

1 The precise quote reads: "Men make their own history, but they do not make it just as they please; they do not make it under circumstances chosen by themselves, but under conditions directly encountered, given and transmitted from the past."

2 Theorists of social movements have yet to make "power" the central component of their analyses of the emergence and development of social movements. One notable exception is Buechler (2000) which uses world system theory, critical theory, and theories of class, race, and gender, to both critique the dominant perspectives and offer an alternative reading of social movements.

3 While the New Deal and the policy aftermath of World War II did indeed facilitate upward mobility of many European ethnics, the process was uneven and benefited some groups more than others depending on the already existing relationship between ethnic groups and the local political machine. However, as I and others have noted, this inchoate, limited, and unstable "social democratic" impulse did not apply to African Americans who were written out of much of the New Deal legislation. Many of the post-war social and economic policies also were exclusionary both in their intent and implementation (Massey and Denton 1993; Quadagno 1994; Valocchi 1994).

4 Taylor and Van Dyke (2005) and Rupp and Taylor (2003) make the case that some forms of drag should be considered legitimate forms of social movement activity.

Notes to Chapter 4

1 Several of my activist narrators referred to manuals and organizing institutes. The bible for many community organizers is Saul Alinsky's *Rules for Radicals* (1972). Saul Alinsky was a labor organizer for the newly established militant labor union, the Congress of Industrial Organizations, in 1930s and 1940s Chicago. Based on his organizing experiences especially in one industrial neighborhood, Back of the Yards, he realized the importance of collective action in neighborhoods as well as on the factory floor. Based in his experiences, he developed a series of guidelines that generations of organizers have used. Also referenced frequently throughout my conversations with activists was Rinku Sen's edited volume, *Stir it Up* (2003). This volume uses examples from a variety of progressive campaigns in the 1980s and 1990s to discuss the process of organizing in a different world from the one Alinsky developed his rules: "characterized by global capitalism, a resurgent conservative movement, and the continued role of racism and sexism." Frequently mentioned organizing institutes that have trained generations of post-1960s organizers is *The Midwest Organizing Academy* (Bobo *et al.* 1991) and the *Center for Community Change*.

2 There is now a fairly large sociological and historical literature on the structure and functioning of the civil rights, feminist, and lesbian and gay movements. Some of this literature has already been discussed under the rubric of intersectionality (e.g. Crenshaw 1995; Moraga and Anzaludua 1984). For the civil rights movement, see Allen (1992)

[1969]; Marable (2007); Hall (1996). For the feminist movement, see Davis (1981); Roth (2004). For the gay and lesbian movement, see Ferguson (2004) and Valocchi (1999).

3 Not surprisingly, the research on the advantages and disadvantages of different social movement strategies and goals is voluminous. For an exceptional treatment of these issues for the progressive movements of the 1960s see Francesca Polletta (2002). Some of the conundrums that accompany movements as they attempt to form coalitions and prioritize goals are dealt with in Stephanie Gilmore's edited volume (2007). An empirically rich and theoretically sophisticated overview of the impact of changing political opportunities and the effects of countermovements on the internal dynamics of movements can be found in Meyer and Staggenborg (1996).

4 Once again, there is a large research literature on the interrelationship between culture and politics as goals of social movements. Some important sources are Rochon (1998) and Bernstein (2003; 1997) and Gamson (1989).

5 This framework is elaborated in Valocchi (2009).

6 A parallel path to the legislative path was the judicial path. In 2004, eight same-sex couples sued the state asserting that the denial of marriage licenses to same-sex couples violated the due process and equal protection clauses of the Connecticut Constitution. In October 2008 the Connecticut Supreme Court agreed with the plaintiffs, and Connecticut became the third state to perform marriages between same-sex couples.

Notes to Chapter 5

1 The early essay that spawned a cottage industry in the United States utilizing the twin concepts of resources and organizations is by McCarthy and Zald (1977). For an evaluation of this "industry" see the essay by Edwards and McCarthy (2005).

2 This understanding of culture is informed by the work of Ann Swidler (1986), who rejects an understanding of culture in terms of coherent value systems across levels of society and instead prefers the metaphor of toolkits to convey the multiple and sometimes contradictory discourses, scripts, and meaning systems that individuals use as decision-making guides or as guides to self-identification.

3 This understanding of organizations as cultural entities is becoming increasingly popular in the study of social movements. Polletta (2008) stresses the interpretive and symbolic components of organizations.

4 In his account of the Battle of Seattle, the mass mobilization prior to and during the meetings of the World Trade Organization in Seattle in 1999, Reed (2005) shows the importance of the internet in all phases of the protests. He also points to the innovations in structures of deliberation and action through the interaction between communication in cyberspace and action in affinity groups.

Notes to Chapter 6

1 For many years scholars have approached these questions using rational actor models of social action and casting recruitment and commitment in terms of individual costs and benefits (Olson 1965). According to these models, movements that are successful in recruiting individuals are those that solve the free rider problem by offering selective incentives to encourage individuals to make short-term sacrifices for long-term collective benefits. These models have been critiqued elsewhere (cf. Hirsch 1990). Suffice to say, that the activist narrators' own accounts of their motivations, sacrifices, and satisfactions require a fuller, more complex, and fundamentally social definition of the human actor.

2 When strain models and relative deprivation approaches fell out of favor in the 1960s, social movement theory and research developed apart from the developments in social psychology. These have recently been brought back into closer dialogue (Stryker, Owens, and White 2000). Also see Klandermans's (1997) innovative analysis of the social psychology of collective action.

3 I use the concept of collective identity to explore the variety of pathways activists take to participation and commitment in Valocchi (2007). Chapter 8 revisits this concept and demonstrates its utility in understanding differences in the strategies, goals, and social movement frames employed by progressive activists.

Notes to Chapter 7

1 This tendency is due to many factors. For the most part, scholars proceed at the level of structure, assuming that structural conditions are the most important factors for explaining recruitment, participation, and exit. As I argued in Chapter 6, this assumption needs to be amended to see individual motivations, biographies, networks, etc. as interacting with structural conditions. Related to this factor, most scholars examine "big" social movements in the same way they examine "little" instances of collective action or a series of campaigns. The separation of these two levels would enable us to see the operation of structural and social psychological factors operating simultaneously.

2 This deep commitment is found in other narrative-centered accounts of social movement participation (Andrews 1991; Downton and Wehr 1997; Teske 1997).

3 McAdam (1988: 206–28) examines these conflicts in the context of the denouement of the 1960s protest wave. For many of these activists, their relationships were "movement" relationships and once the movement was over so were the relationships. McAdam (1988) does not identify the factors that caused some relationships to persist and others to dissolve once the cultural and political supports for activism dried up.

Notes to Chapter 8

1 It is only somewhat hyperbolic to say that "identity" is one of the central and contentious concepts in both the social sciences and the humanities pivoting around different epistemological and theoretical positions about the nature of the social subject and the defining characteristics of modern/postmodern societies. Michel Foucault (1990) and Judith Butler (1990) have been influential in shattering the myth of the coherent subject and seeing identities as forms of power/knowledge. While mindful of the multiplicity of power sources in the postmodern world, Anthony Giddens (1991) and Charles Lemert (1997) have insisted on the constructed coherence of the social subject and the "liberating" aspects of new identities and subjectivities.

References

Abbott, Andrew. 2004. *Methods of Discovery: Heuristics for the Social Sciences*. New York and London: W. W. Norton & Company.

Alinsky, Saul D. 1972. *Rules for Radicals*. New York: Vintage Books.

Allen, Robert L. 1992 [1969]. *Black Awakening in Capitalist Awakening*. Trenton, NJ: Africa World Press, Inc.

Andrews, Molly. 1991. *Lifetimes of Commitment: Aging, Politics, Psychology*. Cambridge: Cambridge University Press.

Battle, Stanley F.1994. *The State of Black Hartford*. Hartford, CT: Urban League of Greater Hartford, Inc.

Benford, Robert D. 2000. "Framing Processes and Social Movements: An Overview and Assessment." *Annual Review of Sociology* 26: 611–39.

Bernstein, Mary. 1997. "Celebration and Suppression: The Strategic Uses of Identity by the Lesbian and Gay Movement." *American Journal of Sociology* 103: 531–65.

——. 2002. "Identities and Politics: Toward a Historical Understanding of the Lesbian and Gay Movement." *Social Science History* 26: 531–81.

——. 2003. "Nothing Ventured, Nothing Gained? Conceptualizing Social Movement 'Success' in the Lesbian and Gay Movement." *Sociological Perspectives* 46: 353–79.

——. 2005. "Identity Politics." *Annual Review of Sociology* 31: 47–74.

Blee, Kathleen M. and Verta Taylor. 2002. "Semi-Structured Interviewing in Social Movement Research." Pp. 92–117 in *Methods of Social Movement Research*. Bert Klandermans and Suzanne Staggenborg eds. Minnesota: University of Minnesota Press.

Bobo, Kim, Jackie Kendall, and Steve Max. 1991. *Organizing for Social Change: A Manual for Activists in the 1990s*. Washington, DC: Seven Locks Press.

Bonelli, John. 1996. "Unifying and Uniting as a Community." Presented at *Different Voices and One Community Conference*.

Bonelli, John and Louise Simmons. 2004. "Coalition Building and Electoral Organizing in the Passage of Anti-Discrimination Laws: The Case of Connecticut." *Journal of Gay and Lesbians Social Services* 16(3–4): 35–53.

Breines, Wini. 1989. *Community and Organization in the New Left, 1962–1968: The Great Refusal*. New Brunswick, NJ: Rutgers University Press.

Buechler, Steven M. 2004. 1995. "New Social Movement Theories." *The Sociological Quarterly* 36: 441–64.

——. 2000. *Social Movements in Advanced Capitalism: The Political Economy and Cultural Construction of Social Activism*. New York and Oxford: Oxford University Press.

———. 2004. "The Strange Career of Strain and Breakdown Theories of Collective Action." Pp. 47–66 in *The Blackwell Companion to Social Movements*. David A. Snow, Sarah A. Soule, and Hanspeter Kriesi. eds. Oxford: Blackwell Publishing Ltd.

Burns, Peter F. 2006. *Electoral Politics Is Not Enough: Racial and Ethnic Minorities and Urban Politics*. Albany, NY: State University of New York Press.

Burstein, Paul. 1985. *Discrimination, Jobs, and Politics: The Struggle for Equal Employment Opportunity since the New Deal*. Chicago: University of Chicago Press.

Butler, Judith. 1990. *Gender Trouble: Feminism and the Subversion of Identity*. New York: Routledge.

Calhoun, Craig. 1993. "'New Social Movements' of the Early Nineteenth Century." *Social Science History* 17: 385–427.

Castells, Manuel. 1983. *The City and the Grassroots: A Cross-Cultural Theory of Urban Social Movements*. Berkeley and Los Angeles: University of California Press.

Clawson, Dan. 2003. *The Next Upsurge: Labor and the New Social Movements*. Ithaca and London: Cornell University Press.

Close, Stacey. 2001. "Fire in the Bones: Hartford's NAACP, Civil Rights and Militancy, 1943–69." *The Journal of Negro History* 86: 228–63.

Cohen, Cathy J. 1997. "Punks, Bulldaggers, and Welfare Queens: The Radical Potential of 'Queer' Politics." *GLQ* 3: 437–65

Cohen, Jean. 1985. "Strategy or Identity: New Theoretical Paradigms and Contemporary Social Movements." *Social Research* 52: 663–716.

Collins, Patricia Hill. 1991. *Black Feminist Thought: Knowledge, Consciousness, and the Politics of Empowerment*. New York and London: Routledge.

———. 2006. "Toward a New Vision: Race, Class, and Gender as Categories of Analysis and Connection." Pp. 243–60 in *Social Class and Stratification: Classical Statements and Theoretical Debates* second edition. Rhonda Levine ed. Oxford: Rowman and Littlefield Inc.

Combahee River Collective. 1981. "A Black Feminist Statement." Pp. 210–18 in *This Bridge Called My Back: Writings by Radical Women of Color*. Cherrie Moraga and Gloria Anzaldua. eds. Watertown, MA: Persephone Press.

Connecticut Economic Resource Center. 2002a. *Harford, Connecticut Town Profile: Labor Force*. www.cerc.com.

———. 2002b. *Hartford, Connecticut Town Profile: Economics*. www.cerc.com

———. 2008. Hartford, *Connecticut Town Profile: Demographics*. www.cerc.com

———. 2006. Hartford, *Connecticut Town Profile: Demographics/Labor Force*. www.cerc.com

Connecticut State Data Center. 2007. *Hartford's Racial/Ethnic Composition*. http://ctsdc.uconn.edu/

Costain, Anne N. 1992. *Inviting Women's Rebellion: A Political Process Interpretation of the Women's Movement*. Baltimore and London: The Johns Hopkins University Press.

Crenshaw, Kimberle. 1995. "Mapping the Margins: Intersectionality, Identity Politics and Violence Against Women." Pp. 357–83 in *Critical Race Theory: The Key Writings That Formed the Movement*, Kimberle Crenshaw, Neil Gotanda, Gary Peller, and Kendall Thomas. New York: The New Press.

Cress, Daniel and David Snow. 1996. "Mobilization at the Margins: Resources, Benefactors, and the Viability of Homeless Social Movement Organizations." *American Sociological Review* 61: 1089–1109.

Croteau, David, William Haynes, and Charlotte Ryan eds. 2005. *Rhyming Hope and History: Activists, Academics, and Social Movement Scholarship*. Minneapolis and London: University of Minnesota Press.

Cruz, Jose E. 1998. *Identity and Power: Puerto Rican Politics and the Challenge of Ethnicity*. Philadelphia: Temple University Press.

Davis, Angela Y. 1981. *Women, Race, and Class*. New York: Random House.

Dawson, Michael C. 2001. *Black Visions: The Roots of African American Political Ideologies*. Chicago and London: University of Chicago Press.

Distelberg, Brian J. 2007. "Organizing Gay People: Hartford, Conn.'s Kalos Society – Gay Liberation Front, 1968–75." Paper presented at the NEASA Conference, Sex/Changes: Historical Transformations of Sex, Gender, and Sexuality, Providence R.I., November 2–3.

Donahue, Barbara. 1999. *Here to Help. Here to Stay. The First 75 Years of the Hartford Foundation for Public Giving*. Hartford: The Hartford Foundation for Public Giving.

Downton, James Jr. and Paul Wehr. 1998. *The Persistent Activist: How Peace Commitment Develops and Survives*. Boulder, CO: Westview Press.

Duberman, Martin B. 1993. *Stonewall*. New York: Penguin Group.

——. 1999. *Left Out: The Politics of Exclusion*. New York: Basic Books.

Dugan, Kimberly B. 2005. *The Struggle over Gay, Lesbian, and Bisexual Rights: Facing Off in Cincinnati*. New York and London: Routledge.

Duggan, Lisa and Nan D. Hunter. 1995. *Sex Wars: Sexual Dissent and Political Culture*. New York: Routledge.

Edwards, Bob and John D. McCarthy. 2004. "Resources and Social Movement Mobilization." Pp. 116–52 in *The Blackwell Companion to Social Movements*. David A. Snow, Sarah A. Soule, and Hanspeter Kriesi. eds. Oxford: Blackwell Publishing Ltd.

Einwohner, Rachel. 1999. "Gender, Class, and Social Movement Outcomes: Identity and Effectiveness in Two Animal Rights Campaigns." *Gender & Society* 13: 56–76.

Fantasia, Rick. 1988. *Cultures of Solidarity: Consciousness, Action, and Contemporary American Workers*. Berkeley: University of California Press.

Feagin, Joe R. and Hernan Vera. 2001. *Liberation Sociology*. Cambridge, MA: Westview Press.

Ferguson, Roderick A. 2004. *Aberrations in Black: Toward a Queer of Color Critique*. Minneapolis, MI: University of Minnesota Press.

Filer, John. 1986. "Hartford Reflections." *Northeast Magazine*, Hartford Courant, March 17.

Fisher, Robert. 1994. *Let the People Decide: Neighborhood Organizing in America*. New York: Twayne Publishers.

Flacks, Richard. 2005. "The Question of Relevance for Social Movement Studies." Pp. 3-19 in *Rhyming Hope and History: Activists, Academics, and Social Movement Scholarship*. David Croteau, William Haynes, and Charlotte Ryan. eds. Minneapolis and London: University of Minnesota Press.

Foucault, Michel. 1990. *The History of Sexuality. Volume 1: An Introduction*. New York: Vintage Books.

Fraser, Bruce. 1988. *The Land of Steady Habits: A Brief History of Connecticut*. Hartford, Connecticut: Connecticut Historical Commission.

Freeman, Jo. 1973. "The Origins of the Women's Liberation Movement." *American Journal of Sociology* 78: 792–811.

Friedman, Debra and Doug McAdam. 1992. "Collective Identity and Activism: Networks, Choices, and the Life of a Social Movement." Pp. 156–73 in *Frontiers in Social*

Movement Theory. Aldon D. Morris and Carol McClurg Mueller. eds. New Haven: Yale University Press.

Gamson, Josh. 1989. "Silence, Death, and the Invisible Enemy: AIDS Activism and Social Movement 'Newness'." *Social Problems* 36: 351–7.

——. 1996. "The Organizational Shaping of Collective Identity: The Case of Lesbian and Gay Film Festivals in New York." *Sociological Forum* 11: 231–61.

——. 1997. "Messages of Exclusion: Gender, Movements, and Symbolic Boundaries." *Gender & Society* 11: 178–99.

Gamson, William. 1992. "The Social Psychology of Collective Action." Pp. 53–76 in *Frontiers in Social Movement Theory*. Aldon Morris and Carol McClurg Mueller eds. New Haven: Yale University Press.

Gamson, William and Andre Modigliani. 1988. "Media Discourse and Public Opinion on Nuclear Power: A Constructionist Approach." *American Journal of Sociology* 95: 1–37.

Ghaziani, Amin. 2008. *The Dividends of Dissent: How Conflict and Culture Work in Lesbian and Gay Marches on Washington*. Chicago and London: University of Chicago Press.

Giddens, Anthony. 1991. *Modernity and Self-Identity: Self and Society in the Late Modern Age*. Stanford: Stanford University Press.

Gilkes, Cheryl Townsend. 1988. "Building in Many Places: Multiple Commitments and Ideologies in Black Women's Community Work." Pp. 53–76 in *Women and the Politics of Empowerment*. Ann Bookman and Sandra Morgen. eds. Philadelphia, PA: Temple University Press.

Gilmore, Stephanie ed. 2008. *Feminist Coalitions: Historical Perspectives on Second-Wave Feminism in the United States*. Urbana: University of Illinois Press.

Gitlin, Todd. 1987. *The Sixties: Years of Hope, Days of Rage*. Toronto and New York: Bantam Books.

——. 1995. *The Twilight of Common Dreams: Why America is Wracked by Culture Wars*. New York: Metropolitan Books.

Glaser, Barney and Anselm Strauss. 1967. *The Discovery of Grounded Theory: Strategies for Qualitative Research*. Chicago: Aldine.

Gould, Deborah B. 2002. "Life during Wartime: Emotions and the Development of ACT UP." *Mobilization* 7: 177–200.

Grele, Ronald J. (with Studs Terkel). 1991. *Envelopes of Sound: The Art of Oral History*. 2nd edition. New York: Praeger.

Gusfield, Joseph. 1962. *Symbolic Crusade: Status Politics and the American Temperance Movement*. Urbana: University of Illinois Press.

Haines, Herbert H. 1984. "Black Radicalization and the Funding of Civil Rights: 1957–70." *Social Problems* 32: 31–43.

——. 1988. *Black Radicals and the Civil Rights Mainstream, 1954–1970*. Knoxville: The University of Tennessee Press.

Harris, Frederick C. 1999. *Something Within: Religion in African-American Political Activism*. New York: Oxford University Press.

Hall, Stuart. 1996. "Who Needs Identity?" Pp. 1–17 in *Questions of Cultural Identity*. Stuart Hall and Paul du Gay eds. London: Sage.

Hirsch, Eric. 1990. "Sacrifice for the Cause: The Impact of Group Processes on Recruitment and Commitment in Protest Movements." *American Sociological Review* 55: 243–54.

Hirsch, Joachim. 1988. "The Crisis of Fordism, Transformation of the 'Keynesian' Security State, and New Social Movements." Pp. 43–55 in *Research in Social Movements, Conflicts and Change* volume 10. Greenwich, CT: Jai Press.

hooks, bell. 1981. *Ain't I a Women: Black Women and Feminism*. Boston: South End Press.

Howard, Judith. 2000. "The Social Psychology of Identities." *Annual Review of Sociology* 26: 367–83.

Hunt, Scott and Robert D. Benford. 2004. "Collective Identity, Solidarity, and Commitment." Pp. 433–58 in the *Blackwell Companion to Social Movements*. David A. Snow, Sarah. A. Soule, and Hanpeter Kriesi. eds. Oxford: Blackwell Publishing.

Isserman, Maurice. 1987. *If I had a Hammer: The Death of the Old Left and the Birth of the New Left*. New York: Basic Books.

Janick, Herbert F. Jr. 1985. *A Diverse People: Connecticut 1914 to the Present*. Chester, CT: Pequot Press.

Jasper, James M. 1997. *The Art of Moral Protest: Culture, Biography, and Creativity in Social Movements*. Chicago: University of Chicago Press.

Jasper, James M. and Jeff Goodwin. 1999. "Trouble in Paradigms." *Sociological Forum* 14: 107–25.

Jenkins, Craig J. and Craig Eckert. 1986. "Channeling Black Insurgency: Elite Patronage and Professional Social Movement Organization in the Development of the Black Movement." *American Sociological Review* 51: 812–29.

Jenkins, Craig J. and Charles Perrow. 1977. "Insurgency of the Powerless: Farm Workers Movements, 1946–72." *American Sociological Review* 42: 249–68.

Johnston, Hank and John A. Noakes. 2005. *Frames of Protest: Social Movements and the Framing Perspective*. Oxford: Rowman and Littlefield Publishers, Inc.

Jones, Mark H. 1995. "When Bootstraps Were Not Enough." *Northeast Magazine of the Hartford Courant*. July 2: E1,4.

——. 2003. "Audacious Alliances." *Hog River Journal* 1 (4): 26–31.

Kern, Bethann. 1992. "The History of Front Street." unpublished manuscript. *The Hartford Studies Collection*, Trinity College Library.

King, Deborah H. 1988. "Multiple Jeopardy, Multiple Consciousness: The Context of a Black Feminist Ideology." *Signs: Journal of Women in Culture and Society* 14: 42–72.

Klandermans, Bert. 1997. *The Social Psychology of Protest*. Oxford: Blackwell Publishers Ltd.

Knapp, Peter J. 2000. *Trinity College in the Twentieth Century: A History*. Hartford, CT: the Trustees of Trinity College.

Kornhauser, William. 1959. *The Politics of Mass Society*. Glencoe, IL: Free Press.

Kriesi, Hanspeter. 2005. "Political Context and Opportunity." Pp. 67–90 in *The Blackwell Companion to Social Movements*. David A. Snow, Sarah A. Soule, and Hanspeter Kriesi. eds. Oxford: Blackwell Publishing Ltd.

Kurtz, Sharon. 2002. *Workplace Justice: Organizing Multi-Identity Movements*. Minneapolis and London: University of Minnesota Press.

Kuzyk, Ivan. 2003. *A Hartford Primer and Field Guide 2nd edition*. Hartford, CT: Cities Data Center at Trinity College.

Lemert, Charles. 1997. *Postmodernism Is Not What You Think*. Malden, MA: Blackwell Publishers.

——. 2005. *Social Things: An Introduction to the Sociological Life*. Oxford: Rowman & Littlefield Publishers, Inc.

Lenzi, Richard. 2003. "Labor and the Left in Hartford, 1890–1960." M.A. Thesis. Department of History, Trinity College.

Lieberson, Stanley. 1980. *A Piece of the Pie: Blacks and White Immigrants Since 1880*. Berkeley: University of California Press.

Liesgang, Jerimarie and Richard Stillson. 2004. "While Paris Was Burning, Hartford Sizzled." *Documentary, 2004 Connecticut Gay and Lesbian Film Festival,* June. Hartford, Connecticut.

Loeb, Paul Rogat. 2004. *The Impossible Will Take a While: A Citizen's Guide to Hope in a Time of Fear*. New York: Basic Books.

Lopez, Steven Henry. 2004. *Reorganizing the Rust Belt: An Inside Study of the American Labor Movement*. Berkeley: University of California Press.

McAdam, Doug. 1982. *Political Process and the Development of Black Insurgency, 1930–1970*. Chicago: The University of Chicago Press.

——.1988. *Freedom Summer*. New York: Oxford University Press.

McAdam, Doug, John D. McCarthy, and Mayer N. Zald. 1988. "Social Movements." Pp. 695–738 in *Handbook of Sociology*. Neil J. Smelser ed. Newbury Park: Sage Publications.

McAdam, Doug, Sidney Tarrow, and Charles Tilly. 2001. *Dynamics of Contention*. Cambridge: Cambridge University Press.

McCarthy, John and Mayer Zald. 1977. "Resource Mobilization and Social Movements: A Partial Theory." *American Journal of Sociology* 82: 1212–41.

Maddison, Sarah and Sean Scalmer. 2006. *Activist Wisdom: Practical Knowledge and Creative Tension in Social Movements*. Sydney, Australia: University of New South Wales Press.

Mansbridge, Jane and Aldon Morris. 2001. *Oppositional Consciousness: The Subjective Roots of Social Protest*. Chicago, IL: University of Chicago Press.

Marable, Manning. 2007. *Race, Reform, and Rebellion: The Second Reconstruction and Beyond in Black America*. 3rd edition. Jackson, MS: University Press of Mississippi.

Marotta, Toby. 1981. *The Politics of Homosexuality*. Boston: Houghton-Mifflin.

Marx, Gary T. and Douglas McAdam. 1994. *Collective Behavior and Social Movements: Process and Structure*. Englewood Cliffs, NJ: Prentice Hall.

Marx, Karl. 1967. *Capital: A Critique of Political Economy volume 1*. New York: International Publishers.

——. 1972. "The Eighteenth Brumaire of Louis Bonaparte." Pp. 436–525 in *The Marx-Engels Reader*. Robert C. Tucker ed. New York: W. W. Norton Inc.

Massey, Douglas S. and Nancy A. Denton. 1993. *American Apartheid: Segregation and the Making of the Underclass*. Cambridge, MA: Harvard University Press.

Melucci, Alberto. 1980. "The New Social Movements: A Theoretical Approach." *Social Science Information* 19: 199–226.

——. 1985. "The Symbolic Challenge of Contemporary Movements." *Social Research* 52: 781–816.

——1989. *Nomads of the Present: Social Movements and Individual Needs in Contemporary Society*. Philadelphia: Temple University Press.

——. 1996. *Challenging Codes: Collective Action in the Information Age*. Cambridge: Cambridge University Press.

Meyer, David and Suzanne Staggenborg. 1996. "Movements, Countermovements, and the Structure of Political Opportunity." *American Journal of Sociology* 101: 1628–60.

Miller, James A. 1994. "Relationship to Culture, Political Structure and the Life Blood of the Black Community." Pp. 38–44 in *The State of Black Hartford*. Stanley F. Battle. ed. Hartford, CT: The Urban League of Greater Hartford, Inc.

Mills, C. Wright. 1956. *The Power Elite*. New York: Oxford University Press.

———. 1959. *The Sociological Imagination*. New York: Oxford University Press.

Montero, Elsa and William J. Mann. 1991. "How the Gay Rights Bill Was Won." *Metroline*. May 3: 16–20.

Moody, Kim. 1988. *An Injury to All: The Decline of American Unionism*: London and New York: Verso.

Moraga, Cherrie and Gloria Anzaldua. 1981. *This Bridge Called My Back: Writings by Radical Women of Color*. Watertown MA: Persephone Press.

Morris, Aldon D. 1981. "The Black Southern Sit-In Movements: An Analysis of Internal Organization." *American Sociological Review* 45: 744–67.

———. 1984. *The Origins of the Civil Rights Movement*. New York: The Free Press.

———. 1993. "Birmingham Confrontation Reconsidered: An Analysis of the Dynamics and Tactics of Mobilization." *American Sociological Review* 58: 621–36.

Morris, Aldon D. and Naomi Braine. 2001. "Social Movements and Oppositional Consciousness." Pp. 20–37 in *Oppositional Consciousness: The Subjective Roots of Social Protest*. Jane Mansbridge and Aldon Morris eds. Chicago, IL: University of Chicago Press.

Morris, Aldon D. and Carol McClurg Mueller. 1992. *Frontiers in Social Movement Theory*. New Haven: Yale University Press.

Morris, Aldon D. and Suzanne Staggenborg. 2005. "Leadership in Social Movements." Pp. 171–96 in *The Blackwell Companion to Social Movements*. David A. Snow, Sarah A. Soule, and Hanspeter. Kriesi. eds. Oxford: Blackwell Publishing.

Naples, Nancy. A. 1998. *Grassroots Warriors: Activist Mothering, Community Work, and the War on Poverty*. Philadelphia: Temple University Press.

Nepstad, Sharon Erickson. 2004. "Persistent Resistance: Commitment and Community in the Plowshares Movement." *Social Problems* 51: 43–60.

Neubeck, Kenneth J. and Richard E. Ratcliff. 1988. "Urban Democracy and the Power of Corporate Capital: Struggles over Downtown Growth and Neighborhood Stagnation in Hartford, Connecticut." Pp. 299–332 in *Business Elites and Urban Development: Case Studies and Critical Perspectives*. Scott Cummings. ed. Albany: State University of New York Press.

Noakes, John A. and Hank Johnston. 2005. "Frames of Protest: A Road Map to a Perspective." Pp. 1–29 in *Frames of Protest: Social Movements and the Framing Perspective*. John A. Noakes and Hank Johnston eds. Oxford: Rowman and Littlefield Publishers, Inc.

Oberschall, Anthony. 1973. *Social Conflict and Social Movements*. Englewood Cliffs, NJ: Prentice-Hall.

Olson, Mancur. 1965. *The Logic of Collective Action*. Cambridge, MA: Harvard University Press.

Pawlowski, Robert E. *c.* 1973. "How the Other Half Lived: An Ethnic History of the Old East Side and South End of Hartford." West Hartford, CT: Northwest Catholic High School.

———. *c.* 1991. *La Gente La Casa: The Development of Hartford's Puerto Rican Community*. Hartford: La Casa de Puerto Rico.

Payne, Charles M. 1995. *I've Got the Light of Freedom: The Organizing Tradition and the Mississippi Freedom Struggle*. Berkeley: University of California Press.

Pearson, Ralph L. 1976. "Interracial Conflict in Twentieth Century Connecticut Cities: The Demographic Factor." *Connecticut History*, January: 1–15.

Pennybacker, Susan and Paul Kershaw. 2004. "Hartford Labor Militants Fight the Spanish Civil War." *Hog River Journal* 2(3): 18–24.

People's History: The Story of Hartford Areas Rally Together. 1995. Hartford, CT: Harford Areas Rally Together Inc.

Piven, Frances Fox and Richard Cloward. 1979. *Poor People's Movements: How They Succeed, Why They Fail.* New York: Vintage Books.

Polletta, Francesca. 2002. *Freedom is an Endless Meeting: Democracy in American Social Movements.* Chicago, IL: University of Chicago Press.

——. 2008. "Culture and Movements." *Annals of the American Academy of Political & Social Science* 619: 78–96.

Polletta, Francesca and James M. Jasper. 2001. "Collective Identity and Social Movements." *Annual Review of Sociology* 27: 283–305.

Quadagno, Jill S. 1994. *The Color of Welfare: How Racism Undermined the War on Poverty.* New York: Oxford University Press.

Reed, Adolph. 1999. *Stirrings in the Jug: Black Politics in the Post-Segregation Era.* Minneapolis: University of Minnesota Press.

Reed, T. V. 2005. *The Art of Protest: Culture and Activism from the Civil Rights Movement to the Streets of Seattle.* Minneapolis and London: University of Minnesota Press.

Regen, Michael. 2007. "A Shift Toward Service Jobs." *Hartford Courant*, September 23: A1,8.

Reger, Jo. 2002. "More Than One Feminism: Organizational Structure and the Construction of Collective Identity." Pp. 171–84 in *Social Movements: Identity, Culture, and the State.* David S. Meyer, Nancy Whittier, and Belinda Robnet. eds. London: Oxford University Press.

Rhomberg, Chris and Louise Simmons. 2005. "Beyond Strike Support: Labor–Community Alliances and Democratic Power in New Haven." *Labor Studies Journal* 30: 21–47.

Riessman, Catherine Kohler. 1993. *Narrative Analysis.* Newbury Park, CA: Sage Publications.

Rimmerman, Craig. A. 2002. *From Identity to Politics: The Lesbian and Gay Movement in the United States.* Philadelphia: Temple University Press.

——. 2008. *The Lesbian and Gay Movements: Assimilation or Liberation?* Boulder, Colorado: Westview Press.

Robnett, Belinda. 2005. "We Don't Agree: Collective Identity Justification Work in Social Movement Organizations." Pp. 201–38 in *Research in Social Movements, Conflicts and Change.* Patrick G. Coy. ed. Amsterdam: Elsevier.

Rochon, Thomas R. 1998. *Culture Moves: Ideas, Activism, and Changing Values.* Princeton, NJ: Princeton University Press.

Roth, Benita. 2004. *Separate Roads to Feminism: Black, Chicana, and White Feminist Movements in America's Second Wave.* Cambridge: Cambridge University Press.

Rubin, Gayle S. 1993. "Thinking Sex: Notes for a Radical Theory of the Politics of Sexuality." Pp. 3–44 in *The Lesbian and Gay Studies Reader.* Henry Abelove, Michele Aina Barale, David M. Halperin. eds. London: Routledge, Inc.

Rupp, Leila J. and Verta Taylor. 1999. "Forging Feminist Identity in an International Movement: A Collective Identity Approach to Twentieth-Century Feminism." *Signs: Journal of Women in Culture and Society* 24: 363–86.

——. 2003. *Drag Queens at the 801 Cabaret.* Chicago: University of Chicago Press.

Ryan, Charlotte. 2005. "Successful Collaboration: Movement Building in the Media Arena." Pp. 115–36 in *Rhyming Hope and History: Activists, Academics, and Social Movement Scholarship.* David Croteau, William Hoynes, and Charlotte Ryan. eds. Minneapolis and London: University of Minnesota Press.

Sacks, Karen Brodkin. 1988. "Gender and Grassroots Leadership," Pp. 77–94 in *Women and the Politics of Empowerment*. Ann Bookman and Sandra Morgen eds. Philadelphia, PA: Temple University Press.

Saul, Arthur Phillip. 1998. "The Hartford Communist Party, 1926–1952." M.A. Thesis. Trinity College, Hartford, Connecticut.

Sen, Rinku. 2003. *Stir It Up: Lessons in Community Organizing and Advocacy*. San Francisco: John Wiley and Sons.

Shaw, Randy. 2001. *The Activist Handbook: A Primer. 2nd ed.* Berkeley and Los Angeles, CA: University of California Press.

Shelby, Tommie. 2005. *We Who Are Dark: The Philosophical Foundations of Black Solidarity*. Cambridge, MA: Harvard University Press.

Shepard, Benjamin and Ronald Hayduk. 2002. *From ACT UP to the WTO: Urban Protest and Community Building in the Era of Globalization*. New York and London: Verso.

Simmons, Louise. B. 1994. *Organizing in Hard Times: Labor and Neighborhoods in Hartford*. Philadelphia, PA: Temple University Press.

——. 1996. "Dilemmas of Progressives in Government: Playing Solomon in an Age of Austerity." *Economic Development Quarterly* 10: 159–71.

——. 1998. "A New Urban Conservativism: The Case of Hartford, Connecticut." *Journal of Urban Affairs* 20: 175–98.

——. 2008 "Does Anyone Care about Poverty and Inequality in Hartford?" Paper Presented at Center for Urban and Global Studies Conference: *Perspectives on the Transformation of Hartford through the Early 21st Century: Local, Regional and Global Perspectives*, Trinity College, Hartford, Connecticut. February 8.

Smelser, Neil J. 1962. *Theory of Collective Behavior*. New York: The Free Press.

Snow, David A. 2001. "Collective Identity and Expressive Forms." Pp. 2212–19 in *International Encyclopedia of Social and Behavioral Sciences*. Neil J. Smelser and Paul B. Baltes eds. Oxford: Elsevier Science Ltd.

Snow, David and Leon Anderson. 1987. "Identity Work Among the Homeless: The Verbal Construction of and Avowal of Personal Identities." *American Journal of Sociology* 92: 1336–71.

Snow, David A. and Robert D. Benford. 1992. "Master Frames and Cycles of Protest." Pp. 133–55 in Aldon Morris and Carol Mueller eds. *Frontiers in Social Movement Theory*. New Haven, CT: Yale University Press.

Snow, David and Doug McAdam. 2000. "Identity Work Processes in the Context of Social Movements: Clarifying the Identity/Movement Nexus." Pp. 41–67 in *Self, Identity, and Social Movements*. Sheldon Stryker, Timothy J. Owens, and Robert W. White eds. Minneapolis: University of Minnesota Press.

Snow, David A., Sarah A. Soule, and Hanspeter Kriesi. 2004. *The Blackwell Companion to Social Movements*. Malden, MA: Blackwell Publishing.

Snow, David A., R. Burke Rochford Jr., Steven K. Worden, and Robert D. Benford 1986. "Frame Alignment Processes, Micromobilization, and Movement Participation." *American Sociological Review* 51: 464–81.

Spivey. Donald. 1994. "Point of Contention: A Historical Perspective on the African-American Presence in Hartford." Pp. 45–61 in *The State of Black Hartford*. Stanley Battle. ed. Hartford, CT: Urban League of Greater Hartford, Inc.

Staggenborg, Suzanne. 1986. "Coalition Work in the Pro-Choice Movement: Organizational and Environmental Obstacles." *Social Problems* 33: 374–90.

——. 1989. "Stability and Innovation in the Women's Movement: A Comparison of Two Movement Organizations." *Social Problems* 36(1): 75–92.

Stave, Bruce. 1979. "Making Hartford Home: An Oral History of 20th Century Ethnic Development in Connecticut's Capital City." Pp. 31–45 in *Hartford, the City and the Region*. Sondra Astor Stave. ed. West Hartford: The University of Hartford.

——. 2006. *Red Brick in the Land of Steady Habits: Creating the University of Connecticut, 1881–2006*. Hanover and London: University Press of New England.

Stave, Bruce M., John F. Sutherland with Aldo Salerno. 1994. *From the Old Country: An Oral History of European Migration to America*. New York: Twayne Publishers.

Steinmetz, George. 1994. "Regulation Theory, Post-Marxism, and the New Social Movements." *Comparative Studies in Society and History* 36: 176–212.

Stockdill, Brett. C. 2003. *Activism against AIDS: At the Intersections of Sexuality, Race, Gender, and Class*. Boulder and London: Lynne Reinner Publishers.

Stryker, Sheldon, Timothy J. Owens, and Robert W. White. 2000. "Social Psychology and Social Movements: Cloudy Past and Bright Future." Pp. 1–17 in *Self, Identity, and Social Movements*. Sheldon Stryker, Timothy J. Owens, and Robert W. White eds. Minneapolis, MN: University of Minnesota.

Swidler, Ann. 1986. "Culture in Action: Symbols and Strategies." *American Sociological Review* 51: 273–86.

Tarrow, Sidney. 1994. *Power in Movement: Social Movements, Collective Action and Politics*. Cambridge: Cambridge University Press.

Taylor, Verta. 1989. "Social Movement Continuity: The Women's Movement in Abeyance." *American Sociological Review* 54: 761–75.

——. 1996. *Rock-a-by Baby: Feminism, Self-Help, and Postpartum Depression*. New York and London: Routledge.

Taylor, Verta and Nella Van Dyke. 2004. "'Get up, Stand up': Tactical Repertoires of Social Movements." Pp. 262–93 in *The Blackwell Companion to Social Movements*. David A. Snow, Sarah A. Soule, and Hanpeter Kriesi. eds. Oxford: Blackwell Publishing.

Taylor, Verta and Nancy Whittier. 1992. "Collective Identity in Social Movement Communities: Lesbian Feminist Mobilization." Pp. 104–29 in *Frontiers in Social Movement Theory*. Aldon D. Morris and Carol McClurg Mueller eds. New Haven, CT: Yale University Press.

——. 1995. "Analytical Approaches to Social Movement Culture: The Culture of the Women's Movement." Pp. 163–87 in *Social Movements and Culture: Social Movements, Protest, and Contention*, volume 4. Hank Johnston and Bert Klandermans. eds. Minneapolis, MN: University of Minnesota Press.

Teske, Nathan. 1997. *Political Activists in America: The Identity Construction Model of Political Participation*. Cambridge: Cambridge University Press.

Tilly, Charles. 1978. *From Mobilization to Revolution*. New York: Random House.

Trinity College Bulletin. 2008. *Catalogue Issue 2008–2009*. Hartford, CT: The Trustees of Trinity College.

Tuckel, Peter, Kurt Schlichting, and Richard Maisel. 2007. "Social, Economic, and Residential Diversity within Hartford's African American Community at the Beginning of the Great Migration." *Journal of Black Studies* 37: 710–36.

U.S. Census Bureau. 2000. *Comprehensive Demographic Report 1970–2000*. Washington, DC: Government Printing Office.

——. 2002. *American FactFinder: Hartford City, CT*. http://factfinder.census.gov.

——. 2005. *American FactFinder: Hartford County, CT*. http://factfinder.census.gov.

——. 2006. *American FactFinder: Hartford County, CT. Selected Statistics by Economic Sector.* http://factfinder.census.gov/servlet.

——.2009. "The Importance of Being 'We': Collective Identity and the Mobilizing Work of Progressive Activists in Hartford, Connecticut." *Mobilization* 14: 65–84.

Valocchi, Stephen. 1994. "The Racial Basis of Capitalism and the State, and the Impact of the New Deal on African Americans." *Social Problems* 41: 347–62.

——. 1996. "A Way of Thinking about the History of Community Organizing." Talk given at the Trinity Center for Neighborhoods. www.trincoll.edu/depts/tcn/valocchi.htm. accessed November 2008.

——. 1999. "The Class-Inflected Nature of Gay Identity." *Social Problems* 46: 207–24.

——. 2001. "Individual Identities, Collective Identities, and Organizational Structure: The Relationship of the Political Left and Gay Liberation in the United States." *Sociological Perspectives* 44: 445–68.

——. 2002. "History, Memory, and the City: Stories of Growing Up in Hartford Connecticut During the Great Depression." *Connecticut History* 41: 41–67.

——. 2007. "Ideology, Organization, and Biography: The Cultural Construction of Identity Talk Among Progressive Activists in Hartford, Connecticut." Pp. 189–217 in *Research in Social Movements, Conflicts and Change.* Vol. 27 Patrick G. Coy ed. Oxford: JAI Press.

Voss, Kim and Rachel Sherman. 2000. "Breaking the Iron Law of Oligarchy: Union Revitalization in the American Labor Movement." *American Journal of Sociology* 106: 303–49.

Walsh, Andrew H. 1996. "For Our City's Welfare: Building a Protestant Establishment in Late Nineteenth Century Hartford." Ph.D. Diss., American Studies Program, Harvard University.

Walsh, Edward J. 1986. "The Role of Target Vulnerabilities in High Technology Protest Movements: The Nuclear Establishment at Three Mile Island." *Sociological Forum* 1: 199–218.

Warner, Michael. 1999. *The Trouble with Normal: Sex, Politics, and the Ethics of Queer Life.* New York: The Free Press.

Weaver, Glenn. 1982. *Hartford: An Illustrated History of Connecticut's Capital.* Woodland Hills, California: Windsor Publications.

Whalen, Jack R. and Richard Flacks. 1989. *Beyond the Barricades: The Sixties Generation Grows Up.* Philadelphia: Temple University Press.

Whittier, Nancy. 1995. *Feminist Generations: The Persistence of the Radical Women's Movement.* Philadelphia: Temple University Press.

Wholley, Owen. 2007. "Collective Identity." *The Blackwell Encyclopedia of Sociology.* George Ritzer ed. Blackwell Reference Online. Accessed 6 June 2007.

Wilson, Tracey Morgan. 1993. "From Assembly Line to Steno Pool: Women Workers at Colt's Firearms and Travelers Insurance Company 1910–55." Ph.D. Diss, Department of History, Brown University.

Wilson, William Julius. 1980. *The Declining Significance of Race: Blacks and Changing American Institutions.* Chicago: University of Chicago Press.

Yow, Valerie Raleigh. 1994. *Recording Oral History: A Practical Guide for Social Scientists.* Thousand Oaks, CA: Sage Publications.

Index

abeyance structures 5, 128–9, 138, 141
action-oriented strategies 61, 62, 64, 68, 69, 70
adoption 56, 77
African Americans: AIDS/HIV interventions 55, 68–9; formal organizations 102; Hartford 36, 38, 39, 44–5, 46; NAACP 44–5; New Deal legislation 171n3; People for a Change 78; politics 47; self-help organizations 44; voting rights 101; *see also* civil rights movement
age 7, 10
agency 3, 14, 18, 32, 33
AIDS activism 51, 63–5, 68–9, 79, 84; *see also* HIV interventions
Alinsky, Saul 58, 73–4, 152, 171n1
Anderson, Leon 142
animal rights 32, 81–2, 107
anomie 15
anti-globalization movement 7, 92, 108, 109, 120–2
anti-racism 5, 7, 59, 61, 70, 135

benevolent control 40–1, 52–3, 166
biography: activist identity 141, 142, 148, 153–4; recruitment and commitment 110, 111–18, 165
"Bishops" 40
Black Caucus 45
black power 148, 149, 150
burnout 5, 124–38; activists' experience of 129–30; betrayal 133–4; scholarship 128–9; strategies to manage 134–8; support structures 130–3, 138, 168

capitalism 6, 34–5, 71
Catholic Worker movement 90, 122, 128–9, 130
Catholicism 48, 49, 119–20, 154–5

churches 19, 48, 49, 112, 119–20, 154; African American 44; gay rights activism 51; Protestant 40; values learned from 163
civil disobedience 21, 70, 79–82, 105, 128–9
civil rights movement 45, 46, 94, 148, 171n2; activist identity 147; goals of activism 60, 63; political opportunity theory 20, 21; radical flank effect 81; resources 19, 87; separatist discourse 148; strategies 70–1; student networks 110–11; unions 105; *see also* African Americans
class: activist burnout 133; activist identity 163; class war 23, 56, 77; Hartford 38–9, 43; identity politics 169n4; intersectionality 28, 118; oppositional consciousness 28, 29; organizational leadership 97
classism 98, 133, 139
Cloward, Richard 101–2, 103
coalitions 59, 61–2, 69, 82, 162, 167; cultural change 67; gay rights activism 51; intra-organizational conflict 98; organizations 95, 99–101; People for a Change 78–9; Puerto Rican activism 47–8
collective action 53, 71, 121, 151–2; critical events 111; cultural resources 90; new social movement theory 30; oppositional consciousness 28; power structures 40; repertoires of 33; resource mobilization theory 18; solidary-based identity 159; strain theory 15, 16, 93–4
collective identity 5, 25–7, 38, 142–61, 165; definition of 142; discursive strategies 70; education and consciousness-raising 72; movement-based 143, 145–51, 157–8, 160; new social movement theory 29; organization-based 143, 147–8, 151–6, 160; sociologists' conception of 74, 83;

solidary-based 143, 153, 156–60; *see also* identity
colleges 48–51, 104; *see also* student activism
colonization 31, 32
commitment 4, 109–10, 123, 163, 165; activist identity 141; critical events 121, 122; intensity of 126–7, 129; plausibility structures 132; social networks 118, 168; tension with personal life 129, 137; women's movement 128
commodification 31, 32
community 90–2, 125, 130
community organizing 5, 7, 9, 55, 58; activist identity 152; education and consciousness-raising 72; legislative and service delivery goals 65; reformism 62–3; resource mobilization framework 22; self-interest 73; solidary-based identity 159; stakeholders 167; *see also* neighborhood organizations
Community Renewal Team (CRT) 46
conflict 5, 10; intra-organizational 98, 125, 133, 148; strain theory 16
Connecticut Coalition for Lesbian and Gay Civil Rights 51
Connecticut Global Action Network 120
consciousness-raising 58, 60, 61, 68, 69, 162; collective action 121; cultural events 95; political 91; solidary-based identity 160; strategies 69–70, 71–5, 79, 83
constraints 53–4; and agency 3; resources 87–8, 132–3
cooptation 1, 4, 21, 101, 102
creative activism 66
critical events 110, 111, 120–2, 141, 163, 165
cultural events 95
cultural goals 60, 64–9, 83
cultural resources 27, 90–2, 93, 162–3, 164, 167
cultural theoretical frameworks 12–13, 23, 24–7, 32, 52, 171n9; college activism 50; culture/structure relationship 170n2; discursive strategies 70; Hartford 37, 38; organizations 44, 45; Puerto Rican activism 46
culture: politics distinction 47; toolkit metaphor 172n2; *see also* organizational culture

deindustrialization 5, 17, 35, 36, 53
democracy 5, 64, 69, 98, 100, 103–4, 147
Democratic Party 21, 78, 119

direct action 58, 70, 79–82, 83; *see also* civil disobedience
disability 135
discrimination 18, 39, 45, 53
discursive strategies 70
disruptive strategies 21, 70, 79–82, 83, 101–2
domestic violence 13
Douglas, Frederick 74
downtown areas 30–1, 37, 43–4, 48, 166
drug addiction 72, 115
drug policy 100–1

economic depression 15, 17, 53
economic growth 15, 16
economic support 132
education: AIDS activism 65; solidary-based identity 160; strategies 71–5, 79, 83; through action 64
elites 34–5, 101, 166; business 30, 41, 42; cooptation by 102; economic 40, 43; elite channeling 21, 41, 46; political 35, 42, 47
emotions 17–18
empathetic understanding 74–5
employment 36, 37, 38–9, 40, 42, 53
empowerment 7, 9, 68, 69, 147; cultural events 95; education and consciousness-raising 71, 72; personal 58, 59; student 148
ethnicity: activist identity 163; biographies of marginality 117–18; entry into collective action 26; Hartford 36; inequalities 6; intersectionality 28, 118; New Deal legislation 171n3; oppositional consciousness 28, 29, 157; solidary-based identity 156; *see also* African Americans; Latinos; Puerto Ricans; race
exclusion 69, 98–9

FACE (Featuring All Colors and Ethnicities) 99, 158
faith 149–50, 155
family socialization 108, 109, 110, 111–12, 114
Fantasia, Rick 111, 121
feminism 5, 7, 88, 98, 148, 171n2; activist identity 26–7, 140, 143, 145–7; Democratic Party 21; goals of activism 60; intersectionality 28, 169n5; National Women's Party 128; recruitment and commitment 110, 113–14; *see also* gender; women's movement
Flacks, Richard 2
flank effect 21, 48, 81–2, 170n7

framing 12–14, 25
Freedom Rides 20
Freedom Summer 110–11
friendships 127, 129, 133
funding 22, 41, 45–6, 84–6, 88–90, 96

Gamson, Josh 152
Gamson, William 13, 143, 147, 151, 156
Gandhi, Mahatma 92
gay activism 5, 7, 9, 86, 135, 171n2; AIDS/
    HIV interventions 55, 68–9; disruptive
    strategies 81; gay film festivals 152; goals
    of activism 59, 60; Hartford 36, 51–2;
    intra-organizational conflict 98; Kwanza
    project 99; new social movement theory
    29; People for a Change 78, 79; radical
    flank effect 82; recruitment and
    commitment 115–16; reformism 62–3;
    resources 88; same-sex marriage 52, 59,
    60, 62–3, 75, 77, 172n6; solidary-based
    identity 158; women's movement 140,
    146; youth dances 95; see also sexuality
gender 7, 10–11, 26; activist identity 163;
    inequalities 6; intersectionality 28, 118;
    oppositional consciousness 28, 29, 157;
    solidary-based identity 156; see also
    feminism; women's movement
gentrification 17
Glaser, Nathan 8
globalization 30, 33, 37
goals 58–9, 60–9, 83, 162, 164, 167; animal
    rights 32; cultural change 60, 64–9, 83;
    education and consciousness-raising 71;
    group-based 60–2, 69; labor movement
    131; organizational structure 23; policy
    change 60, 64–6, 69; reform or radical
    restructuring 60, 62–4, 69
grants 84, 85
grassroots activism 9, 84–5, 95, 101, 103
grievances 31, 32; civil rights movement 19;
    cultural theoretical frameworks 24;
    Hartford 35–6, 37, 53, 166; new social
    movement theory 44; resource
    mobilization theory 18; strain theory 15,
    16, 17, 18
grounded theory 8
Gunnison, Foster Jr. 51

Hartford 3, 5, 35–53, 165–6; African American
    activism 44–5, 46; anti-unionism 41–2;
    benevolent control 38–41, 52–3, 166;
    colleges 48–51; ethnic groups 36, 39; gay
    rights activism 51–2; inequalities 36–7;
    Puerto Rican activism 46–8; racism 149;
    urban tensions 43–4
Hartford Foundation for Public Giving 41,
    46
HIV interventions 52, 55, 63–4, 70, 79, 84; see
    also AIDS activism
homelessness 76
homophobia 6, 98, 133, 158
housing projects 61–2

identity 10, 24, 139–61, 163, 168, 173n1;
    biographies of marginality 116; cultural
    change 68, 69; education and
    consciousness-raising 73; goals of
    activism 61, 69; intersectionality 29;
    movement-based 143, 157–8, 160; new
    social movement theory 29, 31;
    oppositional consciousness 29, 38;
    organization-based 143, 147–8, 151–6,
    160; solidary-based 143, 153, 156–60; see
    also collective identity
identity politics 6–7, 8, 169n4
identity talk 142, 145–6, 150, 151, 152, 163
ideology 91, 92, 93, 99–100
immigrant rights 5, 7, 103, 117
immigration 17, 30, 38, 39, 40, 44; see also
    migration
inequalities 6, 36–7, 65; funding 88; new social
    movement theory 30, 37; oppositional
    consciousness 27–8, 29, 156
insider strategies 70, 75–9
interest group politics 21, 75
internal/self-referential strategies 70–5
intersectionality 28–9, 118, 157, 169n5

Jesuit Volunteer Corps 112–13, 154

Kalos Society 51
King, Martin Luther 81, 92
Kwanza project 99, 158

labor movement 5, 7, 97, 109, 140; coalition
    building 62; critical events 111; education
    through action 64; framing strategies 25;
    Hartford 39, 41–3; motivations of activists
    23; People for a Change 78; political
    opportunity framework 22; progressivism
    104–5; support structures 130–2; see also
    unions
Latinos: AIDS/HIV interventions 55, 68–9;
    biographies of marginality 117; "coming

to activism" 109; Hartford 36, 38, 47; intra-organizational conflict 98; oppositional consciousness 159; voting rights 101; *see also* Puerto Ricans
leadership 64, 87, 96–7
the Left 6, 66, 67, 169n4
legislation: insider strategies 77–8; New Deal 171n3; outsider strategies 81; policy change goals 59, 60, 64–6, 69
lesbian, gay, bisexual and transgender activism 5, 7, 9, 86, 135, 171n2; disruptive strategies 81; gay film festivals 152; goals of activism 59, 60; Hartford 36, 51–2; intra-organizational conflict 98; Kwanza project 99; new social movement theory 29; People for a Change 78, 79; radical flank effect 82; recruitment and commitment 115–16; reformism 62–3; resources 88; same-sex marriage 52, 59, 60, 62–3, 75, 77, 172n6; solidary-based identity 158; women's movement 140, 146; youth dances 95; *see also* sexuality
lesbian, gay, bisexual and transgender rights: AIDS/HIV interventions 55, 68–9
liberation theology 107, 109
lobbying 21, 70, 75–9, 81, 82
local politics 47–8, 62–3, 75, 78
LOCK (Lesbians of Color in Kinship) 158

Maddison, Sarah 2
Malcolm X 81
Mandela, Nelson 82
marginality: activist identity 141, 156, 157, 159; recruitment and commitment 116–17, 118–19, 163; sociology 166
marriage 52, 59, 60, 62–3, 75, 77, 172n6
Marx, Karl 34–5, 37, 43, 48, 54
McAdam, Doug 110, 170n3, 173n3
meaning 3, 23
media campaigns 13, 65
Media Research and Action Project (MRAP) 13
migration 15, 36, 53; *see also* immigration
militants (radicals) 45–6, 48, 53, 81–2, 148, 170n7; *see also* radical restructuring
Mills, C. Wright 34–5, 39, 42, 53, 166
mob behavior 15, 16
moderates 45–6, 48, 53, 81–2, 148, 170n7
Modigliani, André 13
Montgomery Bus Boycott (1956) 20
moral panics 15, 16

Morris, Aldon 21, 27
motivations 23, 115–16
movement-based identity 143, 145–51, 157–8, 160
multi-issue work 8–9, 56, 59, 60, 61

National Association for Advancement of Colored People (NAACP) 44–5
National Women's Party 128
nationalism 6
neighborhood organizations 61–2, 88–9, 153; *see also* community organizing
neighborhood revitalization 43, 44, 48, 166
Nepstad, Sharon Erickson 128–9, 130
New Deal 39, 171n3
new social movement theory 24–5, 29–32, 171n10; discursive strategies 70; Hartford 37, 44; organizations 44, 94

oppositional consciousness 27–9, 32, 48, 165, 168; biographies of marginality 116, 117–18; compared to solidary-based identity 156–7; discursive strategies 70; Hartford 38, 39–40, 41, 53; multidimensional 158, 159, 160
organizational culture 104–5, 164; skills 97
organizational structure 22–3, 57, 105, 163, 164
organizations 86, 93–106, 163, 164–5, 167; critique of formal 101–3; distinguished from social movements 94; Hartford 44, 45, 53; intra-organizational conflict 98, 125, 133, 148; leadership 96–7; organization-based identity 143, 147–8, 151–6, 160
outsider strategies 70, 79–82, 83

peace movement 5, 7, 94; coalition building 62; disruptive strategies 80; recruitment and commitment 121, 122; unions 105
People for a Change (PFC) 78–9, 89–90
Perez, Eddie 47–8
personal lives 124–7, 129, 130, 133, 134–8, 163
personal relationships 134–5, 136
Piven, Frances Fox 101–2, 103
plausibility structures 5, 129–30, 132, 138, 141, 165
Plowshares movement 128–9
policy change 59, 60, 64–6, 69
political Left 6, 66, 67, 169n4

political opportunity theory 19–24, 26, 30, 32, 83, 170n6; action-oriented strategies 70; coalitions 47; Hartford 42, 43, 45, 53; insider strategies 76–7; protest waves/ cycles 20, 49; Puerto Rican activism 46

politics 47–8, 53, 62–3, 75, 92, 140; cultural goals 66, 67–8; culture distinction 47; insider strategies 75–9; People for a Change 78–9; prefigurative 31; Puerto Rican activism 47–8

poverty 5, 76, 149; Hartford 35–6, 43, 53; War on Poverty 45, 68

power 33, 34–5, 52–3, 166, 167, 171n2; critiques of 126; disruptive 101–2; goals of activism 60; importance of 48, 50; intersectionality 28; new social movement theory 31, 37; oppositional consciousness 28; political opportunity structure 42, 76–7; structures of 6, 40, 156–7

prefigurative politics 31

progressivism 6–7, 8, 92, 104–5

protest waves/cycles 20, 49, 53

Protestantism 40, 48, 49, 51

Puerto Ricans: biographies of marginality 117; "coming to activism" 109; Hartford 39, 44, 46–8; oppositional consciousness 159; People for a Change 78; solidary-based identity 156; see also Latinos

queer youth 5, 9, 88, 115–16, 129, 136, 140, 158; see also lesbian, gay, bisexual and transgender activism

race: activist identity 149–51, 153, 163; black power 148, 149, 150; college activism 50; cultural goals 68; drug policies and voting rights 100–1; entry into collective action 26; feminism 146; Hartford 165–6; inequalities 6; intersectionality 28; leadership issues 96; oppositional consciousness 28, 29, 157; queer youth 158; sample of activists 7; solidary-based identity 156, 158; tokenism 10; see also African Americans; civil rights movement; ethnicity; Latinos; Puerto Ricans

racial discrimination 39, 45, 139

racism 6, 19, 61, 98, 135; Hartford 149; institutional 70, 100; internalized 28, 139; intra-organizational conflict 133; resource mobilization theory 18; see also anti-racism

radical flank effect 21, 48, 81–2, 170n7

radical restructuring 60, 62–4, 69, 167

Rapid Voting Rights Restoration Coalition 101

Reader's Feast Café and Bookstore 91–2

recruitment 4, 107–23, 163, 165, 168; activist identity 141; biography 110, 111–18; critical events 110, 111, 120–2; cultural goals 66; insider strategies 75; rational actor models 172n1; social networks 110–11, 118–20

reform 60, 62–4, 69, 167

relative deprivation 38

religion 99, 107, 163; activist identity 149–51, 153–5; Hartford 40, 49

resource mobilization theory 18–19, 21–2, 24, 26, 30, 32, 170n6; action-oriented strategies 70; coalitions 47, 51; college activism 50; Hartford 41, 42, 43; organizations 44, 45; radical flank effect 81

resources 18–19, 53, 87–93, 94, 164, 167; civil rights movement 19, 20, 46, 87; Hartford 41; labor movement 131; non-material 27, 89–90, 91–2, 93, 162–3; oppositional consciousness 156; Puerto Rican activism 46, 47; support structures 132–3, 138

Ryan, Charlotte 13

same-sex marriage 52, 59, 60, 62–3, 75, 77, 172n6

Scalmer, Sean 2

scholarship 1–2, 3, 4, 35, 164, 167, 169n3

schools 19, 91

Seattle protests (1999) 108, 109, 120, 121, 163, 172n4

segregation 18, 19, 39, 44, 87

self-interest 24, 55, 58, 73–4, 152–3, 170n8

service delivery 7, 9, 65, 76, 83

service ethic 6–7

sexism 6, 10–11, 100

sexuality: activist identity 163; entry into collective action 26; inequalities 6; intersectionality 28; oppositional consciousness 28, 29, 157; solidary-based identity 156; see also lesbian, gay, bisexual and transgender activism

Smith, Wilbur 45

Snow, David 142

social change 2, 14–15, 59, 113, 138; cultural goals 64–9; solidary-based identity 160; strain theory 15, 16, 17; strategies 70; transgender activism 52; unions 105

social interaction 23, 24, 90, 91, 165
social justice 5, 6, 89, 105, 114, 147
social networks 87, 91, 94, 165; friendships
  127; political opportunity theory 21;
  recruitment and commitment 110–11,
  115, 116, 118–20, 141, 168; resource
  mobilization theory 19
sociology 14, 16, 33, 34, 166, 170n1
solidarity 4, 55–6, 58–9, 80, 83, 122
solidary-based identity 143, 153, 156–60
strain theory 15–18, 30, 36, 38, 93–4, 170n3
strategies 69–82, 160, 162, 167; burnout 130,
  134–8; insider 70, 75–9; internal/
  self-referential 70–5; outsider 70, 79–82,
  83
Strauss, Anselm 8
stress reduction strategies 131
structure 3, 6, 33, 156–7, 173n1; oppositional
  consciousness 27–8; strain theory 16–17;
  theoretical frameworks 14, 32, 170n2
student activism 94, 104, 110, 140, 148; see
  also colleges
Students for a Democratic Society (SDS) 110
suburbs 36–7, 43, 76
support structures 130–3, 134, 138, 168
synagogues 49, 163

Tarrow, Sidney 22
Taylor, Verta 128, 142
theater 31, 65–7, 70, 74

Three Mile Island nuclear accident 13, 111,
  120
tokenism 10, 86, 98, 135
transgender activism 52; see also lesbian, gay,
  bisexual and transgender activism
Trinity College 50, 51
Twain, Mark 41

unemployment 35–6
unions 39, 41–3, 92, 97, 140; activist identity
  147; Alinsky 171n1; progressivism 104–5;
  support structures 130–2; training 105;
  see also labor movement
United for a Fair Economy 95
University of Connecticut 49–50, 140
University of Hartford 51
urban social movements 30

values 40, 160, 163
veganism 32
Vietnam War 49, 105, 110, 140
voting rights 100–1

Walsh, Edward 111
Warriors for Real Welfare Reform 80
Whittier, Nancy 110, 142
women's movement 22–3, 58, 107; activist
  identity 140, 145–7; ebbs and flows 128;
  participation and commitment 113–14;
  see also feminism; gender